COLLEGE KNOWLEDGE

COLLEGE KNOWLEDGE

What It Really Takes for Students to

Succeed and What We Can Do to Get

Them Ready

David T. Conley

JOSSEY-BASS
A Wiley Imprint
www.josseybass.com

Published by Jossey-Bass
A Wiley Imprint
989 Market Street, San Francisco, CA 94103-1741   www.josseybass.com

Jossey-Bass books and products are available through most bookstores. To contact Jossey-Bass directly, call our Customer Care Department within the U.S. at 800-956-7739, outside the U.S. at 317-572-3986, or fax 317-572-4002.

Jossey-Bass also publishes its books in a variety of electronic formats. Some content that appears in print may not be available in electronic books.

Library of Congress Cataloging-in-Publication Data

Conley, David T., 1948-
 College knowledge : what it really takes for students to succeed and what we can do to get them ready / David T. Conley.-1st ed.
    p. cm. - (The Jossey-Bass education series)
Includes bibliographical references and index.
ISBN-13 978-0-7879-7397-1 (alk. paper)
ISBN-10 0-7879-7397-1 (alk. paper)
ISBN-13 978-0-7879-9675-8 (paperback)
ISBN-10 0-7879-9675-0 (paperback)
1. College student orientation-United States. 2. Academic achievement-United States. I. Title. II. Series.
LB2343.32.C66 2005
378.1'98-dc22
                        2004030569

Printed in the United States of America
FIRST EDITION
HB Printing   10 9 8 7 6
PB Printing   10 9 8 7 6

To Genevieve Conley, Nancy Rose Spector, and Julia Conley,
whose college knowledge is awesome.

CONTENTS

An ever-increasing proportion of high school students in the United States today aspire to college. Yet statistics indicate that the percentage of college students receiving bachelor's degrees has remained relatively constant over the past twenty-five years, that it now takes on average five years to get a four-year college degree, and that somewhere between 30 percent and 60 percent of students now require remedial education upon entry to college, depending on the type of institution they attend. Also over the past twenty-five years, SAT and ACT scores have risen only slightly in math and been relatively constant in reading, high school grade point average has gradually risen, and the proportion of students taking college preparatory courses has grown as well. How do we explain the seeming inconsistencies between these trends?

The answer can be found in part in the distinction between being *college-eligible* and *college-ready.* Because of the unique nature of the U.S. educational system, high schools focus on making students college-eligible—in other words, to enable students to meet admissions requirements. Students become college-eligible primarily by taking courses whose titles have been approved by college admissions offices. However, these students may or may not be college-ready, which is defined as being able to meet the expectations they encounter in entry-level college courses.

When they enter college, they face placement tests that may relegate them to non-credit-bearing courses. They encounter instructors who move through material at a much faster pace than in high school, who expect them to spend much more time on their own outside of class reading and reviewing, who provide feedback that can be much more unvarnished than what the students are used to receiving. They may be expected to support their opinions and assertions and to cite sources properly. They may find their ideas challenged in class discussions and their assumptions about what is true called into question. Students who earned straight A's in high school may receive the first C of their lives.

For the best-prepared students, little of this is a problem. However, for many students, perhaps the majority, such changed expectations catch them by surprise. They may be accustomed to moving through material slowly and methodically, providing the correct answer rather than the thoughtful one, writing as little as possible, and never ever rewriting an assignment. They may think that having an opinion is justification for the opinion in and of itself. They are not used to being challenged to support a contention with evidence. They may not have taken math for a year, science for two years, and a second language for three. For these students, the first year of college can be a very rocky and disconcerting experience.

Why does this disconnect in experiences and expectations exist? To help readers understand what it takes to succeed in college, this book undertakes a thorough examination of the college preparation process, beginning with an overview of how and why we have two distinct and loosely connected systems of secondary and postsecondary education. Understanding that the U.S. education system was designed consciously *not* to have strong linkages between high school and college is key to comprehending the nature of college preparation and the mismatches that can arise between what high schools think students need to know and what colleges expect them to be able to do.

This is not a book about what is wrong with high schools or with high school teaching. Quite the contrary, the large number of students who do succeed in college is an indirect indicator of the heroic accomplishments of high school teachers, who work in a system that provides them little consistent direction on what they should do for or ask from students to help them become college-ready. The book's central goal is to support high school educators—teachers, counselors, and administrators—who already put so much time and energy into preparing their students for college. The book also seeks to be a resource for enterprising parents and students who want to gain greater insight into what they can do to achieve college success. Finally, the book can assist high school and postsecondary faculty members when they sit down together to align more closely the expectations they hold for their students.

The book as a whole draws from a strong research base that has been established over the past two decades identifying what it takes for students to succeed in college, but it is deliberately written in a nontechnical style without in-text citations or footnotes that might distract from the core themes and messages. The Bibliography contains detailed information on the sources employed or referenced in the text as well as additional resources for those who wish to pursue these topics in greater depth.

The central research findings underlying the book are derived from Standards for Success, a research project I designed and directed between 1998 and 2001. This project was sponsored by the Association of American Universities and The Pew Charitable Trusts and conducted by the Center for Educational Policy Research at the University of Oregon in collaboration with the Stanford Institute for Higher Education Research at Stanford University. The initial goal of the research was to identify the specific knowledge and skills necessary for success in entry-level university courses. The project shared that information with secondary educators by sending a copy of its final report, *Understanding University Success,* to every high school in the United States. The ultimate goal of the research was to enable the high schools to prepare more students for success in entry-level college courses by showing high schools the connections between their state content standards and university success standards.

The book consists of three parts. Part One contains six chapters focused on the high school component of the college readiness equation. Each chapter provides information to help everyone engaged in preparing students for postsecondary success to focus their efforts in ways that enable more students to enter college prepared to succeed.

Chapter One examines the purposes of high school and how high schools decipher the college code. It makes the case that high schools are largely on their own to set their standards and expectations and even the content they include in college prep courses.

Chapter Two explores what high school students know about college readiness. Which students aspire to which types of colleges and why, and where do students get their information on college entrance requirements, placement test policies, and annual tuition costs? The chapter explores these issues and many others related to where students learn about college requirements. The primary conclusion is that college preparation is a knowledge-intensive activity and that some students have much greater access to the necessary information than others. Schools have a heightened responsibility to help level the playing field in this area.

Chapter Three outlines the old and new criteria for college success. Whereas college admission was not widely competitive as recently as the late 1970s, this has changed as more students compete for a limited number of slots at the most selective institutions and as more students apply to more colleges each year. This phenomenon has sent shock waves through the admission process, causing institutions that have been selective to tighten their criteria even further and those that have previously not been selective to begin to accept a lower percentage of applicants. Ever more emphasis is placed on merit. Increasingly, students must demonstrate that they belong in college before an institution will admit them. The choices students make in high school are more important than they ever were, and students can make good and bad choices, which in itself is an issue worthy of consideration by high schools.

Chapter Four explains in some detail the existing means by which high school and college are connected and the relative strengths and weaknesses of each. These include Advanced Placement courses, the International Baccalaureate, dual enrollment courses, and the early college high school. These have come into being to provide collegelike experiences to students while they are still in high school. The proliferation of these programs demonstrates the intertwined nature of high school and college teaching and learning. The chapter concludes with a discussion of a means to ascertain how well these programs and the remaining classes in the high school college prep curriculum align with college success standards. The Alignment and Challenge Audit is introduced as an example of a technique that can be used to analyze the content of a high school's curriculum in relation to the Knowledge and Skills for University Success presented in Part Three.

Chapter Five ties together much of what is discussed throughout Part One and paints a picture of a high school designed to prepare students for postsecondary success. The key concept explored in Chapter Five is how intellectual coherence in the curriculum can serve as a framework for progressively more challenging and engaging learning experiences that will more thoroughly prepare high school students for what they will face when they enter college. The senior seminar is presented as a means to achieve this in a number of fields of study. Chapter Six then presents in greater detail what teachers, students, school administrators, and parents can do to help create an intellectually coherent high school environment focused on college success.

In Part Two, the focus shifts to the college experience itself, and particularly the first year of college. Chapter Seven offers a panoramic perspective on the opportunities a college education affords students and the challenges they face taking advantage of those opportunities. Research on college students provides detailed descriptions of what is expected of them, including the amount of time they spend on academic work, the amount and type of reading they are assigned, the number and length of written assignments they are expected to complete, the kinds of thinking they are expected to develop, and the ways they engage in learning.

Chapter Eight offers insights into what really happens during the first year of college, examining the kinds of courses students take and the ways in which the general education component of a college education—the "core"—is changing. A number of examples from diverse institutions serve to illustrate these changing programs of general education. Also considered are the all-important and little-understood placement tests, which can determine where in the curriculum an incoming student is placed and, as a result, dramatically affect time to degree completion and even entry into a major. The chapter concludes with examples of course schedules of typical first-year students at a number of universities in various parts of the country.

The focal point of Chapter Nine is what must be done to create a more aligned educational system. How can state high school content standards and assessments be connected with postsecondary success, and why aren't they already? How is the admissions process likely to change over time? How will data systems that span high school and college create new possibilities for communicating information on student readiness for college? What would a K–16 system of education look like? Finally, what can policymakers, high school educators, postsecondary faculty and administrators, students, and parents do to bring about a better-aligned educational system that leads to enhanced student success?

Part Three of the volume consists primarily of the Knowledge and Skills for University Success standards (KSUS), which are presented by subject area in Chapters Ten through Sixteen. These are a statement of what students need to know and be able to do to succeed in entry-level university courses. They are a blueprint of the cognitive skills, habits of mind, dispositions toward learning, key principles and concepts of the disciplines, important skills, and key content knowledge students need to have mastered. The standards reflect the collective wisdom and insight of hundreds of faculty members who actually teach entry-level courses at research universities. They know of what they speak when they describe what it takes to succeed in these all-important courses and where students struggle the most.

The KSUS standards are broken into chapters organized by discipline, beginning with English. Each chapter contains two sections. First, and perhaps most important, is a presentation in narrative format of the foundational skills needed to excel in the study of the discipline. Second is a detailed listing of the content students should have mastered in order to be successful in entry-level university courses.

Chapter Seventeen contains material that may be of great interest and use to those who wish to understand college success in more practical terms. The chapter consists of student work samples that illustrate the assignments that students do in college classrooms. The work samples translate the standards into actual classroom tasks. This book contains only a representative set of examples drawn from a much larger collection that is available online. The work samples have proven to be very useful both to provide greater definition to the standards and to suggest the types of tasks that are appropriate in high school to facilitate a smoother transition for students to postsecondary education.

Appendix A contains the Checklist for College Readiness, a very detailed self-assessment that allows students to determine how well they have mastered each standard by rating themselves on tasks they are expected to master relative to college success standards. High school teachers can also use this instrument to gauge the challenge level of their courses relative to college readiness standards. Which of the content standards are students being exposed to in a particular high school class? Which are they mastering? Which might they not encounter at all? Such determinations are useful when planning curriculum coverage and seeking better alignment with postsecondary education.

This self-assessment may be appealing to students who wish to gauge how well they are preparing for college success. Although it may be challenging initially to get students to devote the time necessary to complete the assessment, most become intrigued by it once they undertake the task. They get a certain sense of satisfaction when they realize they meet one of the standards, and they find it revealing to think about which ones they still need to master.

The book includes several features designed to help readers make good sense of this information. The first four chapters and Chapter Seven each contain a section entitled "Through the Students' Eyes." These sections tell the continuing stories of three different young people who experience preparation for postsecondary education in three fundamentally different ways, although they attend the same high school and have the same initial aspirations to postsecondary education. Each installment illustrates issues discussed in the chapter in which it appears by demonstrating how these issues play out in the lives of students. The purpose of these sections is to enable readers to connect the content with individual students they may have known and to see how the disconnect between college preparation and college success affects different students differentially.

At the conclusion of each chapter in Part One is a section entitled "Increasing College Success: What We Can Do" that contains ideas and activities that can be undertaken by high schools. All of the listed ideas have been tried at various high schools around the country and have led to improvements in student success in college. Each section contains activities that individual teachers can undertake independently as well as initiatives that require department or school-level organization or endorsement.

Through the content it presents, the standards it defines, the examples of student work it explains, the experiences it describes, the suggestions for action it outlines, and the diagnostic opportunities it offers, this book seeks to enable readers to understand the important elements of college success and to take actions that enable more students to go on to postsecondary education and do well in entry-level college courses. If the contents of this book make it a little easier for more students to succeed, particularly those students who historically have not had access to this type of information, then it will have achieved its objective.

ACKNOWLEDGMENTS

I have been greatly assisted in writing this book by a number of people who have contributed their time, talents, and expertise. Terri Heath, research associate in the Center for Educational Policy Research at the University of Oregon, provided consistent leadership in organizing the contributions of many people and in working with the editors on the student work samples. Her assistance was invaluable in getting this project completed in a timely fashion. She was assisted by Susan Merschel, our office assistant and a future educational star. Doctoral student Peter Mohn conducted extensive background research for the sections on general education and gathered numerous examples of general education programs and of typical schedules for first-year students.

In addition to the involvement of the over four hundred faculty from around the nation who gave their time and expertise to participate in the process to develop the Knowledge and Skills for University Success, a number of faculty members have contributed more directly to specific aspects of the book. Both the Checklist for College Readiness and the comments on student work samples derived largely from college faculty, most of whom I came to know through their previous participation in Standards for Success.

The following individuals provided the rich examples used in the Checklist for College Readiness: for English, George Cusack, University of Oregon; for physics and chemistry, John Halpin, New York University; for social sciences, Richard Hessler, University of Missouri; for the arts, Jen Katz-Bounincontro, University of Oregon; for second languages, Connie Knop, University of Wisconsin; for mathematics, Michel Kovcholovsky, University of Oregon; and for four sections of the natural sciences, Brenda Leicht, University of Iowa.

I also asked a number of faculty members to comment on the student work samples to help guide the reader's understanding of the specific aspects of each work sample that illustrated the skills needed for college success. The following faculty graciously provided commentary, and some also contributed work samples: Richard Askey, University of Wisconsin; John Fry, Trinity College; Connie Knop, University of Wisconsin; Brenda Leicht, University of Iowa; Judith Liskin-Gasparro, University of Iowa; Carol Severino, University of Iowa.

The original manuscript was reviewed by three people whom I respect greatly, and their comments were very useful to me as I made revisions. Mike Riley, superintendent of the Bellevue, Washington, schools, and a former English teacher, went over the manuscript line by line to point out inconsistencies in my argumentation and points that required better exposition. He also encouraged me to illustrate general principles with more explanation, applications, and examples. Andrea Venezia, policy associate at the National Center for Public Policy and Higher Education, offered her usual thorough and thoughtful critique and contributed her expertise on this topic, drawn from her own research. Bob Laird, former director of undergraduate admissions at UC Berkeley, provided the perspective that only someone steeped in admissions could offer.

Finally, I wish to thank the Jossey-Bass team, including Lesley Iura, Kate Gagnon, Pamela Berkman, Sandra Beris, and others who helped improve the original manuscript immeasurably with their tactful suggestions, creative ideas, and skillful management of the editing and publishing process.

ABOUT THE AUTHOR

David T. Conley is professor of educational policy and leadership in the College of Education, University of Oregon. He is the founder and director of the Center for Educational Policy Research at the University of Oregon.

Conley recently completed Standards for Success, a $2.5 million project funded by the Washington, D.C.–based Association of American Universities (AAU) and The Pew Charitable Trusts. This project linked state high school content standards and assessments with university admission and success.

From 1993 through 2000 he designed an entirely new system for the Oregon University System that connected state high school reform and college success. The Proficiency-based Admission Standards System (PASS) employs student proficiency information generated from the state high school assessment system in combination with collections of evidence of student proficiency to determine college readiness and admission.

In 2003, he published *Who Governs Our Schools?* with Teachers College Press. This book analyzes changes in educational policy and governance structures at the federal, state, and local levels.

Conley has received over $7 million in grants and contracts from federal and state governments and foundations over the past ten years to conduct research on a range of policy issues, including adequacy funding, accountability systems, alternative methods of assessment, proficiency-based admission, and high school–college articulation. The results of this research have been published in numerous books, journal articles, technical reports, and conference papers.

Conley received a B.A. with honors in social sciences from the University of California, Berkeley. At the University of Colorado, Boulder, he earned a master's degree in social, multicultural, and bilingual foundations of education and a doctorate in curriculum, administration, and supervision.

Before joining the faculty of the University of Oregon, he served in school-level and central office administrator positions and in an executive position in a state education department in Colorado, and as a teacher and administrator in two public multicultural alternative schools in California.

COLLEGE KNOWLEDGE

From the Current System and the High School of Today to an Aligned, Coherent Program

To understand what it takes to succeed in college, we must first understand how high schools today prepare students for college and the ways in which students are aided or impeded by these practices. Part One undertakes a thorough examination of this process.

Chapter One begins by providing an overview of how and why we have two distinct and loosely connected systems of secondary and postsecondary education. Understanding that American education was designed consciously to have a weak link between high school and college helps us comprehend the range of issues that result from this system. Chapter Two examines how much high school students today actually know about the college admissions process and the college experience. Chapter Three goes on to look at what it takes for students to be successful in their first year of college. Chapter Four reviews some innovative programs currently offered to prepare high school students for college, and Chapter Five describes what the ideal high school program would look like. Finally, Chapter Six offers some recommendations for high schools that wish to provide a coherent program.

Each of the chapters in Part One provides information to help those who prepare students for postsecondary success to focus their efforts and redesign their institutions in ways that will enable more students to reach college and succeed there. In addition, the first four chapters contain a section designed to help readers understand how college preparation is experienced by different types of students as they navigate the current system's labyrinth of requirements. These sections, entitled "Through the Students' Eyes," tell the stories of three different young people who prepare for postsecondary education in three fundamentally different ways, even though they are attending the same high school and have the same aspiration to go on to college. The last section in each of these chapters is entitled "Increasing College Success: What We Can Do." It describes activities that high schools can undertake. All of these activities have been tried at various high schools around the country and have led to improvements in student preparation for college success. Some activities may be undertaken by individual teachers, whereas others require school-level organization or endorsement.

The book draws on research on how students succeed in college, but it is deliberately written in a nontechnical style without in-text citations or footnotes that might distract readers from the core themes and messages. The Bibliography contains detailed information on sources for those who wish to pursue them in greater depth.

Everything presented here is supported by findings accumulated primarily over the past ten years, with much of it derived from the research done for the Knowledge and Skills for University Success (KSUS) standards, which I designed and directed. Sponsored by the Association of American Universities and The Pew Charitable Trusts, the research was conducted by the Center for Educational Policy Research at the University of Oregon in collaboration with the Stanford Institute for Higher Education Research at Stanford University. The purpose was to determine the impediments to successful student transition to college and identify ways in which the transition might be redesigned. The ultimate goal was to find ways to enable more students to prepare appropriately and successfully in high school for successful college matriculation and subsequent success in entry-level college courses. An additional important source for information in Part One on student attitudes toward college readiness is research drawn from the Bridge Project, which was also housed at the Stanford Institute for Higher Education Research. These key sources and others help identify some of the central issues related to high school–college transition and how to make it more successful for all students.

Understanding the System

Preparing for college success is more complicated than it seems. Most parents of high school students (and most high school students and teachers) believe, or at least hope, that the college preparatory curriculum is carefully designed to ready students for success in higher education. Parents would likely be shocked to learn that the relationship between the high school instructional program and college success is imprecise at best. High schools are designed to get students to graduate, and in the case of college-bound students, to make them eligible for admission to college—generally the public university in that state. They are not necessarily designed to enable students to succeed in college.

This lack of a strong connection between secondary and postsecondary education in the United States comes as something of a surprise to many people because they assume that everyone in the education system at all levels must be talking with one another about something as basic and important as the knowledge and skills students require for success at the next level. They may assume, at the very least, that the government makes them do so.

Changing the Focus from College Admission to College Success

In practice, however, the two systems—K–12 and postsecondary—evolved in relative isolation. Although each is clearly engaged in education, each has traditionally seen its purposes and goals as distinctly different from the other's. This worked reasonably well when the proportion of high school students who went on to college was relatively small, when few institutions were truly selective, and when a college degree was not the primary passport to economic success in our society as it is today.

All three of those circumstances have now changed. In surveys conducted by the Bridge Project and Public Agenda, upwards of 90 percent of ninth graders say they plan to attend college. The actual proportion of high school graduates who actually go directly from high school to some form of postsecondary education is closer to two-thirds, and this figure increases to above 75 percent when high school graduates are followed for five years. For the first time in human history, a society has large numbers of students continuing past high school.

The increase in high school graduates has led to greatly increased competition for admission to college, particularly at the most desirable institutions. This phenomenon began in earnest in the late 1970s and has not abated since. The most selective universities have witnessed the greatest increase in the number of applicants competing for a finite number of seats in the entering freshman class. The University of California, Berkeley, for example, now receives over thirty-five thousand applications annually, extends about eighty-five hundred offers of admission, and ends up with about thirty-eight hundred freshmen. Although it is not impossible for students to gain admission to even the most selective institutions, they must pay careful attention to the choices they make throughout high school.

The college degree has become much more important for entry into the labor force and continues to be the critical credential for access to graduate schools in the professions. As more high school students aspire to college and to higher career goals, they need to be prepared for college in ways that give them the skills to complete the baccalaureate degree in a timely fashion and successfully enough to enter the labor market or compete for scarce spaces in graduate school. To do this, they must attain high levels of academic competence, not just complete required courses.

Admission to certain schools, perhaps 5 percent of all colleges, has clearly become increasingly competitive. Requirements have grown more stringent as the number of applications has burgeoned. For students who want to be admitted to those schools, the quest to find the right combination of qualifications to entice the admissions offices has led to almost frenzied activity to demonstrate worthiness. This admissions "arms race" has caused schools, students, and parents to focus entirely on getting into college, often at the expense of looking beyond admission to consider how successful the student will be once there. Student scores on SAT and AP tests, grade point average, class rank, letters of recommendation, and extracurricular activities have become the means to an end: admission.

But what happens after admission? What does the student face in that first college course? What do the faculty at a research university care about? What do they expect students to know and be able to do? Until now, these questions have seldom been asked and even less seldom been answered. Although colleges were willing to offer general platitudes about the "well-prepared" student, few ventured much beyond stating course requirements. Almost none were willing to specify what knowledge and skills students needed to master or develop to survive and prosper in their entry-level courses, although some talked about the importance of generic attributes, such as study skills and time management.

Much has been written about how to run the admissions gauntlet. A veritable cottage industry of books, courses, and private consultants has grown up around what should be a relatively straightforward activity: applying to college. This book is not designed to contribute to the volumes that already provide detailed advice on what it takes to crack Fort Knox and get admitted to America's elite universities. It is not about how to do the right things to get admitted to college but rather about how to do things right in high school so that graduates are prepared to succeed after being admitted. As students spend four years preparing for college, how can they direct their energies to doing things that will not only help them in the admissions process but also equip them to do well academically once they are accepted? Given the time, energy, and ever-increasing dollars that must be devoted to a college education, the time has come to think past admission to academic success.

> **"The time has come to think past admission to academic success."**

This book will help those who teach, guide, assist, and support students preparing for college to know what should be occurring in high school to maximize student college success. At the core of this book is a relatively detailed set of specifications describing what students should know and be able to do to succeed in college. The Knowledge and Skills for University Success (KSUS) standards were developed during a three-year study conducted under the sponsorship of The Pew Charitable Trusts and the Association of American Universities, a national organization composed of sixty of the nation's leading research universities. Its membership list is a who's who of selective universities, twenty-eight of which sponsored or endorsed the standards presented here. The findings were sent to every public high school in the nation in April 2003 in a report entitled *Understanding University Success*. What these standards enable parents, students, and teachers to do is to compare what is occurring in high school classes with what will be expected in university classes.

The book presents four distinct types of information: description of the content knowledge that is important to master; explanation of the broader cognitive skills and "habits of mind" that may be even more important in college than content knowledge; examples of college general education programs, requirements, and student course schedules that were culled from a range of colleges and universities; and finally, documents from real-life university classes, including examples of student work, course outlines, assignments, reading lists, and grading criteria. Subsequent chapters also examine the ways in which the high school experience can be organized to achieve the goal of an intellectually coherent curriculum tied to college success.

It is worth stating explicitly that this book is not intended as a criticism of high school teachers and what they are doing currently to prepare students for college success. In fact, it is likely that many teachers are already doing much of what this book identifies as effective practice. If they were not doing so, no student would arrive in college today with the ability to cope with the demands of introductory courses. As it is, many students make a smooth transition from high school to college, and this is in part due to the efforts of dedicated teachers at high schools who have done their best to offer a challenging education that is well aligned with college admission and success. The book is about the larger system of high school–college articulation and how the high school program of study can better prepare more students for college success.

How High Schools Decipher the College Code Today

Even in schools that succeed in getting large numbers of students admitted to college, a certain amount of doubt exists about what is really needed for college success. And indeed, these schools should have some doubts. The students from the best high schools often go on to the most selective universities, where all the skills discussed in this book are in the greatest demand. These students have the least margin for error when it comes to preparing for college success.

Teachers at these schools decide how to gear their curriculum for college success based on a variety of mechanisms. Of course, they went to college themselves, often to the same selective institutions. They maintain contact with graduates who return to describe the ways in which they were well prepared and areas that could be improved. They may teach Advanced Placement or International Baccalaureate courses specifically designed to connect with postsecondary education's expectations for knowledge in a particular subject. They may even score tests for one of these organizations, and in the process, talk directly with college faculty about their expectations.

These are the lucky ones, the ones who have deciphered the code most clearly. But even these teachers often rely on their instincts when deciding exactly what knowledge and skills to develop in their students, how to structure a course, how to grade student work, and which topics to emphasize. More to the point, precious few schools are composed entirely of teachers with this level of knowledge and sophistication, so the coordination between grade levels or across classes in, say, the school's English department becomes a "best guess" about how to sequence and develop the skills necessary to do well in college. Add to the mix that most high schools now have more than one college-bound track, and providing a program that equips all students to handle entry-level college courses becomes impossibly complex.

In practice, large high schools may end up having one college-prep track that fulfills the requirements of the state university and a second, *real* college-prep track that is designed for students headed to more selective institutions. Perhaps there is nothing inherently wrong with this arrangement, except that many students and parents do not understand the nature of the two-track system and the implications of one or the other.

> **Many students and parents do not understand the nature of the two-track system.**

Even when individual teachers do a good job covering content or developing skills for college success, rarely does the high school's instructional program over four years provide an intellectually coherent experience that cultivates the habits of mind that may be even more important than specific content knowledge. Without a well-designed academic program and curriculum that progresses from ninth through twelfth grade, both in the content covered and the intellectual skills developed, relatively few students will integrate what they learn in high school—find the whole to be greater than the sum of the parts. Many will enter college with pockets of knowledge and skill and then experience difficulty with a curriculum that assumes they already know certain things and can undertake complex cognitive tasks.

The lack of an intellectually coherent program of instruction affects the overall quality and efficiency of preparation. When the English 9 course does not enable students to master what is necessary for English 10, for example, then English 10 may end up being in large measure a repeat of English 9. The net result may be students reworking similar material for two years, and then all of a sudden in their junior year being thrust into a more demanding course. If the challenge level and pacing are not consistent from year to year, then students are not prepared when they reach Advanced Placement courses, for example, where content coverage and mastery is dictated by an external exam. They may avoid AP altogether or struggle mightily adapting to work expectations that are more collegelike in nature.

If the high school–college connection leaves something to be desired at even the best high schools, what is the situation in average schools or those that send few students on to college? These schools have a very difficult time maintaining the level of academic challenge necessary to prepare their students for the rigors of college courses, at least in part because the culture supporting academic achievement is not as well developed in them or as systematically nurtured; in addition, there is little knowledge of what is required for success and it is not widely publicized.

It is difficult for the average high school with little direct information on college practices and expectations to make all the right choices about how best to structure their college preparatory curriculum and ensure an appropriate challenge level in that curriculum. For these schools, which constitute the majority of high schools, the content and challenge level of their college preparatory courses vary considerably. As a result, their graduates vary in the degree to which they are prepared for the demands of college classes.

In Part Two we will examine the nature of the college course of study and its strengths and weaknesses. For now, it is worth noting that high schools have little choice other than to accept the current structure and content of entry-level college courses as a fact of life. Perhaps colleges should change their pedagogy and expectations to match the realities of high schools, but that is not likely to happen anytime soon. It makes more sense for high schools to understand how college courses operate and gear their student preparation accordingly.

Rethinking the Purpose of High School

Many people make the legitimate argument that the purpose of high school is not simply to prepare students for college, that the high school education has inherent value, and that in any event not all students go on to college. This is a powerful argument. This book is not intended to devalue aspects of the high school curriculum that do not directly prepare students for postsecondary education. Instead, it adopts an inclusive perspective by encompassing all forms of postsecondary education. From this perspective, nearly every aspect of the high school curriculum could conceivably be geared to help students prepare for success after high school.

The point of view presented here is simply that if college preparation is one of the purposes of high school, then it should be done as well as possible so that all students who wish to attend college can do so. Given that close to 90 percent of incoming high school freshmen state that their goal is to go to college (although many may not behave that way during high school), the high school program of college preparation should draw on all available information to align itself better with postsecondary success for those students who do ultimately choose to pursue it. Perhaps the key focus in all classes should be life after high school.

> " Close to 90 percent of incoming high school freshmen state that their goal is to go to college. "

More and more students and parents are interested in the degree to which a high school program of instruction is oriented toward college admission, and increasingly, college success. All high schools will be forced to cope with the growing expectation that what they are doing is preparing all their students for college success. Many high schools will find themselves lacking the information, the point of reference, to evaluate how well they are doing this. This book is designed to serve as a guidepost and a frame of reference that teachers and administrators in particular can rely upon while strengthening the connections between high school and college in ways that help more students succeed in college.

Through the Students' Eyes

Throughout this book we will periodically view college preparation, transition, and undergraduate general education from the student perspective to help illustrate how the issues we are discussing actually play out in the lives of young people. We will follow the journeys of three hypothetical students, each a composite of characteristics associated with groups of students who achieve varying degrees of college success. To illustrate the variation that occurs even in a single institution, we assume that all three students attend the same high school.

That school is Westside High, a large comprehensive high school that enrolls nearly sixteen hundred students and is located in a transitional neighborhood in the inner suburban ring of a midsize American city. It has a strong tradition of preparing students for college, and its students have been regularly accepted at some of the more selective universities in the nation. Each year Westside sends a significant number of students to the state's top two public universities and the local community college. Approximately two-thirds of its graduates go on immediately to some form of postsecondary education, with many more attending within several years of graduation.

The composition of the student body at Westside has been changing over the past ten years as the community has become more diverse ethnically and economically. Historically, the community has been home to a largely middle-class group of residents, many of whom worked downtown in professional roles. Many of these families raised their children in the neighborhood and have strong social networks. New arrivals in the community include recent immigrants to the United States as well as families moving in from other states and members of racial minority groups who have relocated from the inner city. The children in these recently arrived families are almost always the first generation to aspire to college, and their parents generally support these aspirations, although they are limited in their knowledge of how to help their children. They depend on the high school to inform them and to ensure their children are being properly prepared for postsecondary education.

Let us begin by acquainting ourselves with our three students as they prepare to enter ninth grade at Westside.

Alicia

Alicia is typical of the students whose families are new to the community. She has a vague idea that she will go to college and is interested in entering the medical profession in some way, but she knows little about what is actually required to achieve these goals. As a freshman, she has one brief meeting with a counselor and participates in a group advising session in which she completes a proposed program of study for her four years of high school. She makes sure she has all the classes she needs to meet local graduation requirements. She is also careful to save space in her schedule for some classes that look like "fun," and to take some business classes, in case she needs to work over the summer or while in college.

As a ninth grader, she is placed into Algebra I based on her middle school math grades. She also takes regular ninth-grade English, geography, a business class, Spanish I, and art. She cannot get into biology because of schedule conflicts, and ends up with a double lunch period. She knows she could be taking a more challenging math class, but she also kind of likes being able to get most of her homework done during the school day.

DERRICK

Derrick is in many ways what people would describe as a typical high school student. He is at least as interested in sports as in academics. His parents moved to the community from the city about ten years ago, primarily for the schools, and Derrick attended elementary and middle school in the district. He has an older brother and sister, each of whom graduated from Westside and went on to college. His brother went to the local community college, where he obtained a certificate in computer-assisted drafting, and he now works for a local engineering firm. His sister is attending a four-year college in the metropolitan area where she is in her sixth year and nearing completion of a degree in political science with hopes of becoming a high school social studies teacher. Her time in college was extended because she had to take remedial courses as a freshman and had particular difficulty with the college writing requirement, although she is now an accomplished writer. She feels that she learned about college readiness "the hard way."

Derrick wants to attend college on an athletic scholarship. Like Alicia, he sets up his schedule largely as he has been advised to do by his counselor during a group advising session. His parents review his schedule and compare it to the courses taken by their other two children. Derrick's goal is to take the minimum necessary to get into college. Also like Alicia, he takes core academic courses, although he begins with a geometry course in addition to freshman English, geography, Spanish, and biology. For electives, he takes tech ed and a computer class. He is hoping to participate in the school's athletic trainer program, which is offered in conjunction with the local community college and lets students serve internships as athletic trainers. He also plans to play three sports this year, which will limit the amount of time he has available for homework.

Teresa

Teresa, our final student, has a laser-sharp focus on her future. She knows she wants to become an aerospace engineer, and perhaps work for NASA some day. She has demonstrated keen analytic abilities all her life and has already participated in a summer camp where she learned about the space program. She knows she wants to attend an out-of-state university, one that will prepare her well for the graduate education she believes she will need to achieve her professional goals. Teresa also has parents who fully support her in this vision. Both are college-educated and work in professional fields. Her mother also arranges her work schedule to allow her to volunteer a half-day a week in the high school's career center, where she helps students prepare to make the transition out of high school. In the process, Teresa's mother has learned a great deal about the college admissions process.

Teresa's schedule looks different from that of the other two students. She begins her mathematics with Algebra II, having been accelerated in her middle school mathematics studies. She is a student in the high school's International Baccalaureate school-within-a-school program. This program shapes her schedule significantly and reduces her options and choices. She has only one elective, and she uses it to continue orchestra, which is offered at a time that allows the many IB students with musical backgrounds and training to participate. She is in Spanish III, having taken two years of Spanish in middle school. The International Baccalaurate curriculum determines the rest of her schedule, which consists of these courses: Global Geography, Global Literature, Cultural Aesthetics, and Global History.

Teresa has set her sights on membership in National Honor Society as well as the full IB diploma and has already researched the community service requirements of both. Through her parents, she makes contact with a local firm with a specialty in optics and a subcontract from NASA, and she inquires about an internship with this company. Last summer she participated in a creative writing workshop where she received instruction from a well-known short story writer. She plans to enroll next summer in another Space Camp, in Alabama, where she will learn more about NASA and the space program.

Each of these students starts high school with the same hypothetical opportunity to prepare for college, yet an observer can already perceive differences in how successful each will be. Unfortunately, the choices they make and those the school makes for them over the next four years will further affect their preparation. We will check back with these students in the next chapter to follow their progress.

Increasing College Success: What We Can Do

Each chapter in Part One of the volume concludes by raising issues and asking questions related to the topics it has discussed. These discussion points also suggest ways for educators and others to begin to make the kinds of changes that will lead to college success for more of their students. Some of the suggestions are quite broad, others specific. The intent is not to offer a detailed, one-size-fits-all action plan. Although an action plan will be necessary, it will have to be adapted to the context of each school.

The brief suggestions are meant to stimulate further thought about the current situation and the assumptions present in a school or school system. The suggestions can serve as tools to gauge the degree to which alignment may be an issue locally. Based on such an analysis, a school staff, in partnership with central administration of the district, might decide to delve more deeply into the alignment issues raised by these questions.

Questions

- To what degree is the high school's program of instruction consciously designed to achieve some specified set of aims versus being the accumulation of historical precedent, tradition, and teacher and community preferences?

- How is the school's program aligned with its purposes?

- Are the purposes conveyed to students and parents?

Actions

Members of the school community can ask these questions to examine the fundamental purposes of the high school education. This can lead them to reconsider the courses offered, their purposes and goals, and the school's culture. The ultimate goal is to be able to articulate clearly and concisely what the high school stands for and what it commits itself to accomplish for all students, and particularly the role of college readiness in the school's program of instruction.

Questions

- How does the emphasis on meeting college admission requirements support or inhibit an emphasis on readiness for college success?

- Who determines which skills are taught in which classes?

- How stable are these skills over multiple sections of courses with the same name?

- How dependent is the instruction in these skills on a particular teacher, and how much do the knowledge and skills taught in the same class change when one teacher leaves and a new one arrives?

Actions

These questions need to be asked because college prep courses can, over time, come to lose their connection with their ultimate goal: college success. To respond to these questions, a more introspective examination of the content of courses is needed, both individually and cumulatively, to determine how they really prepare students to succeed in college. It may be that the courses do have the potential to prepare students adequately, but no one has ever asked the right questions or developed an adequate means to determine which of them prepare for college success rather than just admission. The method most likely to be employed here is content analysis of course syllabi. This method will be discussed later in more detail. At this point, it is most important to consider the purposes for, content of, and variance present in college preparation courses.

Questions

- How are expectations different for different groups of students?

- In what ways do the expectations of all students progress over the four years of high school so that they better approximate college expectations by the end of senior year?

Actions

To understand better the ways in which the high school is challenging different students, student schedules, disaggregated by type of student, must be analyzed. The school should pay special attention to the schedules of students in poverty and those from groups traditionally underrepresented in college. The analysis should note whether students are taking a full load of classes all four years, how many math, science, and social science courses they take, and the number of advanced courses in which they are enrolled. If these students are dramatically underrepresented in key college prep courses, this is strong evidence that the proportion of them going on to postsecondary education from the high school is unlikely to increase in the foreseeable future.

High schools need to examine the college preparation program over all four years to determine its coherence, the connections between classes, the types of cognitive skills developed systematically, and the cultivation of the habits of mind that will enable students not only to succeed academically in college but to get the most out of the experience. These issues too will be addressed in greater detail later. Suffice it to say now that, for a school conducting a general inventory of its goals and program of instruction, these issues are worth considering in general terms during this initial review and then in greater detail as changes are made to the curriculum.

What High School Students Know About College Readiness

Although the connection between high school and college may be tenuous and unclear at times, a great deal of research has been conducted on what high schools do and do not do to prepare students for college and the effects of different forms of preparation. This information is useful to understand how high schools can help students better prepare for postsecondary education, but perhaps is even more valuable for what it tells us about the distance yet to travel to get all students to understand what they should be doing.

The Bridge Project

A study conducted from 1996 to 2002 by the Bridge Project at the Stanford Institute for Higher Education Research gives us some insight into what today's students know about college entrance requirements. The project studied twenty-five high schools in six states (California, Georgia, Illinois, Maryland, Oregon, and Texas), surveying over 2,000 students and a similar number of parents. Illustrative of the findings are the results from its study of 450 students at three high schools in or near Sacramento, California. Students here were similar to those elsewhere in terms of how well they understood what they needed to do to be ready for college. In fact, the California example is probably a best-case scenario, because the structure and requirements of postsecondary education in the state are among the most clearly articulated in the nation. If California students are having difficulties understanding a system with clear distinctions between the University of California, California State University, and community college systems, then it can be assumed that students in states with less clearly hierarchical systems of postsecondary education will be having at least as much difficulty as California students.

Student Aspirations

These three schools were quite diverse in the race and ethnicity of their populations. About a quarter of the students were White, the rest were members of a range of racial and ethnic groups. The income level was predominantly middle class and lower. All students were surveyed, and some participated in focus groups where they discussed in depth their perceptions of what it takes to be college-ready and how they had acquired their knowledge and opinions of college readiness and requirements.

First, the survey asked ninth and eleventh graders to indicate all the types of colleges to which they aspired. At one California high school, researchers found that 20 percent of ninth graders aspired to attend the local community college, but by eleventh grade the number had doubled to 40 percent. The proportion aspiring to the local campus of the California State University system increased by about 8 percent between ninth and eleventh grade, while 51 percent of ninth graders aspired to attend the nearest University of California campus, Davis. This number decreased by eleventh grade to 45 percent, but those aspiring to other UC campuses increased by 10 percent. The researchers found that less than 12 percent of these students knew the course requirements for the selective public university closest to them. As a point of comparison, of students surveyed in one other state in the study, less than 3 percent of them knew the requirements for the selective university closest to them.

These changes in aspirations over time are a manifestation of students being able to assess realistically their prospects for getting into college. The number of students planning on community college increased as more students recognized that they had not taken the course of study required to apply to state universities or that their grade point average (GPA) would not be high enough to be competitive. In fact, the higher a student's GPA, the less likely he or she was to be interested in going to a community college, and vice versa. The "crossover point" for all groups—where aspirations shifted from community college to four-year institutions—was between B– and B. All racial groups were planning about equally to go to community college.

Where Students Get Information on College Requirements

Most students at the high schools studied gained their information about college from their parents and teachers. Although counselors remain a potentially important source of information, more than half of the ninth graders surveyed had not yet talked with a counselor about college. The percent talking to counselors increased to 77 percent in eleventh grade, but by that time most had already made decisions and taken courses that defined their postsecondary options significantly. Older siblings and friends who attended college also were a source of information for those households of which they were a part.

> **"Most students gained their information about college from their parents and teachers."**

It turns out that teachers are very important college advisers. Students get information about state university requirements in particular from teachers as well as counselors. Much of this advising is informal, not necessarily a part of the curriculum or the teacher's responsibility. At the same time, teachers feel unsure about their knowledge of college requirements outside their state institutions. They are even less clear about the content and uses of college placement tests. This affects both the advice they are able to give students and their ability to prepare students for such tests. Teacher knowledge of educational costs and requirements for private and out-of-state institutions tends to be very uneven as well.

Student Knowledge of Curricular Requirements

How knowledgeable are students about curricular requirements for college admission? In 2003, Greene and Forster published a national study of students who had graduated from high school. They determined that only 32 percent of graduates had taken four years of English, three years of math, two years each of natural science, social science, and foreign language, and had reached the "basic" level of performance on the National Assessment of Educational Progress (NAEP). This level of preparation is consistent with potential success in college. However, nearly twice this number of students enroll in college directly upon graduation, according to the U.S. Department of Education, National Center for Education Statistics. Greene and Forster's finding suggests that many students do not fully understand what courses they must take and skills they must develop in high school to become college-ready.

Student knowledge of curricular requirements as determined by the Bridge study varied considerably. For example, 31 percent of ninth graders knew they needed to take three years of math to apply to UC Davis, and 51 percent of eleventh graders were aware of the requirement. The percentage of ninth graders who knew UC Davis has a two-year science requirement was 32 percent, but by eleventh grade only 30 percent could state this correctly. Nearly half of ninth graders, 47 percent, stated correctly that UC Davis has a two-year foreign language requirement, while 54 percent of eleventh graders knew this.

If only half of the eleventh graders knew there was a three-year math requirement for the UC system, this means that the other half may not have planned their high school program of study to include three years of math. Although the UC system is intended for the top 12 percent of qualified students, students who are unaware of course requirements have no chance of getting into the qualified pool in the first place. When students are unaware of complex course requirements and sequences, it is easy for them not to take a course they need or not to remain in the sequence, thereby losing the opportunity to be eligible for admission to certain schools. Such students often find that their options to apply to college are limited because of these choices (and nonchoices). It can come as quite a shock to them and to their parents when they do find out.

> **"Students who are unaware of course requirements have no chance of getting into the qualified pool in the first place."**

Student Knowledge of Placement Test Policies

Although students at these three high schools were fairly knowledgeable about admissions requirements, at least in terms of the number of years they had to take courses in specific subject areas, they were largely unaware of placement test policies and content. Placement tests are important because they determine where in the college curriculum sequence students will begin their studies. Low scores can result in their being required to take remedial work, being barred from certain courses they may wish to take as freshmen, or being required to retake courses that duplicate much of the content they already mastered in high school. Concomitantly, a high placement score can open access to more challenging courses and help a student move through the college curriculum more quickly, efficiently, and economically.

Only 10 percent of ninth graders knew that UC Davis had both an English and a math placement test. That number increased to 24 percent of eleventh graders. Students were somewhat more familiar with the CSU placement test requirements. Seventeen percent of ninth graders knew CSU had both an English and math placement test, and that figure rose to 40 percent by eleventh grade. One problem with students not being aware of the math placement test policy is that they are more likely not to take math during their senior year of high school, and then may do poorly on the placement test because they have been away from math for a year. Further confounding the problem is that placement tests often assess knowledge and skills slightly or significantly different from what is taught in high school college preparatory courses; in addition, colleges do not release the items they put on their tests or otherwise make this information available to high schools. Placement tests and strategies to help students prepare better for them are discussed in greater detail in Chapter Eight.

Student Knowledge of Tuition Costs

When it came to estimating the cost of a college education, students' assumptions were not close to the actual costs. Students were asked in the ninth and eleventh grades to estimate the annual costs of tuition at UC Davis, campuses in the CSU system, and the local community college. Their estimates ranged from an average by ninth graders of $40,000 for UC Davis, when actual tuition costs there were $4,000, to an average by eleventh graders of $6,000 for the local community college, when tuition was $300 at the time. Ninth graders similarly thought that tuition at a CSU campus was $40,000, when in fact it was $2,000. Students reduced their estimates somewhat by eleventh grade, at which point they thought the CSU system cost $20,000. However, these estimates were still at least five times more than the actual costs.

The closest cost estimates came from students at high-performing high schools and students in the highest academic track. African Americans and Southeast Asians had the least accurate (that is, highest) estimates of tuition costs. Students with more accurate estimates also got more information from parents. Those speaking primarily with teachers and counselors were half as likely to have a close estimate.

College Preparation: A Knowledge-Intensive Activity

The bottom line is this: college preparation is knowledge-intensive. Requirements are complicated, and there are often special additional requirements for specific institutions and exceptions for others that are not immediately evident. The economically well-off are more likely to have this knowledge than working-class families or families whose children are the first generation to attend college.

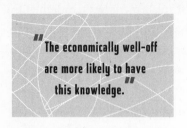

"The economically well-off are more likely to have this knowledge."

Specialized information on admissions testing is needed and often lacking, as is awareness of costs of a college education and financial aid opportunities. Fewer high schools have the resources or programs to make students aware of how to navigate the confusing processes of admission and financial aid. Without such prior knowledge, students frequently have problems registering for tests, miss deadlines, are unaware of test preparation options, or do not take advantage of fee-waiver programs. Lack of knowledge of the true costs of college tends to diminish the pool of potential applicants who believe they can afford college in the first place. If they think college is totally out of reach, they do not even attempt to find out how to apply for admission and financial aid.

The admission testing requirements for the UC system illustrate the problem. In addition to the SAT, students must take two SAT II tests. They also benefit from taking AP courses, which receive an extra weighting when GPAs are calculated, and from taking AP tests, because applicants to the more popular UC campuses need good scores on those tests to have a realistic chance of being admitted. A high school student could easily end up taking six or seven different tests during the junior and senior years, each requiring separate registration, testing dates, preparation, and fees.

The effects of this system are most severe on first-generation students who lack familiarity with the entire process. They often have unrealistic expectations, particularly about the financial aid they are likely to receive. They gain much of their information anecdotally, not through official channels. They tend to change their goals and plans rapidly. Going to college may not have been a lifelong goal, and other family priorities may easily intercede. The choice of institution, in particular, is subject to considerable negotiation and rapid fluctuation.

It takes only one mistake in the entire chain of events for the college application process to derail for these students. Increasingly, even community colleges require students to meet deadlines and complete applications comparable to those of four-year colleges. If they are unaware of these requirements, students can end up being locked out of postsecondary education altogether.

Recommendations for Improving Student Awareness

The Bridge Project study made recommendations for how high schools could help all students, and first-generation college-goers in particular, achieve their goal of participating in postsecondary education.

First, the high school curriculum needs to be simplified so that students cannot make bad choices. In particular, most high school courses should be designed to meet a college requirement. Although this does not necessarily mean eliminating elective programs, it does suggest that even elective courses should contribute to postsecondary readiness. Once again, if postsecondary readiness is defined as including community college, many electives can help more students prepare to succeed, particularly if elective teachers are communicating regularly with and coordinating with their postsecondary counterparts.

> "The high school curriculum needs to be simplified so that students cannot make bad choices."

In addition to making students aware of the knowledge and skills necessary for college success, high schools increasingly have a responsibility to offer programs or access to information that helps students, particularly first-generation college-goers, gain the knowledge and skills specific to the admissions process, primarily admissions testing and financial aid requirements and procedures.

All students should be signed up automatically for the PSAT and SAT, or PLAN and ACT. School time should be allotted during which they can fill out the forms and eligible students can apply for fee waivers. Dual-enrollment programs can give students a taste of college work while still in high school, and often get them onto a college campus, thereby making the college experience more real. More high schools and even some states are making Advanced Placement tests available to all students who wish to take them, thereby increasing the pool of those who may earn college credit while in high school and making more students competitive at a wider range of colleges and universities.

Volunteer-staffed career centers located in or near counseling centers are a popular mechanism to create access to college information in cash-strapped districts. Some high schools build career-planning units into the curriculum, using this time to make sure all students conduct college searches and research requirements. It is a gradual, difficult, and continuous process to ensure that high school students are aware of what it takes to be admitted to and succeed in college.

These highlights from the Bridge Project's more extensive findings are meant to illustrate some of the issues and challenges students face as they prepare for college and that high schools face as they seek to prepare students for college. The first lesson is that college preparation in the United States is knowledge-intensive, and much of that knowledge is not readily available in one place. Parents with several children who attended college will tell you that, for the first child, they were at the mercy of others for information. They had to sort out what was accurate and important from what was inaccurate and unimportant. They had to learn a whole complex set of requirements and deadlines. They had to figure out how an entire system operated. By the second child, they were much more confident. This works fine—as long as the family has access to necessary information to help avoid mistakes with the first child and also has a second child who can benefit from lessons learned with the first. Many families do not conform to this model and suffer as a result.

> **College preparation is knowledge-intensive, and much of that knowledge is not readily available in one place.**

Many parents do become experts in how the system operates, but the Bridge Project research found that, in general, knowledge of the entire college admissions process is more prevalent among the more privileged. High schools have few systematic means to ensure that all students have this knowledge and even fewer resources to devote to those who are most in need of it. This study focused only on basic admissions information and did not investigate challenges associated with admissions tests (for example, the SAT and SAT II), including student registration problems, knowledge of deadlines, preparation options, fee waivers, or the entire financial aid process, including the infamous federal Free Application for Financial Student Assistance (FAFSA). When these are added in, it becomes clear that navigating the shoals of the admissions process requires a map or a pilot.

Although high schools are somewhat limited in their ability to tackle this problem alone, they are aided by the increasing availability of information on the Internet, where new one-stop portals are cropping up with increasing frequency. These Web sites offer information on and links to other sites covering admissions and financial aid as well as many other aspects of college life (and many commercial products designed to help in one or more of the areas featured by the portal). Several important Web sites at which to begin to gather information include the College Board (creators of the SAT, PSAT, and AP tests) and ACT (formerly

American College Testing), the U.S. Department of Education financial aid site, the Princeton Review (an organization devoted primarily to test preparation), and the Pathways to College Network.

Thanks to this availability of information, more and more parents are becoming competent in the admissions process. Some may be willing to help out in a volunteer capacity, even after their own children have left high school. Some realize what a waste it is to spend so much time and energy developing this needed knowledge and then not share it with others. More high schools are turning to parents and other volunteers to staff career centers that provide college admission information, in addition to resources on careers and other options.

As long as education in the United States continues to be divided into secondary education controlled by some fifteen thousand local school districts and postsecondary education consisting of over four thousand distinct institutions with independently developed requirements, new high school students and their parents will have to be educated each year in the workings of this complex system. Each year roughly one-quarter of the high schools' student body graduates, and all their knowledge of the admissions process goes with them. The schools must then start over with a new group, who need to learn all the same lessons. High schools are not well equipped for this challenge in an age when education funding for services such as college counseling is being reduced while at the same time more students are setting college attendance as a goal.

The task was easier when only 20 to 30 percent of students chose college right out of high school. These students had their own well-defined, separate curriculum taught by teachers who often worked only with the college-bound. High schools even had one or more counselors devoted strictly to college counseling, writing letters of recommendation, being in touch with admissions officers, remaining current on college admissions information, and the like.

Now, far fewer high schools offer any of these services. Counselors may cycle with students through four years, and as a result, go several years without needing to keep up with new college admission issues and information. Counselors are assigned so many students that they become acquainted primarily with those aggressive enough to seek them out or troubled enough to demand their time and energy.

> "Counselors are assigned to so many students that they become acquainted primarily with those aggressive enough to seek them out."

With the (thankful) elimination of low-level English and math courses in many high schools as a result of state education reforms, nearly all courses may now bear titles that allow them to meet college entrance requirements. But they may not be rigorous enough to prepare students for college success. As a result, ownership for college prep may be everywhere and nowhere in today's high school.

Through the Students' Eyes

The students we met in Chapter One—Alicia, Derrick, and Teresa—are now completing ninth grade and preparing for tenth. They have many issues to consider as they make their choices.

Alicia has enjoyed her freshman year. She has never spent more than an hour or so a night on homework, which has been fine because she has been able to help out her parents with their business in the evenings or baby-sit for her younger sister.

When it comes time in the spring to sign up for sophomore classes next fall, she fills out her schedule largely based on what her teachers tell her to do. She does not do well in Algebra I, and her teacher suggests that she re-take it before moving on with math. She could try again to get into biology, but her friends tell her how hard it is, so she finds a general science course that will fit her schedule and allow her to be with many of her friends. She did quite well in English, and her teacher suggests an honors course, which she considers briefly but then abandons when it conflicts with a business class she wants to take. As a result, she decides to continue in regular sophomore English and American history, which are required of all sophomores. She found Spanish boring, so she decides to take a year off foreign language study; this will allow her to continue the double lunch period that has worked out so well this year.

When she reviews her new schedule, it seems to her that she will be taking a full load. Her parents spend about five minutes with her going over it. They ask her what her teachers and counselor thought of it. Although she had not actually talked with a counselor, she implies that everyone thinks the schedule is fine. Based on this general assurance, her parents approve the schedule and sign the form the school requires for the schedule to be processed.

DERRICK

Derrick has had a great ninth-grade year, at least as judged by his athletic performance. He has tolerated his coursework and managed B's for most classes, with a couple of C's and an A in tech ed. He wants to lighten his academic load even further next year, but his sister, on a visit home, rings the alarm bell with his parents, who insist he drop by the career center and at least get some information on the NCAA requirements for eligibility for athletic scholarships. With this information in hand, he devises a schedule that will keep him on track to meet his local high school graduation requirements and NCAA regulations, although he does so in a very half-hearted fashion.

Here is a peek ahead to Derrick's sophomore year. By about three weeks into tenth grade, he has figured out that the geometry course he is taking is graded in a way that is so dependent on homework assignments that he can get D's on the tests and still get a low B for the course. He figures out that he can do his math homework during his first period English course when he is supposed to be discussing course readings or rewriting the short essays that the students are to write every several weeks. The system works well enough, but he has a distinct feeling of panic when the first big test approaches and he realizes he does not really understand any of the math concepts he has been taught; he can only complete certain problems that conform to certain patterns. "Oh, well," he thinks. "I can still get a C here and not have it be a problem. Besides, this is the last math class I'm going to have to take, since I've already met the graduation requirement, and I think it's all the math I need for college admission, too." He means to check if he is correct in this last assumption, but he does not get around to it.

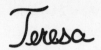

Teresa

Teresa's freshman year has been a whirlwind of activity, in many ways not unlike her middle school experience, which had been packed with extracurricular activities and participation in special events and activities in addition to her accelerated classes in math and foreign languages. There are few mysteries in her sophomore schedule either. Most of it is relatively predetermined. The IB diploma requirements include Global Literature II and the Arts, Comparative Values and Belief Systems, and the Global Independent Project.

On top of these, she considers adding an honors chemistry course, in anticipation of an AP physics class junior year. Her main concern with her choice of science courses is maintaining her 4.0 grade point average. Should she take the honors chemistry course, whose instructor rarely gives A's, or the regular chemistry course, where she will be pretty much assured an A? She and her parents ponder her strategy.

Her parents do a bit more investigation to find out how much value an honors course will really have on her transcript. They consult a friend who has connections in the admissions office of a private college in another state and ask her to pose the question there. They also seek the opinion of a private consultant who helps students prepare college admission applications and essays. Although they had not intended to contact the consultant until the summer between Teresa's sophomore and junior years, they know that the difference in course titles on a transcript is important. Furthermore, they have in mind that Teresa could take a college chemistry course during her senior year as well at a local college, if this will help strengthen her position.

This information-gathering goes on for two weeks, during which time the family has several discussions about the pros and cons of each strategy in the context of Teresa's overall planned program of study. In the end, they choose the honors course, but not before a subtle conversation with one of the school's assistant principals to inquire about how to appeal a grade.

During this time, they become even more familiar with terms from the admissions world, such as "indexing," "two-stage review," and "comprehensive review." They find out what the average SAT score and GPA are for incoming first-time freshmen at several of the colleges in which Teresa has shown an interest. They also check cost and financial aid policies, where they learn about "need-blind," merit-based policies, and when and how to fill out the FAFSA.

They also review the sequence of admissions tests and decide to have Teresa take the PSAT during her sophomore year primarily as a practice, having learned that the scores for PSAT tests are not communicated to college no matter how many times it is taken, whereas colleges now get the scores for all SAT tests a student takes. Better for her to learn about the format of admissions tests on the PSAT, they think, and then take the SAT only once or twice. They decide to enroll her in a test-prep course offered by a retired counselor who had been Westside's college counselor for many years before that position was eliminated in budget cuts.

Increasing College Success: What We Can Do

Increasing students' knowledge of what it takes to succeed in college requires an ongoing effort by everyone involved in their schooling. Getting this information equally to all students will require a reorganization of roles in the schools and an acceptance of responsibility by them for ensuring that all students make the right decisions and take the right actions to become college-ready. Here are some key questions and suggestions for ways to approach this complex and multifaceted challenge.

Questions

- How aware of college entrance requirements are middle-school students and their parents? How are they made aware of requirements?

- Who is responsible for ensuring that students have the necessary knowledge to make appropriate decisions?

Actions

Middle schools should determine how well eighth graders who are preparing their high school schedules know the basic course requirements for admission to the state's public university system. To accomplish this, class time will need to be allocated or group meetings with counselors will need to be scheduled to project the eighth graders' high school schedule over four years. High school and middle school counselors should organize and conduct such advising sessions jointly. To check student knowledge, a brief quiz on college admission requirements should be administered shortly after the planning session, with students provided the correct answers immediately after completing the quiz. The school should tally the quiz results each year to determine if student knowledge of college requirements is increasing. If it is not, the school should consider including an advisory period for second-semester eighth graders to orient students to high school and college requirements and help them construct schedules designed to enable them to be postsecondary-ready by the end of high school.

Questions

- How do students choose their high school courses?
- Are students prepared to make intelligent choices about the courses?
- Do parents understand the implications of choices made?

Actions

Several states have moved in the direction of establishing a "default" high school curriculum. If a high school pursues this strategy, the default curriculum should consist of courses required for admission to the state's public university system. All incoming students should be enrolled in such a curriculum unless their parents specifically opt them out of it. The high school should ensure that the opt-out options are equivalently challenging. When combined with enhanced middle school orientation, advising, and preplanning, fewer students are likely to have schedules that inadvertently prevent them from being college-ready.

Questions

- Where do students learn about college requirements?
- How does the high school ensure that those students least likely to be knowledgeable about college requirements gain the necessary information?

Actions

High schools can develop much more systematic, required programs on the intricacies of college knowledge. Such a unit, in which all sophomores would be required to participate, would include the following: information on admissions testing and sign-up deadlines; course requirements for admission to more selective and less selective postsecondary institutions; costs for a public or private postsecondary education, including examples of common forms of financial aid; placement testing policies; ways to earn college credit while still in high school; and typical college freshman schedules at a number of colleges and universities.

Question

- How can students explore postsecondary choices to become familiar with the range of options open to them and to understand what they must do to be able to take advantage of those options?

Actions

Given the limited availability of counselors, high schools can transfer some of the responsibility for doling out college information to career centers, where students can access information on postsecondary education options and requirements. Such centers may be staffed by individuals who are knowledgeable about what it takes to succeed in college, not just admission requirements. Some of these individuals may be volunteers or hourly workers, including retired educators and conceivably even students from local colleges who first receive some additional training from their college. The ever-increasing availability of information on the Internet and specialized computer software to help students select colleges helps support the work of volunteers and makes it less necessary to rely exclusively on counselors, who can still play a pivotal role overseeing the career center as well as the traditional role of meeting with individual students who need personalized guidance.

All students could access the career center at least annually through required assignments in language arts classes to conduct research on various aspects of college requirements. The career center, in partnership with the school's library media center, would be the primary resource for students to complete the research projects.

Questions

- To what degree do teachers know the requirements of the state's public colleges and universities?

- To what degree do teachers know the specific knowledge and skills associated with student success in college courses?

Actions

Given the pivotal role teachers can play in the college advising process, schools need to determine how well-prepared their teachers are to advise students on college entrance requirements. Closely related is the understanding teachers have of the knowledge and skills students must master for college success.

To improve their knowledge, teachers should be provided annually with a packet and list of Web sites with key information on requirements for admission to local and state institutions. This information should be briefly reviewed annually at a faculty meeting where teachers are also provided data on how well recent graduates of the high school have fared in postsecondary education, including how many enrolled in some form of postsecondary education and how well those who enrolled performed in entry-level college courses in English, math, and science.

The Old and New Criteria for College Success

chapter
THREE

When it comes to college admission, everyone is familiar with the basics. Students must take certain courses, receive adequate grades, and for selective institutions, take and score acceptably on admissions tests. This system, by its very familiarity, lulls many into a sense of complacency and a belief that students who meet the standards are ready to succeed in college. This is not necessarily the case, however, as figures documenting remediation and completion rates indicate. How did we arrive at this situation, and what can high schools do differently now to help more students prepare for success, not just admission?

The Evolution of Admissions Criteria

The high school college preparation program traces its roots to the late nineteenth and early twentieth centuries. The basic structure of the American high school was largely locked into place by the 1920s, when some 5 percent of high school students routinely went on to college. These were mostly from the upper economic classes, and although entrance tests were given, merit-based admission was not a dominant concept. The purpose of higher education, particularly in the Ivy League schools, was as much to develop the character traits necessary to assume one's destined position of leadership in society as it was to acquire academic knowledge and skills or economically marketable skills.

In such an environment, academic readiness for college success was determined as much by the preparatory school the student attended as by the courses taken and the grades received. Courses varied greatly in title and content, number of sessions, length of time of sessions, and grading scales. Gradually, through the efforts of the Carnegie Corporation, the Carnegie unit began to standardize both high school and college course length and titles. The Carnegie unit came to be defined most basically as one class meeting daily for fifty minutes per day for thirty-six weeks. The Carnegie Corporation allowed schools and colleges that agreed to use the Carnegie unit to become members of its pension plan, TIAA-CREF. Over time, this process led to the course titles and requirements that have become so familiar, as well as the length of the school semester.

As standardization spread among high schools, colleges were better able to judge the suitability of high school courses for their admission purposes. The process of approving course titles and their attendant value in Carnegie units became the dominant form of quality control that colleges applied to the high school college prep curriculum. To this day, state university systems still have some form of high school course approval process in place to determine which course titles can be used to meet their entrance requirements.

However, the course approval process was never a very effective means to control the content, challenge level, and grading practices of college prep courses. Those courses varied dramatically then and continue to vary today, even among schools in the same district. This phenomenon is a result of the highly decentralized governance structure of U.S. public K–12 education, where school boards in over fifteen thousand local school districts make final decisions on instructional policies, programs, and practices. This local autonomy is highly prized and jealously guarded.

In addition, each high school can establish the goals and purposes of its instructional program and how it chooses to accommodate the aspirations of the students it is responsible for educating. Some districts delegate authority to each high school to determine its academic program, but even in those that do not decentralize these decisions, little direct oversight exists. Therefore, in practice, schools and individual teachers are largely free to do as they please when it comes to course content, expectations, grading practices, challenge level, and alignment with college success criteria. This is often described as being responsive to the local community.

As long as there was no requirement or compelling need for all students to be equally prepared academically for college and comparable economic opportunities existed for those who did not go on to college, this kind of variety was relatively harmless. However, in the post–World War II educational system, near-universal high school graduation became a key goal. The high school graduation rate, as measured by several U.S. Department of Education longitudinal studies, increased throughout the twentieth century, rising from around 5 percent at the beginning of the century to something above 80 percent by the end. More students were thus eligible for college, and more set their sights on college. College attendance exploded in the late 1940s and early 1950s in response to the G.I. Bill, and it has continued to increase ever since.

In this new educational environment, academic accomplishment is at least in theory more important than economic class background or the prep school one attended as a prerequisite to college participation and success. As universities have seen their applicant pools expand, the admissions process has become much more focused on well-prepared students. Unfortunately, colleges have not provided any greater insight into what constitutes a well-prepared student, even though their course and grade point average requirements have gradually increased.

> **"Academic accomplishment is at least in theory more important than economic class."**

University admissions processes long assumed that most applicants came from relatively similar academic programs—the college prep program or school. But this began to change as more students from a wider range of high schools and economic backgrounds began to apply to college. The proliferation of the college preparatory track into essentially all American high schools by the late 1950s helped create an ever-expanding pool of students who applied to college in record numbers. High schools were encouraged in the 1950s by influential higher education leaders to become more "comprehensive" in nature. In practice, this meant that all large high schools offered at least three curricular tracks: vocational, general education, and college preparation.

As the number of college prep courses increased, so did the variation in content and quality among them. No longer did a cadre of teachers handpick those who would be allowed entry into the necessary courses. This increase eventually led to differing challenge levels even among college prep courses. Students could choose from regular, honors, and Advanced Placement courses in the same subject area.

The combination of more students seeking to attend college and more high schools offering college prep programs of study led to gradual changes in the admissions process, which increasingly emphasized academic preparation, high school achievement, and scholarly merit. State universities in particular began to rely on *indexes*, which combined student grade point average with their score on a national admissions test, such as the ACT or SAT. When scores on a combination of the two measures met or exceeded a designated threshold, the student was admitted without further examination.

Private colleges and universities continued to rely on somewhat broader criteria, searching for well-rounded students who possessed a variety of characteristics valued by the institution, and of course, the all-important "legacy" applicant, whose family members had previously attended the institution. Here as well, though, academic competence became an increasingly important component of all admission decisions.

The 1980s saw an acceleration of the competitiveness and emphasis on academic achievement. This occurred in part because many states implemented high school reforms requiring students to take an increased number of academic courses. At the same time, many high schools abandoned the experimentation with curriculum, schedules, and grades that had occurred since the 1970s and returned to traditional academic models.

As the reforms of the 1980s steered more students into classes that met college entrance requirements, the number of students professing college as their post–high school goal grew dramatically. Student GPAs continued to rise, a trend that began in the 1960s and persists to the present day. Meanwhile, SAT and ACT scores dipped in the 1970s, leveled out in the 1980s, and began a slow, small increase in math in the 1990s while English scores remained relatively unchanged.

The increasing number of students who met GPA and minimum course requirements caused university admissions officers to pay closer attention to the composition of the high school transcript and the number and type of academic courses that applicants took. Next, they scrutinized more closely the challenge level of the academic courses. Were they honors courses? In what other ways did the students demonstrate intellectual rigor? Gradually, more weight was placed on Advanced Placement (AP) courses, and more recently, on the International Baccalaureate (IB) program. The effect of increased emphasis on AP has been particularly striking. An outstanding student in the mid-1980s might have taken one or two AP courses. Now, the transcripts of comparable students commonly contain five or six such courses.

What the AP program and later the IB program possessed were course content geared to college course expectations and external examinations, which were not graded by the classroom teacher at the school where the students took the course. The advantage for admissions officers was that these exams provided an externally referenced judgment of academic performance that was independent of the GPA and class rank, both of which were becoming less reliable measures of absolute academic achievement, although they still worked reasonably well as a means to identify the very best students.

State academic content standards, developed in the 1990s for the most part, could conceivably have been a tool to help align the content of college prep courses and the desire of colleges for the best-prepared students possible. However, almost without exception, the standards that states developed did not connect with postsecondary success. State standards development processes were geared toward creating "well-educated citizens" and ensuring that all students were prepared to enter the workforce, not necessarily college. The standards were not anti-college; they just did not give college much thought. The result has been that state standards and their accompanying assessments have had little effect on the college preparatory curriculum and have not necessarily served to increase the number of students who are prepared for postsecondary education.

> **Almost without exception, the standards that states developed did not connect with postsecondary success.**

Although about three-quarters of all postsecondary institutions admit all qualified candidates, only a third of admitted students graduate in four years from the institution in which they enroll as freshmen, according to data from the National Center for Education Statistics. The data indicate that well over six hundred thousand students each year leave college before receiving a degree or take longer than four years to graduate. The *High School and Beyond* study found that remediation rates at all but the most selective institutions approach the 40 percent mark, with over 60 percent of community college students who wish to participate in a college transfer program having to take at least one remedial course. Somewhere along the line, students are not getting the message about what they need to do to succeed in college, although they do figure out what they need to do to be admitted.

What the Research Shows to Be Most Important for College Success

According to the *1998 High School Transcript Study* and the *High School and Beyond* study conducted by the federal government that followed students through high school and college, the single most important factor in determining college success is the academic challenge of the courses students take in high school. This is particularly true for students from racial and ethnic minority groups. African-American and Latino students' college degree completion rates are more positively affected than that of any other group by a high-quality, academically intense high school curriculum.

> **"The single most important factor in determining college success is the academic challenge of the courses students take in high school."**

The subject in the curriculum that is most predictive of college success is the level of mathematics completed. Students who take a course beyond Algebra II, for example, such as trigonometry or pre-calculus, are more than twice as likely to graduate from college than those who do not. Students who take a mathematics course during the last year of high school and then another immediately in the first year of college are more successful in the college math course than students who take a year off from mathematics in high school or wait to resume math studies in college until after the freshman year. In other words, continuity is important in mathematics. In addition, success in college chemistry and physics is affected by students' math skills. An interruption of math in high school can have large-scale ripple effects when a student reaches college.

These findings, although useful, do not illuminate the specific knowledge and skills that students require. How important, relatively speaking, are all of the things students are taught in high school math, for example? Are problem solving and mathematical reasoning more important than number sense and measurement, or are they equally important? What elements of algebra are key foundational elements that must be mastered to do well in other branches of mathematics and other college courses outside of mathematics? What about other key subjects and skills? How well are students expected to write? What kinds of writing are they expected to do? How important are research skills? How are they judged? What are the expectations associated with college courses in literature, humanities, science, history, second languages, and other disciplines? (These questions will be addressed throughout the rest of the book as the outline and elements of a standards-based system for college success are introduced in the next several chapters, the specific knowledge and skills are enumerated subsequently, the first year of college is examined in detail, and finally, examples of students' work and tasks from college classes are presented.)

In English, research conducted by Clifford Adelman for the U.S. Department of Education in 1999 validated the importance of four years of courses in this area but did not address issues of content or sequence. Although essentially every college has long required four years of high school English, none specifies what must be included in those course titles as they do for mathematics courses.

Although high school English courses vary significantly, many emphasize literature, poetry, and expressive writing. Significantly less time is spent on expository writing or informational texts. High school English is currently taught largely by teachers who majored in English in college themselves, and it seems to be designed with college English as its reference point, not broader literacy preparation for success in college more generally.

To understand what students should learn in English, we must move beyond the 1995 federal *High School and Beyond* study and the 1999 *Answers in the Toolbox* report of course titles and make our first foray into the Knowledge and Skills for University Success (KSUS) findings on those required in entry-level college courses.

According to this research, the high school language arts curriculum should be clearly focused on reading progressively more complex and challenging books and texts from a wide range of literary traditions and textual styles. Deep understanding of a few texts, not all of them necessarily literary, in addition to awareness of the characteristics of a wide range of publications, can help prepare students for the type of analysis they will be expected to undertake in college. When students engage in a four-year sequence of language arts courses that is carefully designed around and focused on expanding their repertoire of skills to analyze literary and informational texts, they acquire more of the tools and habits of mind they will need to succeed in entry-level college courses across the disciplines.

Writing is one of the great challenges. For someone to learn to write, that person must write a lot. He or she must also receive feedback on the quality of the writing. This is time-consuming and particularly difficult to manage for high school teachers, who find themselves stretched thinner as they are called on to enable more students to meet state standards without concomitant increases in resources. Writing often suffers when class size

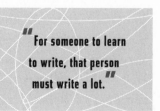

"For someone to learn to write, that person must write a lot."

grows larger. Students write less, or they learn primarily how to mimic state scoring rubrics, what some call "six-paragraph writing."

More important from the perspective of college readiness, students may not fully comprehend how complex and challenging it is to write well. They may never grasp how difficult, time-consuming, and demanding it is. Accustomed to receiving A's on all their writing assignments and little or no critical feedback, they are shocked when they receive a C on their first college writing assignment, along with copious feedback on the paper's deficiencies.

How Too Much Choice Can Be a Bad Thing

Perhaps the greatest pitfall for high school students is the range of course and scheduling choices available to them. This is not generally perceived as a problem of great magnitude by students or even their teachers. It can be, however, when it results in students making poor choices or choices that close off their options when they did not intend to do so.

The philosophical position that students should be allowed to choose their own path through high school can be traced to the comprehensive high school movement of the postwar era. Ironically, the primary proponent of the comprehensive high school was James B. Conant, president of Harvard, who saw it as a way to accommodate all types of students in one institution of secondary education but most surely not to prepare them all for college. *The American High School Today,* his 1959 publication, was highly influential at a time when high school enrollments were burgeoning and more students than ever were graduating.

> **The choices they made as freshmen or sophomores often constrained their college options.**

Conant's concept, as adopted by many school districts, led to high schools where students had significant latitude to construct the schedules they wished. Although many students took advantage of the choices available to them to construct interesting and stimulating programs of study, many more sought to avoid difficult and challenging coursework. Because relatively few students then (as now) truly understood what was required for college admission, the choices they made as freshmen or sophomores often constrained their college options or even took them out of the running for college admission altogether.

To this day, many students construct schedules with uneven academic content, particularly in the twelfth grade. When these students fail to take math, science, second language, or other core academic courses in their senior year, they either fail to become eligible for college or struggle when they next attempt one of these courses in college. Ironically, choice has come to limit rather than increase options for many high school students who wish to go on to college.

Through the Students' Eyes

Let us check in again with our three students who are journeying through high school, picking them up as they move through their junior year. This is an all-important time because it is the last full year for which high school grades are reported to admissions offices when students apply to college.

Alicia seems to be doing less and less homework each year. When her parents ask her about this, she tells them that she is getting it all done at school. Her grades have been a mix of B's and C's, with nothing to indicate a real problem, and her parents have not heard anything negative from teachers or school personnel, so they have assumed that everything is going well. In any event, Alicia is a wonderful daughter, which is how they see her on a daily basis. They believe she will go to college. Does not everyone who wants to go to college in the United States get a chance to do so? Is not that what high school does—prepare children for college?

Alicia has found herself most interested in courses that enable her to remain with the group of girls and boys with whom she has become close during the past two years. As someone new to the community, this affiliation has been particularly important. These students have selected classes based on how much homework they would have; the less homework, the better. They also like classes where they can socialize to some degree. They have favored an array of elective courses that became open to them when they completed their high school diploma requirements of two years each of math and science. Alicia has been quite content with her schedule, although even she has noticed she has hardly been writing at all anymore. Once when she tries to remember a concept from algebra—the commutative property—she realizes that math knowledge tends to slip away without frequent use and review. But she is not worried about that right now.

DERRICK

Derrick is getting through high school on charm and a smile. He can be counted on in class discussions to crack up the class with his imitations of teachers and other students. He can be seen in the lunchroom and commons chatting casually with his teachers as they pass by. Everyone knows him, and most folks like him.

One of the fringe benefits of this status is that Derrick has gotten a little help along the way. Although no one has ever changed a grade for Derrick or let him get by with lesser work, he has been helped in many small ways to "just get by." For example, he has been allowed to make up work at the end of the year to raise his grade and to file papers as a form of extra credit. He has learned the fine art of not putting any more effort than is necessary into schoolwork. His older sister catches wind of this approach and tries to get her mother and father's attention after failing to get Derrick to wise up. But his parents take the attitude that Derrick's grades are good enough to get him into college. Where is the problem with a "get along, go along" attitude in high school? In short, no one has a real handle on what Derrick knows and does not know. And since he has not really gotten interested in anything outside of sports, it has been even more difficult to determine whether he might need more knowledge and skill in any one area in order to be able to succeed in the future. He does his homework, more or less, does not cut classes, and gets decent grades—which is much more than can be said for a lot of kids, his parents believe.

Derrick has known that the SATs are important because he has to achieve designated minimum scores in order to meet NCAA eligibility requirements. Yet amazingly, when the time to take them approaches, he does almost nothing to prepare. He borrows an SAT test prep book from the career center about two weeks before the test, largely because he has seen a number of his friends with copies of it. When he does take the test, many questions seem strange and some appear unusually easy. He leaves the test not knowing how to judge his performance, but in talking with friends who take the test he is relieved to find that they have similar reactions. He assumes his scores will be "good enough" and does not sign up to take the test again.

Although he has heard from a couple of colleges informally, there has not yet been the rush that he had anticipated to have him declare his intentions. He feels sure his senior year will be the capper to his career and at that time he will get the attention of the big universities where he wants most to play. He feels confident that college will more or less take care of itself if he can just keep improving his athletic performance as he has done over the previous two years.

However, by late in his junior year Derrick's dream to make it to a Division I NCAA school begins to derail. Although he has excelled on his high school teams and a number of colleges have expressed interest in him, none are Division I. He is good but not that good, it seems. This presents him with an unanticipated dilemma. He is not really all that interested in attending college if he cannot be part of the "big time," and neither he nor his parents have done much planning for this eventuality. Should he go to college, and if he goes, should he play athletics at an institution where he will not be on a scholarship or on a path toward a professional career?

Teresa

Teresa's junior year has been her hardest, which is saying something considering how challenging her first two years were. All her academic courses this year are either AP or IB, with the exception of music, so she is well prepared for the high-stakes tests associated with these courses that are administered in a short period of time during the spring of her junior year.

She has really worked on her time management and on determining where she should put her energy. She has realized that she is not a great writer but is determined to improve her writing, because she knows writing will be important at many points on her road to NASA and her goal of participating in the space program. Her solution is relatively simple: she asks her parents to read all of her writing and to edit with a sharp pen everything she writes. At first this results in some hurt feelings, because she thinks her writing is better than her parents apparently think it is, particularly her mother, who majored in English literature in college and has written extensively throughout her career. Once the initial conflict subsides, however, Teresa notices that her work begins to take on greater clarity, that her word choice is expanding, and that she is describing details more precisely. This measurable improvement in her writing encourages her to write even more, although it does not prevent her from relapsing periodically into her old practice of putting off a paper until the last minute and then writing in "stream of consciousness" style, which was her problem to begin with. What is frustrating for her mother is that Teresa's teachers do not seem to grade these papers much differently than those where she demonstrates better writing fundamentals.

Although her days are full, she decides it is important to volunteer in the math center to help students who need tutoring. This will help her get the community service hours she needs for National Honor Society and International Baccalaureate. This will also keep her familiar with basic algebra and geometry, which are emphasized on the SAT and ACT. These are not her only motivations, though. She also thinks it will be fun, because she has heard from a couple of her friends who have already volunteered that they enjoyed it.

Increasing College Success: What We Can Do

The structure and content of the high school program of instruction is critically important to college success. The program can be designed in ways that help students make good decisions, ensure that they learn the right content, and help them develop the habits of mind necessary to succeed in postsecondary education. The following questions and suggested actions can help a high school consider how well it achieves these aims.

Questions

- How much variance exists among the classes that make up the college preparatory curriculum?
- Do differences reflect valid choices about different ways to master the knowledge and skills needed for college success?

Actions

Examining differences between courses in a department or across departments is one of the more challenging tasks to undertake in a high school. This activity should not be attempted unless a level of trust and agreement exists among faculty committed to work to improve college readiness at the school.

Assuming such conditions are in place, the analysis process can begin in a relatively general fashion. Subsequent chapters describe more detailed analysis techniques. However, the first activity can be to make a simple inventory of the key goals, objectives, and content covered in each college prep course. This information can be displayed in tabular format without identifying individual faculty or mandating one way as the correct way. Eventually, agreement will have to be reached on the correct way, but for now it is sufficient simply to note the range of approaches employed, content emphasized, and conceptions of the purpose of each course that is analyzed.

Questions

- Do teachers employ grading techniques that encourage students to master the requisite skills for college success and to mature intellectually, rather than simply to complete the assigned tasks?

Actions

Grading practices are the ultimate expression of decentralization and are difficult to discuss. Here again, the goal initially is to catalogue techniques rather than anoint one method as the correct one. The ultimate goal is to institute quality control measures to ensure that grading practices are consistent schoolwide and are connected to performance levels, so that a grade means roughly the same thing regardless of the class in which it is earned in terms of mastery of content knowledge and development of key cognitive skills needed for college success.

Part of the challenge in moving toward the agreement that grades will focus on academic performance is to define which measures will be included and which will not. Elements of the grading system that are really measures of behavior and attitude more than performance are particularly suspect. Reaching agreement and definition in this area will require considerable discussion of the desired performance levels and the acceptable assessment techniques that can contribute to a grade and will likely lead to a general set of grading criteria as well as much more public accountability for grading practices.

As already noted, algebra and writing are key foundational skills for college success. The grading criteria in these areas in particular need to be clear, consistent, and linked to mastery. It is even possible to incorporate measures of these areas beyond the courses where they are initially taught, so that students receive continuing feedback on their knowledge of algebra in subsequent math and science classes and their skills as writers in the social sciences, for example. If grading criteria for these key areas are consistent schoolwide and are developmental over four years of high school, students will seek to continue to consolidate and master these skills.

Questions

- How much writing and what kinds of writing are students expected to produce in any given semester and over the course of four years?

- How is the quality of writing expected to develop in complexity and mastery of conventions?

- What styles of writing are developed and emphasized?

- What kind of systematic feedback do students receive on their writing and ways to improve?

Actions

Evidence suggests that high school and postsecondary faculty have different perceptions of what is most important in student writing, with high school teachers favoring student expression and postsecondary faculty emphasizing mastery of conventions as a platform for expression. The differences may not be as great as they appear in survey results, but few high schools have developed comprehensive writing expectations that span disciplines, courses in a discipline, and grade levels. Such an instructional framework for writing development can be a key component of improving student readiness for college.

Faculty can begin by conducting an inventory of the number of pages students usually write each year and over four years. The inventory should also enumerate the kinds of writing assignments students are given in order to determine if the writing skills being taught are consistent with college success and if there is a reasonable balance between developing expression and mastering conventions. In the senior year, writing assignments should begin to parallel entry-level college courses in frequency, length, and performance expectations, as will be outlined in later chapters of this book.

Having completed the inventory, faculty should identify at least one writing assignment each year on which students will receive detailed feedback and that they will be expected to rewrite and resubmit, based on the feedback. The assignment should be scored against the same criteria schoolwide, and student performance on the assignment should be reported cumulatively and compared on a yearly basis.

Doing this will require detailed planning on where the necessary skills will be taught, where the assignment will be required, who will score it, and how teachers will be trained to score reliably. All of these activities, however, will lead to a more integrated, articulated writing program.

Questions

- To what degree are the courses contained in the language arts sequence actually a developmental curriculum?
- What skills are systematically developed over four years?
- Which language arts skills must also be developed or supported elsewhere in the curriculum?

Actions

Considering the importance of reading and writing across the college curriculum, the high school language arts sequence is critical to college success. However, seldom are these courses designed as a true sequence in which skills are developed systematically at a mastery level and built upon subsequently. In fact, often teachers do not coordinate between language arts courses.

Several steps can be taken to transform language arts classes into a more coherent curriculum. Much of the reading in college is informational texts, not literature, and students receive little formal instruction in language arts courses on reading informational texts. One key activity is to determine where in the curriculum students are taught and evaluated on their skills with informational texts. If the amount of instruction is inadequate, an interdisciplinary task force will need to determine how the responsibility for teaching how to read informational texts is apportioned throughout the curriculum and what role language arts courses will play in teaching these skills.

Equally important are the core readings to which all students are exposed throughout the course of four years of language arts instruction. These need to be selected carefully and systematically and agreed on by all language arts teachers so that instruction systematically builds with each subsequent piece of literature. The most desirable works are those that can be referenced in other classes or that help students gain insight into broader social, cultural, philosophical, historical, and scientific issues. Such a list can be developed at the district or individual school level. College literature syllabi can serve as valuable reference points when judging which readings should be included at each level of the high school curriculum. These syllabi are available through the Web site associated with this book (http://www.s4s.org) or directly online from many colleges and universities.

Current Strategies to Increase College Readiness

Although the point is made throughout this book that the connection between high school and college in the United States is not well articulated, educators are resourceful people and they have devised many programs and strategies to link the two systems. Faced with the necessity of inventing connections between two educational systems that do not have many, they have been remarkably innovative.

How Nongovernmental Organizations and State Programs Bridge the Gap

Admissions-testing organizations are important innovators in connecting high school and college. The two most dominant are the College Board, makers of the SAT (formerly the Scholastic Aptitude Test or Scholastic Assessment Test and now just an acronym), the Preliminary SAT (PSAT), and the Advanced Placement (AP) tests, and ACT (formerly American College Testing), which offers the ACT admissions test and other admissions-related assessments. Independent of state and federal government and controlled by large nonprofit organizations, such entities are not found in other countries, where government control over college admissions testing is the norm. Both of these organizations have gone beyond admissions testing to develop programs to facilitate the transition between high school and college. The College Board has a long history of providing courses of study designed to smooth the transition through its Advanced Placement program, which introduces college-level work into high schools. ACT offers a sequence of tests, EXPLORE, PLAN, and ACT, that are to be taken in eighth, tenth, and eleventh grades and provide students with ongoing information on college readiness while they can still do something about it through the courses they choose to take. Other innovations, such as the International Baccalaureate program, postsecondary options programs that allow students to begin taking college courses while still in high school, and more recently, early or middle college high schools, also seek to enhance college readiness and success by offering collegelike experiences at the high school level.

Advanced Placement

The Advanced Placement (AP) program has been offered by the College Board since the late 1950s. It has been one of the most readily available means for high schools to increase the academic challenge of their college prep curriculum. Advanced Placement offers thirty-four courses in nineteen subject areas that have several advantages over classes such as high school honors courses. First and foremost, each of these courses is linked to an AP examination. The exam is designed to test student knowledge and skill up through what is needed in the first year of college study. Many colleges acknowledge the high challenge level of AP exams by awarding credit or waiving certain prerequisite course requirements for students whose scores on the exams reach designated levels.

" More than three-quarters of a million high school students take over a million AP exams annually. "

More than three-quarters of a million high school students take over a million AP exams annually, and the number is increasing at a dramatic rate.

The exams themselves are an interesting and challenging combination of multiple-choice questions and more complex tasks that involve extended writing or problem solving. The results from the two exam components are combined into one score on a five-point scale. This format favors students who develop mastery of content knowledge and key concepts as well as analytic and writing skills consistent with college work. Therefore, AP courses that are properly taught improve students' readiness for college success rather than simply allow them to earn college credit. This creates an incentive for AP teachers to build a challenging curriculum clearly focused on the knowledge and skills necessary for college success.

Advanced Placement has its own culture. The College Board offers training for those who teach or plan to teach AP courses. This training helps teachers understand the expectations associated with each AP course. Teachers can also compare teaching techniques and strategies during these sessions. Many AP teachers also are trained to score the exams, which are administered annually. These training sessions become a form of professional development; teachers read student work from around the country, which helps them gauge better the performance of their own students, and talk with colleagues about best practices in their classrooms.

The cumulative effect of the AP program, when it works properly, is to create a set of standards in each AP classroom that is calibrated against the AP exams. Ideally, this supports relatively consistent teaching and expectations across all AP classrooms. The exams reinforce this course uniformity. This is the closest U.S. education comes to a common program of instruction.

However, this is a best-case description of AP, one that requires several pieces to be in place for it to occur. First, AP teachers must have deep content knowledge of the subject they are teaching. The courses put greater demands on them to understand their subject area and be able to explain more complex concepts to students than do traditional courses.

Second, teachers must be committed to orienting their instruction toward the AP exam. Because many college and university admissions officers value AP course titles on a high school transcript, high schools may be tempted to offer AP without encouraging or requiring students to take the exam or without concern for how the students will score on the exam. This can lead to a curriculum in an AP-titled course that is decidedly not AP in nature, with the result that few students take or pass the course's AP exam.

Third, the courses should be open to all students who might benefit from them. Some schools restrict admission to AP classes based on teacher recommendations or grades in particular courses. Evidence compiled by the College Board suggests that schools that set strict prerequisites for AP enrollment exclude many students who could benefit from AP.

Advanced Placement courses also face two challenges when it comes to fitting into the typical high school's curriculum. Courses at most high schools are designed as a sequence through which the typical student will progress, and this sequence does not lead to an AP course. Overlaid on the sequence are honors courses, which may exist at each grade level or only at the end of the sequence.

Advanced Placement takes students who have completed the typical sequence in an accelerated fashion or stands in place of the terminal course in the sequence. Thus, a large high school may have senior English, honors English, and AP English all existing in parallel. Although there is nothing inherently wrong with this arrangement, it does result in different expectations for students at similar points in their intellectual development.

> "A large high school may have senior English, honors English, and AP English all existing in parallel."

Another limitation of the AP model is that, although each individual course is challenging, collectively the courses lack coherence. The very strength of AP—its focus on one course of study and an associated exam—is therefore also potentially its greatest weakness. When students take three, four, or five AP courses in succession, nothing in the design helps them make connections among these experiences. They work hard in each course, but their efforts are not necessarily complementary or connected across disciplines. Writing skills learned and tested in one AP class are not necessarily employed in another. Ways of knowing and thinking necessary to excel in one area of study do not readily transfer to another. Teachers who teach AP in one disciplinary area are not expected to coordinate instruction with those who teach AP in other areas. In fact, it would be difficult to have them do so.

Similarly, the work done in high school classes taken before the AP course may not necessarily prepare students for the rigors of AP. It is not uncommon for students to experience difficulty in an AP course, not because they are intellectually incapable of mastering the content but because they have not been expected to work at that level or pace before.

High schools do not usually design their four-year instructional programs to be intellectually coherent. The focus is more on content coverage than on student development; classes and requirements do not consciously develop student cognitive abilities or key learning skills. However, when AP courses are given as capstone courses at the end of a carefully designed sequence that develops students' key knowledge and skills, these classes can help ready the students for college success. The advantage of conceiving AP as a capstone for the curriculum is that the entire four years of the high school experience can then be aligned and organized around students progressively mastering core skills and concepts. Many of these are identified in the Knowledge and Skills for University Success (KSUS) standards, which are presented and discussed in detail in Chapters Ten through Sixteen. These standards can be introduced in ninth grade and developed each year, culminating in AP courses that reflect entry-level college course expectations.

Particularly important are the KSUS foundational skills, the higher-level cognitive capabilities that are critical for college success. A well-conceived high school curriculum that focuses on these foundational skills can use AP courses to cultivate critical and analytical thinking and problem solving, for example, across the entire range of AP courses offered. Such an approach helps create coherence among AP courses and gives a focus and intellectual integrity to the overall high school program of instruction.

When the high school program is well-designed and coherent, it accomplishes two goals. First, all students achieve some mastery of the core KSUS skills over the course of their high school education. Even if they do not go directly to college they benefit, because they acquire the foundational knowledge and skills that they can develop further at some later date. In essence, the door to college participation will be held open a bit wider for these students. Second, teachers can connect assignments and assessments. This way, they can ensure that all students are aware of the key skills for college success and understand that the mastery of these skills is necessary to succeed across a range of courses.

In consequence, one of the key drawbacks of the AP model—namely, that only a limited percentage of students get access to the courses, and by implication, gain knowledge of what is required for college success—is overcome. All students pursue college readiness as they proceed through high school. In addition, when students do take AP courses, they are ready for them, intellectually and in habits of mind. Neither the courses nor the exams in which they culminate are overwhelming to the students. The transition from high school to college is smoothed for all students, and postsecondary success becomes more likely.

Thus, although Advanced Placement will never meet the needs of all high school students or become the means by which all are made college-ready, it can help high schools create challenging, coherent programs of instruction. When AP courses serve as the capstone for an integrated, coherent curriculum, there may be significant changes in all subject areas, but perhaps most in English and social studies, two subjects where less agreement exists about content to be taught and skills to be developed. In other areas, such as math and foreign languages, a clearer focus

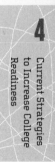

may result in different skills being emphasized to a greater degree in the sequence of courses. For AP to succeed as a capstone, there must be significant curricular reengineering as well as a willingness among faculty to work together to agree on the key knowledge and skills each will develop and how expectations will increase as students progress through their four years at high school.

SpringBoard

SpringBoard is another product of the College Board, which, in addition to the AP program and tests, also offers the SAT and PSAT tests. SpringBoard, however, is not a test. It is an integrated college-readiness program that includes standards that describe what students should know and be able to do from seventh through twelfth grade in order to be prepared for college, provides instructional units of increasing complexity to develop the key knowledge and skills they will need for college success, and offers diagnostic testing at all six levels that lets students and teachers alike know if the students are on track in developing the college readiness skills they will need.

The program is based on the College Board Standards for College Success. These are organized in six levels, spanning middle and high school education.. They can be an important tool for school districts seeking to ensure that college preparation appropriately begins in middle school to put students on the path to achieving full college readiness by the end of twelfth grade. The College Board Standards for College Success include many of the key elements of the Knowledge and Skills for University Success standards.

SpringBoard sets a level of expectation and challenge that is consistent across all educational environments where it is employed. In this way, an entire school can calibrate its curriculum to a common and appropriate standard of college readiness. This is especially important in schools or school districts that have not historically sent a large proportion of students to college. In such settings, expectations are often based on assumptions about what students are capable of or interested in doing. Over time, these assumptions can become self-fulfilling prophecies as students fall to the level that is expected of them. SpringBoard ensures that the key components for college success, such as writing and reasoning, are being developed systematically in all courses where the program is in place.

> **"** An entire school can calibrate its curriculum to a common and appropriate standard of college readiness. **"**

Because the SpringBoard program also includes professional development and continuing online assistance to teachers via "mentors," it can serve as the vehicle for whole-school improvement in institutions that do not have the resources to support large-scale projects of this nature. The school and school district do not have to create and staff a major design effort and develop necessary materials or conduct training sessions. Thus, SpringBoard can be a tool for small schools and low-performing schools in particular that wish to implement a set of high standards tied to college success.

By using an "instructional loop," teachers can build cycles of instruction around the College Board Standards for College Success. The instructional loop consists of a model unit of instruction where student skill and progress are gauged through embedded assessments and diagnostic assessments. These two types of assessments in combination allow teachers and students to know with greater certainty how well students have mastered content knowledge and grown cognitively. This complete program of instruction provides a framework in which teachers can express their individual creativity. They can also adapt lessons for the needs of specific student populations without straying from the key standards. Teachers can have greater confidence that students have been taught specified materials, and more detailed diagnostic assessment tells them how well students know the taught material. This allows for clearer focus on the key knowledge and skills necessary for college readiness.

ACT Testing Sequence

ACT offers a unique sequence of tests to help students gauge their college readiness and general academic skill. Beginning with the EXPLORE test in eighth grade, students receive feedback on their skills in English, reading, math, and science. Then in tenth grade, student take the PLAN test, which is the precursor to the ACT test, which is required by many colleges for admission and which most students take in the junior year or early in the senior year. These three instruments allow students to gauge their readiness for college and make better decisions about the courses they should be taking throughout high school, and even in middle school.

In combination, these instruments make up ACT's Educational Planning and Assessment System (EPAS), which is designed to provide longitudinal information on student readiness for college. The program has four components to help educators ensure they are working to prepare students for postsecondary success. Student planning is facilitated with tools that help students identify their career and educational goals and develop plans to pursue them. Teachers are provided support material to help students make the necessary transitions from middle to high school and from high school to college by connecting results from the three tests with the ACT Standards for Transition and linking these to the classroom. The three assessments, EXPLORE, PLAN, and ACT, generate the critical data on student performance to help inform school decisions on instruction. Finally, an academic information management and monitoring system provides teachers and administrators with data on student academic progress relative to EPAS levels.

International Baccalaureate

The International Baccalaureate (IB) began operation in 1970 as a means to meet the needs of students who moved between various countries as they completed their education. The IB is designed to lead to a diploma that will be accepted and valued in many countries, each of which has its own national education system. The IB Diploma Programme can be a stand-alone high school program or the culmination of a three-program sequence offered by the International Baccalaureate Organization, with the other two occurring at the middle and elementary levels. The IB Diploma Programme was designed to address issues of specialization required by some national systems and the breadth expected in others without attempting to replicate any particular national system.

> "The IB is designed to lead to a diploma that will be accepted and valued in many countries."

IB emphasizes a broad general education that results in mastery of basic knowledge and critical thinking skills necessary for university studies; international understanding that creates citizens committed to a more peaceful, productive world; and student choice in a balanced framework. The program particularly emphasizes the development of habits of mind and ways of knowing that may be more important for college success than any specific disciplinary knowledge. Over four hundred schools in the United States currently offer the diploma program.

IB epitomizes the coherent curriculum focused on postsecondary success. At its core are three key elements: the extended essay; the Theory of Knowledge course; and a commitment to creativity, action, and service. These are expressed as requirements at various points in the program. The curriculum itself consists of six groups:

- First language, including the study of world literature
- Second language, including modern languages and classical languages
- Individuals and societies, including history, geography, economics, philosophy, psychology, anthropology, business, and information technology
- Experimental sciences, including biology, chemistry, physics, environmental sciences, and design technology
- Mathematics and computer science
- The arts

The IB program at the high school level is concentrated in the junior and senior years. In addition, as already noted, the two other IB programs—the Middle Years Programme and the Primary Years Programme—extend the IB curriculum down into the earlier grades. Although schools are free to offer their choice of IB courses, the nature of the high school IB program requires traditional high schools to commit to creating what amounts to a school within a school. The IB program is more intellectually coherent than the program of instruction in the remainder of the high school. Contributing to this coherence is a series of tasks students must complete as they move through the program that require them to integrate and reflect on what they have been learning. Two of these, the Theory of Knowledge course and the extended essay, are in addition to the exams given at the end of the IB course sequence.

The Theory of Knowledge course is interdisciplinary, drawing on both pragmatic and philosophical aspects of teaching and learning. Students learn to think about knowledge differently, to consider the limitations of the knowledge systems that they have studied in earlier courses and reflect on the more fundamental truths and knowledge on which many areas of study are based. The course encourages students to question and examine everything they have learned elsewhere. They must write an essay of twelve hundred to sixteen hundred words on a topic selected from among ten prescribed by the IB organization. Students also make a ten-minute class presentation and write a self-evaluation in which they describe their presentation and answer questions provided by the IB organization that vary from year to year.

The extended essay is a four-thousand-word (maximum) paper that requires students to investigate a topic of interest and become more familiar with methods of research and standards of writing associated with university-level study. Students conduct research and write the essay outside of class time. Usually, students either research a topic of interest (chosen from one of twenty-two subject areas) or analyze or critique a piece of literature (chosen from fifty literature classes). They are supervised by an adult, usually the IB teacher, as they plan and manage this complex task but are on their own to complete the project successfully. The essay is assessed based on general criteria related to the appropriateness of the research question and the cognitive sophistication and quality of the analysis and presentation, which is weighted double, and on how well the chosen topic is managed in the context of the subject matter being researched. Several raters may score the essay, including teachers at the school and community members trained in the scoring criteria.

The IB Diploma Programme has a community service requirement as well, which is designed to get students to interact with their communities and test their capabilities in real-world settings. They give back to the community even as they learn more about themselves and develop the maturity and self-directedness they will need to succeed in postsecondary studies.

In addition to these school-based requirements and a set curriculum from which IB schools must select their courses (or develop their own syllabi for approval), the IB is built around external end-of-course exams that align with the major courses. Students may elect to take none, one, some, or all of the exams. To receive the "full IB," students must pass exams in six subject areas. Passing an exam in a particular subject yields a certificate in that area. Students are free to select the areas in which they wish to take an exam. Many colleges award credit for each exam that a student passes with a score of four or higher on a seven-point scale.

There is much more to the IB Diploma Programme than can be explained in the brief summary here. The curricular requirements in particular are designed to balance breadth and depth. They anticipate well university general education requirements. In fact, many IB students describe their first year in college as one in which they encounter little for which they are not prepared intellectually. A quality IB program, properly implemented and managed, can be a powerful experience that prepares students well for the transition to postsecondary education.

Dual Enrollment and Postsecondary Options

According to the Education Commission of the States, all states except three have instituted some type of program that allows high school students to enroll in courses that carry both high school and college credit. The courses may be offered at the postsecondary institution, taught on the high school campus, or offered on the Internet. In some states, the course must be taught by a college instructor; in others, high school teachers may teach such courses. The main attraction for high school students and their parents appears to be financial: if college credit can be earned while the student is still in high school, this may ultimately decrease the total cost of a college education. In addition, needless to say, admissions officers look favorably on transcripts that contain evidence that a student has already completed college work successfully.

Other reasons exist for students to participate in these courses, however. Dual enrollment courses, particularly those taught on a college campus, give them a realistic picture of what will actually be expected of them in college. When they take a college class on a college campus, they can precisely gauge their own readiness to take on college-level work. Can they handle the pace and intellectual demand? Can they function effectively in a classroom in which they will be more anonymous than they were in high school? Can they accept being in an environment where many other people are as talented and knowledgeable as they are? Can they manage their time outside of class in ways that allow them to complete assignments successfully? All of these lessons may be learned when they take a college course while still in high school.

> "Dual enrollment courses give a realistic picture of what will actually be expected in college."

As already noted, another variation on this approach is to have college classes taught on the high school campus, often by a postsecondary faculty member but sometimes by a high school teacher. This approach is particularly efficient, because students do not need to move physically to a new campus to experience a higher level of challenge. The practice does raise questions about what constitutes a high school course as opposed to a college course and the differences between the two. But it is beneficial because it familiarizes students with the academic demands of such courses without their having to cope with the cultural changes or scheduling and transportation problems involved in going to a college campus for instruction.

4

Current Strategies to Increase College Readiness

One issue that is rarely addressed systematically is grading criteria. Unlike AP and IB courses, these courses have no agreed-upon or common assessments. The result is that individual teacher judgment predominates. If the course is taught by a college faculty member at the college, high school students taking it will be graded as college students are. If it is taught on the high school campus, students may be assessed against the standards of high school work. This variance in assessment leads to a concomitant variance in student knowledge and skill that is greater than in courses linked to external assessments, such as AP and IB. As a result, colleges and universities around the nation may have greater concerns about what a grade earned in some dual enrollment courses really means.

In addition, although some states have well-defined criteria for participation in dual enrollment programs, others have no criteria at all, leaving it up to students alone to determine their readiness for college and the courses that might be most useful to them. However, as more students participate in dual enrollment programs, colleges and universities are learning how to accommodate them better, although some do so grudgingly. Most colleges have someone responsible for enrolling high school students and coordinating their participation and providing information on which courses are open to them under what circumstances. Some even go so far as to offer advising and support to high school students who come to their campus. These institutions see it as in their interest to have high school students succeed and feel positive about their campus, the goal being for them to enroll eventually as full-time students.

Since forty-seven states offer some form of dual enrollment or postsecondary option program, it is likely that any high school can offer a dual enrollment option. The trick is integrating the dual enrollment option into the college prep curriculum. Do the dual enrollment courses meet student needs that the high school was previously unable to meet or do they inadvertently compete with the high school's own curriculum? A well-sequenced dual enrollment program will provide students with an additional goal and help them point their high school program of study toward taking a college-level course during the senior year.

Ideally, the faculty from the high school and the postsecondary institution will meet and coordinate each other's programs so that the last high school course the students take aligns with the entry-level course at the postsecondary institution. High school teachers can then provide assignments and cover material of increasing complexity and cognitive challenge in the exit-level high school class, knowing that the college course will pick up where they leave off, providing students a smoother transition through the dual enrollment program.

Early, or Middle, College High Schools

A recent phenomenon aimed at increasing student success in college and easing the transition to postsecondary education is termed the *early college high school*. Based on the premise that high school students are often ready for college-level work, the early college high school incorporates the equivalent of the first two years of college study into the last two years of high school so that students graduate with both a diploma and an associate degree.

> "Early college high school incorporates the equivalent of the first two years of college study into the last two years of high school."

Early college high schools are often located on two- or four-year college campuses so that students can take college courses easily and conveniently. This arrangement creates certain cultural challenges, but they have in practice proven quite manageable. Students who participate in early college high school programs tend to be interested in progressing academically and not as concerned with some of the social aspects of high school; indeed, such schools lack the normal activities commonly associated with high school, such as prom and homecoming.

It is perhaps in part for this reason that early college high school programs have been favored by children whose parents are recent immigrants to the United States or who otherwise may be underserved at the traditional high school. These students are not necessarily the highest academic performers in traditional high school settings, but they prove quite capable in the early college high school structure because they are motivated and focused in their pursuit of a college education.

These programs raise an issue that also comes up with dual enrollment programs: What is a high school course and what is a college course? Particularly when high school students take high school classes on a college campus or college courses on a high school campus, it becomes more likely that the lines between high school and college courses begin to blur. Some may argue that this is a good thing, but the underlying issue remains. What is the distinguishing factor between the two?

Here is another place where a clear set of standards associated with entry-level college courses can be helpful. If the content and challenge of entry-level college courses can be determined with some precision, it becomes much easier to distinguish between a high school and a college course. This is particularly important when college credit is awarded to high school students. How can the postsecondary

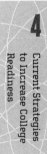

4

Current Strategies to Increase College Readiness

institution ensure its quality standards so that a college credit continues to mean something? A systematic process to determine the standards a course meets helps determine if it is properly a high school or college course.

The Knowledge and Skills for University Success standards can be a particularly useful resource here. These standards specify knowledge, skills, and cognitive challenges, so they clarify what students need to do. When accompanied by student work samples, the standards illustrate in even greater detail what college-level work looks like and how it is different from high school work. This helps faculty and students in each institution design learning experiences appropriate to the students' assumed level of intellectual development.

Early college high schools have great potential because they allow for a truly seamless transition from secondary to postsecondary education. Whether they will ever appeal to more than a minority of high school students is not yet clear, for they lack the social and cultural elements that define the high school experience for most. They have already demonstrated that they fill an important niche for students who do not fit into the traditional high school well and want to move more quickly to life after high school. These schools can also teach regular high schools important lessons about how to articulate the curriculum so that the high school and college experiences become more continuous and the transition from high school to college is less abrupt.

The Alignment and Challenge Audit

How can a school know if its curriculum is properly aligned with college expectations and sets the right level of challenge? Currently, this is largely a matter of opinion among faculty members in the school. However, with the availability of standards that identify what it takes to succeed in entry-level college classes, it is now possible to analyze the content of a high school's curriculum against these standards to determine the degree to which it develops the necessary knowledge and skills.

The Alignment and Challenge Audit is a methodology that was pioneered by the University of Oregon's Center for Educational Policy Research and created as an extension of research conducted to develop the KSUS standards. The process gathers and analyzes data on the content of the college prep curriculum at a high school or group of high schools and compares this content to the KSUS college success standards. Key course documents are analyzed to determine how well the curriculum, as represented by the documents, matches up with college success standards. The degree to which the curriculum enables students to meet these standards is a measure of the degree to which the high school is preparing them for postsecondary success.

The Alignment and Challenge Audit also helps identify the gap between the espoused curriculum—that is, what the school says it is doing—and the enacted curriculum, or what teachers are actually doing. The enacted curriculum occurs in private and is not subject to review or examination. As a result, it is much harder to articulate the high school curriculum; teachers may reteach material students already know and disagree about what knowledge students should master in each course as they progress through the curriculum.

"Teachers may reteach material students already know."

Several steps are involved in the audit. First, the school submits key information from each college prep course, including course outlines and syllabi along with course objectives, and where they exist, the prerequisite learning needed to succeed in the course. In addition, tests and assignments are submitted along with grading criteria to determine how performance is judged. The main topics covered in the course textbook and any supplemental readings or materials are also collected. Representative examples of student work from major assignments or papers are included whenever possible to provide a more holistic picture of how the program of instruction is expressed in student learning.

This first step, collecting information, is not as straightforward as it may seem. Many high school courses do not clearly document in writing what they are attempting to accomplish, or what knowledge and skills students need coming in or will master by the end. Grading systems are point-based but rarely provide much insight into the specific cognitive skills being assessed. Even knowing the course text tells less than one would wish, since the teacher may only use parts of it or may supplement it with materials that do not show up on the syllabus. Almost no district has a common template or format for writing course outlines and syllabi, so teachers' practices diverge widely. In addition, some teachers view their course outlines as private property and are fearful about making them public, believing they may be subject to some sort of judgment or even punishment. A few classes do not have even a minimally informative outline or syllabus.

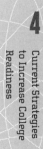

4

Current Strategies to Increase College Readiness

After all the available data are collected, the audit process converts the accumulated documents into electronic form, enters them into a database, and codes them on a number of dimensions, including subject area, course title, grade level at which the subject is taught, and other similar information. The documents are then ready for online analysis, at which time they are rated by university faculty members who have been trained to make reliable judgments about the elements of a course that align with or fail to align with the KSUS standards. The raters look at two dimensions of each document: First, does it align with one or more KSUS standards, and if it does, at what cognitive level? Second, is it at a sufficiently challenging level to set students on a pathway for college readiness if the skill is mastered as stated in the document or demonstrated in the work sample?

These judgments yield profiles or maps of each subject area by accumulating the scores from the courses in that subject area. Although it is certainly possible to examine how individual courses align with college success, the most important determination is how well the instructional program as a whole does so. The profile identifies areas that are covered well and those where students would not receive adequate instruction or would not be challenged at a sufficient level.

Armed with this information, a school-level task force can make recommendations for curricular and instructional changes, at the course, department, and school level. The intent is to adjust the total instructional program so that all students receive an appropriately challenging education that prepares them for postsecondary education and lifelong learning. Annual updating allows faculty to gauge the degree to which alignment is being achieved. The online database of all course outlines and assignments may be used in several capacities, including inventorying the amounts and types of writing being assigned. This ability to examine courses across disciplines also opens the door to better interdisciplinary planning, such as coordinating assignments between physics and calculus classes, or developing humanities-type assignments that link language arts, history, and art.

What schools often discover when they go through the Alignment and Challenge Audit process is that no one is really responsible for teaching students how to read informational texts. Similarly, the use of charts, graphs, tables, and visual aids is not specifically addressed in the curriculum, and instructors often assume that students know how to cope with these devices. Knowledge of statistics may be assumed in some courses, but few students actually master basic concepts of statistics. Math instruction may reteach basic algebraic concepts in several different courses. This is not a bad thing if the lessons are designed in an intentional fashion to deepen understanding of the concepts, but such intentionality is not necessarily present and students may end up simply reviewing material they already know at some level. Students are often assumed to have mastered basic concepts of number sense and measurement, but this may not be the case in practice.

Of course, the audit does more than discover problems or even suggest opportunities. It also identifies areas of excellence and places where the curriculum is appropriately aligned and balanced to support college success. This act of affirmation alone may be reason enough to conduct an audit, because faculty often go literally years without knowing for certain how well their classes are truly addressing college readiness. This celebratory dimension of the audit can also be shared with the community (and even the students) to help instill confidence that what students are learning is appropriate and necessary.

Through the Students' Eyes

Our three students are now in their senior year, a time of hope and dreams, but also a time for taking stock of the options available to them. Each is coping with the challenges of preparing for the impending transition from high school to college—and from child to young adult—in a different way.

Alicia

Alicia's grades level off during her senior year. By now her parents are no longer looking at her schedule or even paying much attention to her grades. Although they still want her to go to college, they do not know what to do to get her to do the things they imagine must be necessary to achieve that goal. Should her grades be better? When and where should she apply to college? Are there forms to fill out to get financial aid? Is the family even eligible for financial aid?

At the same time, they continue to appreciate Alicia's help in the business and with the younger children. They did not push her when she decided to take a reduced schedule in her senior year because she was well on the way to meeting the local graduation requirements. She needed only an English class and U.S. government to graduate. During the year, she also takes a

peer-counseling course where she works with freshmen and sophomores who are having problems outside of school. Her fourth class is titled Office Assistant, and she does quite well in it thanks to her positive attitude and experience helping in her parents' business.

Alicia misses the deadline for the SAT, and the college application process seems overwhelming to her. She makes an appointment with her counselor to try to figure out what to do next, but the meeting somehow ends up becoming a review of her transcript to verify that she has met all the high school graduation requirements. She never gets her questions about the college application or financial aid processes answered. She goes into the career center several times, but she is never sure what the volunteer staff there actually do, so she takes copies of college promotional material and that is as far as the process goes for her.

Her parents continue to believe that the school will make sure their daughter does everything she needs to do to go to college. After all, is this not a school that sends most of its graduates to college? Had not Alicia signed up for the college preparatory schedule as a freshman? Would not someone let them know if things were not going well?

DERRICK

When the full realization of his situation dawns on him sometime during his senior year, it occurs to Derrick that he has inadvertently made all the right choices necessary to keep the college option open. He is scrambling now, because he realizes he will have to select the college that will have him, not necessarily the one that he might want. His grades are good enough for him to apply to the state university in a neighboring community, and he meets its entrance requirements for courses taken, but his sister counsels against such a choice. She knows that Derrick will get lost in a large school and will have a difficult time with a curriculum that would be much faster paced than what he is used to. She feels he needs a campus with some support systems to help him develop more fully the skills he needs to succeed academically and where he can perhaps plug some of the holes in his content knowledge by taking remedial courses.

After a family meeting, Derrick decides he will apply to a Division III liberal arts college out of state in addition to the local state university. The out-of-state school is small, it touts the support it provides to incoming freshmen, and it appears that his family will be eligible for some amount of financial aid, including reduced tuition, loans, and work-study for Derrick. His sister cautions him that he will not be able to get away with studying twenty minutes every other day as he has done through much of high school, but Derrick just smiles as if to say that everything will be all right.

Teresa

Teresa somehow survives the second semester of her junior year, which includes three AP exams, two IB exams, and her first attempt at the SAT. When she receives her AP scores, she is pleased to learn she has gotten all fours, which will most likely qualify for college credit. Her IB scores are comparable, a five and a six on the seven-point IB scale. She is reasonably certain she will receive college credit for these scores, but that has little effect on the composition of her senior year schedule.

She continues in the IB curriculum, which includes Twentieth-Century Global History, Twentieth-Century Global Literature, Theory of Knowledge, Senior IB Research Project, and a community service apprenticeship in the area of global information and communication systems. The only problem is that she has already completed the entire high school math and science curriculum sequence, which means she has three basic choices.

She can shorten her schedule, as Alicia has done. She can take some elective courses, as Derrick has done. Or she can pursue additional challenges, academic or otherwise, in and out of the school. She chooses a combination of the latter two. She takes the painting and sculpture course that has interested her for several years but never seemed to fit into her schedule. She also takes advantage of her state's dual enrollment program to take a course entitled Physics for Scientists, which is offered by the local community college. This more advanced course will give her a better idea if she really wants to pursue the intensive science studies in college that will be necessary if she remains committed to a career in aerospace. Her summer experiences at Space

4

Current Strategies
to Increase College
Readiness

Camp have already helped her get a good idea of what is really required for such a career.

She also manages to devote considerable energy to her IB senior project, an innovative examination of new techniques astronomers around the world are using to share data to find planets orbiting distant stars. The project gives her a chance to apply some of what she has been learning in her science and math classes and further develop her increasing interest in telecommunications systems. The research project's large written elements allow her to put her much-improved writing skills to good use. Although the project takes up evening and weekend time, she enjoys the challenge as well as the opportunity to meet the various members of the scientific community she consults or contacts via the Internet on various aspects of the project. She even has an e-mail exchange with a former astronaut whose background is in stellar cartography.

Fall of her senior year is taken up with college applications, for which she and her parents work out a plan. She follows much of the advice so readily available from numerous publications, and even meets once with a professional college admissions adviser, who assures her she has done everything right. She allows adequate time to compose the essays required by some colleges and is quite pleased that she has been working most of the past three years to improve her writing, which now has a clear voice. She actually enjoys the reflection and introspection some of the essays invite. She is also able to complete the applications with little difficulty, because she and her mother have kept meticulous records of everything she has accomplished. The process, although time-consuming, is not unpleasant. If anything, it is an occasion for a celebration of her achievements in high school.

The schools to which she applies are all ones where she will be challenged academically and also be able to engage actively in learning. She seeks environments where students are encouraged to express and justify their opinions, question conventional wisdom and explore complex topics, and undertake significant research even if they might fall short of total success. She has a pretty good idea of what college is like and what will be expected of her, and she is not threatened by the choices she faces or the complexity of the college selection and application process.

She knows she will be successful in college and is looking forward to it. She is ready.

Increasing College Success: What We Can Do

Many of the strategies high schools use to improve college readiness today require schoolwide action. Examples include the IB program, early college high schools, postsecondary options programs, and taking the Alignment and Challenge Audit. Some strategies are more departmentally based, with Advanced Placement courses being the best example. The actions suggested here to increase college success begin with those that can be conducted on the departmental or school level, and then go on to include several that are schoolwide.

Question

• Are the AP courses the logical culmination of a sequence of courses, or do they stand separate from the rest of the curriculum so that few students are properly prepared to attempt them?

Actions

Advanced Placement courses are added to a high school curriculum for a variety of reasons, including parental pressure and individual teacher preference or interest. Rarely do high schools formally design their program of study so that it leads to AP courses in a systematic fashion.

A school can begin by conducting a formal inventory of the number and type of AP courses it offers, then determine their relationship to the courses that precede them. The goal is to discover the underlying logic and structure of the curriculum to determine its ability to get large numbers of students to high levels of learning.

Questions

• Are there bottlenecks that prevent students from moving along to AP-level courses?

• Are some AP courses missing?

• Who is participating in AP courses and tests?

• What trends can be identified in terms of the types of students in AP courses?

- Do students feel unprepared? If so, why?

- Can study groups be organized or encouraged outside of class?

Actions

These issues can be addressed by reviewing the number of students taking AP tests as a percentage of all students enrolled in AP courses. The goal should be for the number to be as close to 100 percent as possible. If students are not taking the test, the reasons why need to be determined.

The faculty can review the types of AP courses offered. In subject areas where none is offered, they should determine why. They should distinguish between situations where resources are not available and those where there is an unwillingness to make the curricular changes necessary to accommodate an AP course in that area.

Options for students to participate in online AP courses should be examined; AP can help extend the curriculum of small high schools in particular. The high school can help students enroll and provide additional support, including on-campus study centers and tutoring by students from local postsecondary institutions to help support students with their online studies.

Questions

- What is the trend on AP scores over several years? Are student scores increasing or holding steady?

- If scores are not improving, has the alignment of AP course content with exam content been examined?

- Do the teachers who are teaching the courses have the necessary academic training as well as knowledge about the AP curriculum and system?

Actions

The school should consider having teachers participate in the training necessary to become qualified to score AP exams. This training enables teachers to participate (with compensation) during the summers reading the constructed response (essays, document analyses, and so on) portions of AP exams. AP teachers at the school generally and those certified as AP scorers should be connected to the larger AP community through the Internet (http://apcentral.collegeboard.com) and through participation in other annual AP activities.

Questions

- For schools that do not already have IB programs, what is the fit of IB with the school's structure and culture?
- Could IB be incorporated into the school? If not, are there elements of IB that would improve the challenge level at the school?

Actions

The school should conduct a review of the IB Diploma Programme course requirements and content to determine if it could adapt any of the strategies employed by IB to improve curricular coherence and alignment with postsecondary demands. For example, perhaps a senior paper requirement could be instituted schoolwide.

Question

- How can the ACT sequence of tests (EXPLORE, PLAN, ACT) be used as a means to provide better feedback to students on their college readiness and to the school on how well it is preparing students for college?

Actions

The high school and middle school must work in conjunction to administer the test sequence at the three designated levels. More importantly, the faculty must cooperate to make necessary changes in instruction based on how well students are performing on the tests, which provide relatively detailed summaries of the skill areas where students are proficient and where they need additional help in order to be college-ready. Ideally, the tests are provided to all students at no costs to the student or their parents. Where this is not feasible, fee waivers for those unable to pay should be instituted so that all students take the tests.

Questions

- How can a full range of appropriate postsecondary options be made available to students?
- How can students know when they are ready to take a postsecondary course?
- How well can students judge their readiness for postsecondary courses while still in high school?

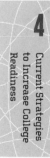

4

Current Strategies to Increase College Readiness

Actions

An important first step is to develop more direct relationships with local postsecondary institutions with the aim of creating as many opportunities as possible for students to take college classes or to have such classes offered on the high school campus. This can be a difficult process because the lines of communication between high schools and colleges are often not direct. There may need to be a district effort, but individual high school faculty members can also connect with individual faculty members at a local postsecondary institution in order to build some initial bridges and conversations about shared expectations for student success.

Questions

- How are the alignment with college success and the challenge level of the curriculum determined?
- What are the school's current beliefs about the alignment that exists with college success? What are these beliefs based on?

Actions

A high school might consider conducting an Alignment and Challenge Audit. The audit can be managed by faculty with guidance from the University of Oregon's Center for Educational Policy Research (http://cepr.uoregon.edu) or it can be conducted by an external consultant. A scaled-down version can even be conducted by faculty members themselves. Regardless of who is conducting the audit, it is necessary to convert all documents to electronic format and store them centrally, both for analysis purposes and to create a compendium of the taught curriculum. The audit should be repeated every two years to gauge curriculum drift. Once a curriculum is aligned to a proper challenge level, the audits can be conducted less frequently.

Another advantage of creating this database is that it allows departments to review easily and conveniently the content of all courses in the department and across departments when they are considering curricular changes or textbook adoptions. Similarly, individual teachers can compare their practices with those of their peers by examining what is listed in the database for other courses with the same title, as well as for courses that precede or follow theirs. The database can also be a powerful tool to develop a more intellectually coherent curriculum by making it convenient to assemble information on current tasks, expectations, and grading criteria.

What Does a High School That Prepares Its Students for College Success Look Like?

Ⓗigh schools designed to prepare all students for college success look dramatically different from those that prepare only a portion of students. These high schools have certain key characteristics. The most important and perhaps the most often overlooked is an intellectually coherent program of study based on a curriculum that grows progressively more challenging over the years. In practice, most high school course sequences do little more than introduce new material in similar ways at all grade levels. Students are confronted with a steady stream of new dates and events to memorize, new equations and concepts to use to solve practice problems, new books and short stories to read and react to, and new vocabulary, laws, and rules in the sciences and second languages. Key skills, such as writing, are not nurtured with progressively more challenging assignments tied to a common scoring system to ensure that the same skills are developed and new skills are mastered and that students mature intellectually.

How Intellectually Coherent Is Today's High School?

High schools today provide learning in discrete units with little connection across the day or across the years. High school English, in particular, tends to be four unrelated consecutive courses in which students read a variety of pieces of literature with no obvious connection among them and sometimes write and sometimes do not; some classes may even venture off into media studies or pop culture, if the teacher is so moved. High school English has no culminating exam or required set of exit skills. In fact, findings from the 1998 National Assessment of Educational Progress suggest that only about a quarter of twelfth graders reach a level of writing defined as proficient by the test and that the percentage that reached this level did not increase appreciably from fourth to eighth to twelfth grade.

Mathematics courses may seem better connected. In practice, key skills such as mathematical reasoning and problem solving are not always developed consistently over the four years of high school. Instead, each course largely follows the same pattern of introducing new material, algorithms, or methods, having students practice them in homework, and then reviewing the homework in class. Examinations may be limited to ascertaining if material has been understood and if students can apply what they have just learned to a range of problems previously introduced and practiced.

According to findings from the Third International Mathematics and Science Study, when U.S. math teaching is compared to mathematics instruction in other nations that excel in international comparisons, students in U.S. classes do not engage actively in problem solving or develop deep understanding of mathematical concepts. As a result, few come away from high school realizing that math is a symbolic language that is used to understand the natural world. Students may emerge from four years of high school mathematics with the ability to factor equations and graph quadratics, but they have little insight into what these phenomena represent at a deeper level, why these are important things to know, and how this knowledge might be put to use.

As for science, the college prep curriculum consists almost exclusively of biology, chemistry, and physics, often with a choice between regular and AP versions. The critique of these courses is that, once again, they tend to emphasize memorization of terms over understanding of concepts. Although basic vocabulary is certainly important to mastering the sciences, much of the same vocabulary is reintroduced and reexplained in entry-level college courses. In addition, general education science requirements in college may be fulfilled by courses in a wide range of scientific fields. General principles of scientific inquiry and scientific thinking are as important as specific content knowledge.

> **"They tend to emphasize memorization of terms over understanding of concepts."**

In sum, the purpose of the high school science sequence is unclear. Is it to prepare students for additional study in biology, chemistry, or physics? Is it to introduce these disciplines as stepping-stones to new disciplines, such as geology and astronomy? Is it simply to cover terminology and topics? How do the three science disciplines taught in high school relate to one another or to parallel concepts taught in the mathematics curriculum? And where do students learn to "think like scientists?" Where do they develop the key understandings of the scientific method as a mode of inquiry, not as an algorithm to be followed in a mechanical step-by-step fashion?

An intriguing question to ask is how high school math and science courses prepare students for studies that lead to careers in engineering, for example. The proportion of American students enrolled in engineering programs has declined over the past twenty years, although the career possibilities in the field of engineering continue to grow. Given the U.S. economy's evolution toward design work and away from low value-added manufacturing, American college graduates who close off engineering as an option lose access to a range of well-paying positions and careers. What can be done to encourage more students to pursue careers in engineering when so many students leave high school with math and science phobias that cause them to eliminate any field that requires such knowledge?

Because high school courses are viewed by students as being concerned with mastery of content knowledge alone, they may enter college assuming that, having received good grades in high school, they have a grasp of necessary foundational knowledge of the disciplines needed to do well in college courses. They are often unprepared for the more conceptually oriented curriculum they encounter. This mismatch in worldviews, in ways of thinking about a discipline, leads to jarring disconnects and frustrations for students and instructors alike.

Although many high schools do strive to challenge students to engage at deeper levels, the structure of the curriculum and the emphasis on simply completing required courses creates the wrong mentality. Students enter college expecting assignments and tests with clear right and wrong answers that do not require much interpretation or even much thinking. When interpretation is required, they often assume that any kind of interpretation will be acceptable and are surprised and even offended when they are told that they must apply certain disciplinary rules of

> **Students enter college expecting assignments and tests with clear right and wrong answers that do not require much interpretation or even much thinking.**

5

What Does a High
School That Prepares
Its Students for College
Success Look Like?

thinking and analysis in order for their argument to be considered worthwhile or correct. In other words, they have completed the introduction to the discipline without developing the habits of mind necessary to engage fully in the study and understanding of that discipline.

Developing an Intellectually Coherent Program

To design a high school instructional program so that it systematically prepares students for success in postsecondary education requires clear agreement on the exit standards students are expected to meet. Here is where the Knowledge and Skills for University Success standards become so important. Without general agreement on the outcome, it is impossible to specify the content of the program. Once such agreement is achieved, the high school faculty can move forward with the process of designing an intellectually coherent, developmentally progressive program of study.

Create Exit Standards

To begin, they design a set of culminating exams, projects, or requirements that students must accomplish successfully for their program of study to be considered complete. These activities are discipline-specific, or if integrated, have standards for each of the disciplines that a project addresses. These culminating projects or demonstrations integrate the content knowledge expected from students who are prepared to enter college with the thinking skills and habits of mind that will be required of them shortly. The projects also require the personal characteristics, such as independent work, initiative, sustained effort, inquisitiveness, and attention to detail and quality, that will serve students well in the postsecondary environment.

The activities are designed to provide information both to the college and to the student. A student may be able to complete a task successfully and demonstrate requisite knowledge and skill, but in the process indicate problems with time management, independent work, or ability to function as a member of a team, for example. Although the student might earn a good grade, she might also receive feedback suggesting problems if she pursues similar strategies in college and specifying ways to avoid them. This type of diagnostic feedback can help students and parents alike anticipate pitfalls that can be expected to occur once the student begins college and works more independently.

It is not easy to develop culminating activities that have intellectual challenge and coherence. Senior projects, although increasing in popularity, can devolve into elaborate "show and tell" rituals where students are not necessarily challenged to demonstrate college-level thinking. The scoring guides used demand particular scrutiny to determine how the mix of criteria included have been selected. Ideally, they will reflect the kinds of expectations consistent with college readiness as one key component, and students will be provided unflinching feedback on the quality of their projects.

One strategy for designing or improving culminating activities is for high school teachers to work jointly with local college and university faculty. Although this is difficult to do for a variety of reasons, an increasing number of schools are connecting across the high school–college boundary. Community colleges have been the most willing partners, but postsecondary institutions of all types have increased their connections to high schools over the past decade as well.

Using the KSUS standards as a common point of departure, cross-level teams can then review examples of actual student work taken from classes in high school and college to determine how the expectations for students are complementary and how they are not. Ultimately, the two groups can rate each other's papers with ease and reliability. Faculty in both institutions then know how their colleagues are thinking and what they expect of students. These commonly held definitions then serve as cognitive frameworks for planning courses at each institution that lead to more seamless transitions for students. The courses connect the exit level of high school and the entry level of college. Students are able to continue to build more complex skills that may require years, not semesters, to master.

Ongoing communication across institutional boundaries using the language of student learning as a common point of reference can facilitate more student movement across those boundaries as well. This means in practice that it is easier to identify when students are really ready for postsecondary studies as opposed to when they have simply run out of classes to take at high school. This standards-based relationship also allows greater coteaching and team teaching of classes, which might be conducted for half a semester in a high school and half at a college, or half-time by an instructor from each level. In other words, the door opens to a range of innovative practices that result in better connections and smoother transitions from high school to college.

One simple benefit of this model is that students are motivated to work right until the end of high school, rather than view the senior year as a time for a

5

What Does a High
School That Prepares
Its Students for College
Success Look Like?

> **"Students are motivated to work right until the end of high school."**

well-earned vacation. The goal is not to make students miserable by never allowing them any time off but rather to help them keep their skills sharp and their intellectual development on track. As noted in earlier chapters, students who do not take math in their senior year have greater difficulty with college math than students who do. The "senior slump" is a real phenomenon, and anything that can alleviate it is likely to contribute to greater college success.

Look Back at the Entire Curriculum

Once basic agreement on exit and entrance expectations and a challenging assessment system focused on culminating activities are in place, the next step is to look at the high school curriculum for the entire four years leading up to the exit standards. This arduous work is at the heart of any successful alignment activity. It is framed by a series of key questions that must be asked about each course, including these:

- How does this course contribute to students acquiring the knowledge and skills necessary to meet the exit standards?

- How does this course develop the intellectual maturity of students in a developmentally appropriate fashion?

- How does this course connect with those before and after it in a way that does not repeat material but that identifies and reinforces key concepts and knowledge previously learned and anticipates skills yet to be mastered?

- Is the challenge level of the material appropriate in relation to the intellectual development of the students who will take the course?

- Is the pace of the work and the expected student production on a trajectory to have them ready for what they will face in college?

- Does the course address at least one of the overarching skills, such as writing, reasoning, problem solving, or inquisitiveness?

- If the course is part of a sequence, is there a plan for the "handoff" of students from one level to another, both as they enter and as they exit the course?

5

What Does a High
School That Prepares
Its Students for College
Success Look Like?

A high school curriculum designed around these focusing questions begins to move in the all-important direction of intellectual coherence. Such a program is organized around carefully selected key cognitive skills and abilities, such as those listed previously. None would be more important than writing, reasoning, and problem solving. Any high school program of instruction built on these will have great potential to develop in students the key capabilities they will need for college success.

What Would an Intellectually Coherent Program of Study Look Like?

This section presents detailed descriptions of the components of an intellectually coherent program of instruction for English, math, science, the social sciences, second languages, and the arts. This discussion also touches on the knowledge, skills, and habits of mind by discipline often lacking when students enter college. The overview presented here can help create a blueprint for coverage and coherence in the high school curriculum.

English

In English, the intellectually coherent college preparation curriculum should consist of a set of texts that are explored in depth and a broad collection of readings designed to expose young people to a variety of styles and genres. The core texts should be read for deep comprehension of author intent, style, voice, and use of literary devices. Students should develop progressively greater insight into and mastery of the analytic processes used to comprehend text and create personal meaning. In the process, they should learn how to use effectively such skills as annotation and close reading. They become adept at identifying an author's basic beliefs and perspectives, point of view, attitudes, and values. As they read works from different historical periods, they are able to place them into a historical context and explain how that context influenced the author's assumptions and goals in the work.

As they read and discuss a range of pieces carefully selected from a variety of literary traditions and genres, they should become progressively more proficient at comprehending the characteristics of genres, the type of language each employs, how literature across cultures contains unifying themes and archetypes, and the ways authors create a particular mood through a variety of techniques. In the process, students are able to demonstrate familiarity with the major literary periods of English and American literature and a more general awareness of literary traditions from beyond the English-speaking world.

The exact texts chosen for students to master can vary. It is more important for them to understand how to analyze at least one text thoroughly and be able to generalize those skills to new texts. The students need to be able to explain their understanding in a reasoned fashion; construct their own arguments; agree, disagree, summarize, critique; and formulate a personal response.

When they go on to write about their observations and insights, they need a set of writing skills that should be developed continuously and progressively over four years of high school. Although writing should most certainly occur and be developed in English courses, it should also be an integral part of an intellectually coherent high school curriculum focused on college success, one in which students write frequently in a variety of courses and on a variety of topics and subjects across disciplines while employing several writing genres. Students who are prepared to write successfully in high school begin by having mastered grammar and usage well enough that these do not interfere with reader understanding. Although perfect mastery may not be necessary, students should show marked improvement in their grammatical precision and use of proper conventions of the English language. These are not ends in themselves, but important tools that allow the proficient writer to construct meaning clearly and efficiently.

As they progress in writing over four years of high school and in a variety of courses in addition to English, students should learn to articulate a position through their writing and advance an argument using evidence. They should become adept at distinguishing between public knowledge and their own personal opinions, be able to compare and contrast points of view and buttress an argument, anticipate and address counterarguments. They should be able to visualize the audience for whom they are writing and adjust their writing accordingly by properly selecting between informal and formal styles, expressions, and vocabulary, among other choices.

When writing an expository essay, they should routinely employ supporting evidence, quotations, paraphrases, citations, and other primary and secondary source material as appropriate. Such essays may also require the use of charts, tables, and other graphic elements to summarize data, trends, or phenomena. Such writing should be largely free from any apparent bias and anticipate and address biases the reader may bring to the topic.

5

What Does a High
School That Prepares
Its Students for College
Success Look Like?

Students should make it a habit to edit and rewrite their work regularly and thoroughly. This is both a skill and an attitude. A goal should be to have students view writing as a craft, not a mechanical process. They should routinely rewrite a piece of work two and three times, with feedback in the interim from the teacher, from fellow students, and even from community members specially recruited for their expertise in writing or editing. The more feedback students receive, including from one another, the better they will understand that writing is a multistep process and that few pieces of writing can be submitted as a finished work after one draft only.

Two other sets of skills that need to be developed throughout the curriculum and can be integrated with English courses are research skills and critical thinking skills. Reference has already been made to the importance of critical thinking in a number of disciplines. In addition, students need formal, progressively more complex experiences in researching. In a coherent program, students learn to formulate research questions, refine them, develop research plans, and find out what is already known about a topic. They learn how to identify claims and assertions in the writing and research on a topic, and how to verify their truthfulness and determine their usefulness. They work extensively with and are able to differentiate between primary and secondary sources.

As students conduct research, they can be made much more aware of the concept of plagiarism and the specific rules that govern the use of material created by other people. Writing research papers offers numerous opportunities to see real-world examples of the line between citation, summary and paraphrase, and plagiarism. Particularly as students work on the Internet, cutting and pasting source material, they can be taught about plagiarism. Working with the Internet can also help them to analyze source material critically so that they come to understand how to use these sources and that all are not equally credible or even equivalent to published sources.

A coherent program of instruction should emphasize progressively more challenging opportunities for students to discuss how their personal experiences and values affect their

> **Students who are confident critical thinkers can more easily formulate and express original ideas.**

opinions, perceptions, and interpretations of taught materials. Students who are confident critical thinkers can more easily formulate and express original ideas, are prepared to support their arguments and provide evidence for their assertions, realize when they are overgeneralizing or where the limits of their generalizations lie, know when they are advocating a thinly supported idea or line of reasoning.

These students are able to engage in vigorous intellectual give-and-take without either feeling hurt or needing to be right all the time. They can accept critiques of their written work or their line of reasoning without viewing such feedback as a personal attack. They can respect the perspectives and lines of argumentation of those with whom they do not agree. In short, such students are prepared to enter a community where these habits of mind are the ground rules for interaction inside and outside the classroom.

Steps Faculty Can Take in English

To accomplish these goals, a high school's English department faculty members will need to agree on the texts to be taught at each grade level, the purpose of teaching each text, the types of analysis that students will do on these foundational texts, how these texts will connect with one another and how students will make linkages among them, what genres they represent, and what themes and archetypes they illustrate and develop.

Furthermore, the school's faculty as a whole will have to come to agreement on expectations and standards for student writing, starting with examples of the type of work they are expected to produce by the time they graduate. These exemplar papers should be created for all the major writing genres students are expected to employ, regardless of the class or discipline in which the writing is to occur. Accompanying the exemplars should be a common scoring guide, with adaptations for specific genres. Teachers should agree to use the appropriate version of the scoring guide as the baseline instrument for evaluating all student writing. Faculty members also have to agree on the number of pages of writing to assign in each course, the quality of feedback to be provided by number of pages, and the number of pages students will write during their four high school years.

In addition, there should be guidelines for proofreading and editing and requirements for grammatical and spelling accuracy; all teachers should agree to apply these to all writing. In essence, the school should produce an explicit set of writing standards that results in all students having the same general expectations applied to their writing. These standards should be designed so that students are expected to write in a progressively more complex and technically accurate fashion each year. This developmental progression simply serves to emphasize that expectations for writing proficiency are high in college, and that such abilities take time to develop.

In a coherent program, research projects become a more central part of the curriculum in English and elsewhere. Here again, a developmental sequence should lead students from relatively simple, straightforward research projects to more complex projects in which they develop more of the skills described in the KSUS standards. Although the resulting research papers need not become ever longer, they should become progressively more complex. According to data collected by the National Survey of Student Engagement (see Chapter Seven for more on this survey), college research papers are generally shorter than twenty pages, most frequently in the five- to ten-page range. Providing students with extensive experience writing many five- to ten-page papers over four years is superior to having them write one twenty-page paper during the senior year.

The culmination of this program of study in English should be a senior-level seminar-type course specifically designed to emulate the demands of college classrooms. It is worth noting that this concept is a radical departure from the current structure of the high school, and as a result, would be among the more difficult practices to implement. However, given the current critiques of the senior year and the need to try something different to keep students more engaged during the final year of high school, it may be time to consider this kind of fundamental change.

Here is a brief look at what the seminar in English might look like. (More on senior seminars is provided at the end of the chapter in "A Note About Senior Seminars.") It may be team-taught with a writer, poet, or faculty member from a local postsecondary institution. Its content should emphasize analytic thinking, critiquing of student writing, and the free exchange of ideas among class members and instructors. The pace of readings and writing assignments should be consistent with what students will encounter in a typical college course, and students should be expected to write and rewrite pieces regularly and present them for discussion and debate.

The course should yield information about student skill level, intellectual development, and work habits necessary for college success. This kind of information is useful to both students and parents as students prepare to make the transition to college. The performance of students in this course as a means to demonstrate understanding and mastery of these skills and habits can also be useful to admissions and placement offices, which can use information of this nature

5

What Does a High
School That Prepares
Its Students for College
Success Look Like?

in what is known as a comprehensive review process or in the process of placing a student into an initial English course. For these reasons, the final course evaluation should contain a narrative component in addition to any letter grade assigned. The narrative would help students understand their strengths relative to college readiness in English and areas where they need to add skills or change behaviors.

Mathematics

Although it may be hard to believe, university faculty across a range of institutions that participated in the Standards for Success research indicated that incoming students do not have a firm grasp of basic mathematical operations, including adding and subtracting fractions by finding a common denominator, reducing terms, dividing without using a calculator, using exponents and scientific notation, understanding relative magnitude, knowing the correct order of arithmetic operations, and demonstrating the ability to use the associative, commutative, and distributive laws, for example. Although students are almost always taught these skills and concepts, they apparently do not practice them enough to develop the ability to employ them automatically and consistently. Yet a high school program of study that helps students consolidate these often-overlooked skills is basic to university success.

> "Incoming students do not have a firm grasp of basic mathematical operations."

In addition to these basic skills are algebraic concepts. Algebra must be mastered in order to move on to higher forms of mathematics. Algebra is conceptually rich, and although the ability to solve equations accurately is, of course, of great importance, understanding the principles that underlie various algebraic operations is at least as important at this stage of students' mathematical understanding.

Algebra has a relatively clearly defined set of concepts and skills that students are expected to learn more or less universally. University mathematics courses assume that students have mastered the basic means for stating and manipulating equations, which is at the heart of algebra. A successful high school mathematics program should therefore strive for both mastery and deeper understanding of algebra. These dual goals can be achieved through instruction that engages students in tasks that require thinking and reflection about the methods used to solve a problem in addition to solving it. Students should understand algebra well enough to apply it procedurally and conceptually to a range of common problems,

5

What Does a High School That Prepares Its Students for College Success Look Like?

knowing, for example, to apply a linear equation to solve a distance-time problem, a quadratic equation to explain the motion of a falling object, and an exponential function to determine compound interest rates.

High school graduates should also understand basic trigonometric principles. They should know the definition of sine, cosine, and tangent using right triangle geometry and similarity relations. They should be able to relate a trigonometric function in its standard form to a corresponding graph of the function, recognize graphs of periodic functions, and know identities for sum and difference of angles.

Similarly, in geometry, the high school program of study should give all college-bound students a basic understanding of both plane and solid geometry, properties of similarity and congruence, and techniques for figuring the area and perimeter of basic figures. The math program should seek to help students develop deeper understandings of the ideas behind simple geometric proofs, and students should be able to produce simple proofs in writing. Students also need to know basic formulas for volume and surface area for three-dimensional objects and to be able to visualize solids and surfaces in three dimensions. They should be able to apply their knowledge of analytic geometry to real-world problems that use the properties of right triangles, and understand the ways these principles are used in various real-world applications. Finally, students should understand the basic relationships between geometry and algebra—for example, that geometric figures can be described algebraically.

The content knowledge students master in a high school program of instruction should be viewed by them and their teachers alike as simply a set of tools to serve a sophisticated goal—the development of mathematical reasoning. The ability to think systematically and logically is perhaps the single most important skill they can gain from a study of mathematics; it opens the door to numerous other areas of study in college.

> "The ability to think systematically and logically is perhaps the single most important skill they can gain from a study of mathematics."

The types of reasoning skills that a high school mathematics program should develop include the ability to formulate inductive and deductive lines of logic for use in basic mathematical arguments. Students should be able to represent mathematical problems in multiple formats, such as analytic, numerical, and geometrical. They should be able to solve a wide range of multistep problems, have at their command a variety of strategies to revise their approaches to solving such problems, and understand how proofs and counterproofs are useful in approaching problem solving.

As students develop intellectual maturity and sophistication, they should become adept at understanding the underlying structure and purposes of mathematics as an abstract symbol system that represents and explains relationships in the real world. Students should become adept at applying appropriate mathematical principles to a broad range of complex real-world problems as well as recognize where mathematical reasoning is applied to such problems in the natural sciences, social sciences, and public policy issues. Making connections between mathematics and other disciplines becomes increasingly important, because most students use their math knowledge to pursue majors in college that employ math as a tool for study, not as an end in itself.

Steps Faculty Can Take in Mathematics

A coherent high school mathematics program gears students toward the progressively more complex application and use of mathematical knowledge and reasoning to understand and seek solutions to real-world problems. For example, carbon dating, amortization tables, predator-prey models, and ocean wave formation and motion all require application of mathematical knowledge. Studies in these areas can range from population dispersion to economic development, habitat preservation, and coastal erosion; these can engage students as well as introduce them to the problems and issues involved in archeology, economics, population biology, and oceanography. Often, students today have little awareness that mathematics is an important prerequisite for study in these fields and many others.

In a coherent mathematics program, these ultimate connections can be made in a capstone seminar course that does not focus on new knowledge but instead on integrated application of knowledge students already have. A mathematics senior seminar might begin by ensuring that all students have mastered fundamental computational skills, then go on to more challenging content, including algebra, geometry, trigonometry, and some calculus.

The mathematics seminar should be problem-based. Experts from the community in areas such as engineering, agriculture, and banking can serve as partners in the development of appropriately complex and challenging problems that students can address in such a seminar. The problems can link mathematical and scientific knowledge, particularly as a means to connect these disciplines to the field of engineering. As with the English seminar described previously, the goal is for students to receive in-depth feedback and diagnostic information on their college readiness, both in content knowledge and in the habits of mind associated with mathematical thinking.

It is worth making two additional observations about subjects that a high school mathematics program needs to include to prepare students properly for college success. One is statistics. In the Standards for Success research, mathematics faculty indicated that knowledge of statistics was not a prerequisite for success in entry-level college mathematics courses. However, professors in the natural and social sciences stressed that knowledge of basic statistical concepts and techniques contributes greatly to student success in a wide range of entry-level courses in those two broad areas of the college general education curriculum.

The other subject is calculus. This is becoming a hotly disputed topic. Calculus, as taught in college, is adapted to the context in which it is being applied. Therefore, it is possible for at least four different versions to be offered, even at the entry level: calculus for engineers, calculus for physicists and scientists, calculus for business students, and calculus for mathematicians. Each department offers its own spin and emphasis on the most important topics. High school calculus, although clearly the most difficult mathematics course now offered in most high schools, may turn out not to be the best-suited course for transition from high school to college or the course best aligned with calculus as taught by college faculty.

If a high school chooses to retain calculus as its signature mathematics course, the school needs to ensure that it is being taught in ways that connect well with the various conceptions of calculus that exist in the postsecondary world. At the least, it would be prudent to alert students and parents to the fact that calculus as taught at the high school level is often not well aligned with courses at the postsecondary level. Work is under way at the national level to ensure that the AP calculus courses are more closely aligned with postsecondary expectations. In the future, these courses may serve as a reference point that regular calculus courses can use to ensure proper alignment.

Science

What should a well-designed science curriculum that prepares students for college success look like? Such a program would be much more closely connected and integrated with the high school mathematics program than is the case in most high schools today. Mathematics knowledge and understanding have been identified by university faculty participating in the Standards for Success research as among the

5

What Does a High School That Prepares Its Students for College Success Look Like?

most important foundational skills for success in entry-level college science courses. Mathematical principles and techniques are necessary to conduct the investigations that are at the heart of the scientific method. When students cannot employ these tools, they are limited in their ability to comprehend the concepts and principles presented in college science courses.

The foundational math content knowledge needed for success in science roughly parallels that described previously for mathematics. Mastery of algebra is perhaps the single most important set of skills, although an understanding of the relationships between algebra and geometry is important for understanding a range of topics and problems in the sciences. Problem-solving skills are even more important in the sciences, so students who can employ various mathematical strategies to solve scientific problems are more successful. Knowledge of statistics plays an important role in the sciences as a means to understand a wide range of natural phenomena. Science is much more concerned with the use of number systems for measurement purposes, so students benefit if they can select appropriate units of measure for the problem at hand, know how to estimate, and understand the metric system as well as the U.S. system and be able to convert between the two.

Biology, chemistry, and physics, the backbone of most high school science programs, remain necessary but probably not sufficient for an intellectually coherent program of study. The program should focus on the basic foundational elements of these subjects as well as the tools needed to conduct investigations in each. In biology, the general structure and function of cells is perhaps the single most important piece of knowledge that incoming college students should have. Also important is a basic understanding of genetic principles, the organization and classification of living organisms, and the concepts of biological change and evolution of species. If students understand key vocabulary, processes, and principles in these areas, they stand a much greater chance of moving through college science courses successfully.

In a coherent program of study, students master key chemistry concepts, including the physical and chemical properties of compounds, mixtures, and solutions and the composition of matter. Students need to become familiar with the periodic table, understand principles of atomic structure and bonding, and be able to apply principles that explain chemical reactions.

In physics, high school students need to understand basic principles and laws. They should learn concepts of energy and motion, the concepts that govern the effects of forces on objects, the properties of matter, and basic laws governing conservation

5

What Does a High
School That Prepares
Its Students for College
Success Look Like?

of energy and electrical and magnetic forces. Students should also be introduced to concepts from modern physics, such as the theory of special relativity.

Finally, an area that is often undeveloped in high school is the role of science in society. Students may learn science as a series of terms and laws to memorize. Science is taught as if it somehow floated above society at a different plane of objectivity, detached from the real world. This perspective makes it difficult for students to understand that science and scientific theory are not absolutes, and that they should be challenged and questioned. In a coherent program of study, students should learn how scientific theory in-fluences the ways people think, how societies for-mulate problems and solutions in response to scientific beliefs, and how governments use sci-ence to make decisions about important public policy issues. They should understand that in college and in the real world, scientific disciplines do not have boundaries between them in the same way that high school courses do and that most modern science is multidisciplinary in nature.

> "Students often learn science as a series of terms and laws to memorize."

Students should be encouraged to understand that simply because a scientific finding is made, it does not mean that society is ready to embrace the results and implications. Throughout history, science has often been in conflict with other so-cial institutions, and it continues to be. Simply knowing "the truth" is not enough when it comes to changing widely held cultural beliefs, but over time science often does result in big shifts in societal beliefs and behaviors.

Perhaps most important and in some ways the most challenging to develop is the mindset of student-as-scientist, referred to by university faculty as learning to "think like a scientist." At the heart of this perspective lies inquisitiveness and genuine curiosity about how the natural world is ordered and how it functions. A coherent program of study would foster in high school students the ability to think experimentally, to think about how a problem could be investigated experimen-tally and how the scientific process could be employed as a means to gain insight into a problem. When students bring this mindset to problems in college science courses, they are more likely to develop the deeper insights and understanding of how scientific principles are used to solve scientific problems. They are more likely to comprehend the relationship between a formula and its real-world application—for example, that photosynthesis is not just a chemical reaction but rather the driving force behind all plant life on the planet.

A high school may choose to continue to organize its curriculum in a three-course sequence consisting of biology, chemistry, and physics. The problem with this arrangement is that the courses are often prerequisites to one another but do not necessarily or automatically build on the content taught in each course. In practice what occurs is that the smaller pool of students who make it to physics includes those who have also taken more advanced mathematics courses. The possible advantages and opportunities presented by this linkage, however, are rarely exploited. Science and math teachers seldom coordinate or integrate their curriculum or assign projects that require application of skills from one subject area to solve a problem in the other. Nor are direct connections made between chemistry and physics courses or biology and chemistry courses. Even less frequent is the kind of interdisciplinary connections that would cause students to combine biological, mathematical, and geographical knowledge to understand issues in population biology or ecology, for example.

Steps Faculty Can Take in Science

At the very least, a more intellectually coherent high school program would make systematic connections between the science and mathematics curricula. It would emphasize the scientific method and scientific thinking throughout the science course sequence and seek to develop more sophisticated applications of scientific thinking to real-world problems that require thoughtful solutions based on understanding and application of key concepts and principles from scientific disciplines.

> "A more intellectually coherent high school program would make systematic connections between the science and mathematics curricula."

Science labs can be useful tools in the pursuit of these goals, but are not automatically so. If lab work consists largely of undertaking experiments that are supposed to yield only one possible result and then completing an exercise in a lab manual, students quickly become conditioned to follow the steps in the manual and write up whatever results they obtain, whether the results make sense or not. This is the antithesis of scientific thinking, and leads to counterproductive habits of mind that limit ability to apply concepts to solve new problems.

One alternative is to develop a course series that introduces and builds on the same basic scientific knowledge and principles from the natural sciences each year but becomes increasingly more complex and conceptual, and requires applications that approximate ever more closely the ways in which scientists think and behave. Such a sequence of courses could certainly include biology, chemistry, and physics but might also allow investigations in environmental sciences and additional disciplines, such as astronomy and geology. This broader overview with a continued focus on foundational concepts, principles, and terminology can equip students to enter a much larger array of college science courses successfully.

The National Science Foundation (NSF) has funded and continues to fund development of innovative, interdisciplinary science curricula that could possibly achieve the goals described here. The goal of such a curriculum is to introduce students to core concepts in inquiry, the physical sciences, the life sciences, and the earth-space sciences. The curriculum development is framed conceptually by the National Science Education Standards developed in 1995 by the National Committee on Science Education Standards and Assessment of the National Research Council. Key objectives are to engage students in integrated study across the disciplines and to explore science and technology from a personal and social perspective. The goal is to create rigorous, coherent alternatives to the traditional science sequence that simultaneously enable students to meet college entrance requirements while developing the habits of mind necessary for postsecondary success, such as interdisciplinary thinking, an understanding of science in society, and the ability to think like a scientist.

Another strategy for achieving a more coherent science program resembles that suggested for English and math—a capstone seminar for students who have completed three years of science. The seminar would only be possible for students who already have a thorough foundational knowledge of mathematics and the sciences that they could draw on to formulate, analyze, and solve complex problems. For example, a seminar could be organized around one or two problems that require application of physics, chemistry, and mathematics, the solution of which would be presented for public review. How do chemicals react to produce energy so that students could create a self-propelled vehicle that could travel a specified distance with a mixture of fuels the students must define and quantify? The students would also explain the formulas they employed to calculate all relevant variables in the experiment. Some studies may emphasize greater understanding of the interaction between science and society by exploring vexing public policy questions where scientific knowledge could play a role in solving the problem and proposing technically accurate and feasible solutions. For example, students might combine their

5

What Does a High
School That Prepares
Its Students for College
Success Look Like?

knowledge of chemistry and biology to devise antipollution strategies that could be employed locally. The final products, the proposals, should include analyses that are both scientifically valid and politically viable.

As noted in the earlier section on the mathematics seminar, there is great potential to connect science and mathematics in ways that get students thinking about careers, particularly in various branches of engineering, and particularly students from groups who are historically underrepresented in engineering. The seminar approach, with its potential for group learning and other nontraditional instructional methods, can provide positive, motivating experiences for those who would not otherwise see the sciences or engineering as potential college majors or careers.

Social Sciences

The social sciences present an interesting challenge. They are a collection of disciplines that employ different methodologies and are founded on different theories and laws. Although it is certainly possible to make connections among the social sciences, they do not necessarily group together in the same fashion as the natural sciences or mathematics. Geography and civics, for example, must be consciously connected. Similarly, the strategies and analytic tools used to conduct historical research are quite different from those employed in the modern study of economic systems.

This does not automatically mean that a high school program of study in the social sciences cannot be made intellectually coherent and challenging in a developmentally appropriate fashion. It does mean that a great deal more thought and planning is required than occurs currently in most high schools. The most common current sequence of social science courses over four years is geography, world history, U.S. history, and civics. However, they are taught in sequence without being sequential. In other words, geographic knowledge is rarely built on systematically in subsequent courses. World history is not necessarily taught as a precursor to understanding U.S. history. Some individual teachers do a good job of making connections, but here as in other disciplines the high school program itself does not. A civics class intended largely for high school seniors is not necessarily designed as a forum in which students hone skills developed over four years of high school to understand systems of government in their historical and geographical, context. It is simply the course they take their senior year.

Further complicating matters is that students can select among social science courses in a wide range of disciplines when they reach college, far more than high schools could possibly offer on an introductory basis. Therefore, high schools should concentrate on core knowledge from key social sciences in combination with the foundational cognitive skills required to succeed in any of them.

Those foundational skills include much of what students should master in English and mathematics. College students studying the social sciences are expected to exercise skills referenced previously in English, including reading for meaning, writing frequently, conducting research, and interpreting charts and graphs. Mathematics is becoming an integral part of the social sciences, with economics being one of the best examples. Knowledge of basic statistics is useful in a number of social science disciplines including geography, sociology, and psychology.

Each discipline has its own knowledge base of concepts, terminology, and key factual elements with which students should be familiar. As high school students work toward mastery of these disciplinary frameworks, they should also strive to develop understandings of the key organizing concepts of these disciplines. An understanding of the flow of history and the different ways history can be interpreted thematically should be developed in tandem with mastery of key factual information that is deemed critical to understanding the discipline.

In a coherent program of study, the key cognitive skill to be developed in the social sciences is analytic thinking. The bedrock of analytic thinking is solid reading skills, particularly the ability to read an article or document closely, with attention to nuance. Close reading allows students to draw inferences by identifying main points and distinguishing them from supportive statements or illustrative details. Perhaps just as important, students know they have understood what they have read.

> **The key cognitive skill to be developed in the social sciences is analytic thinking.**

In a coherent program of study, students should gather information not as an end in itself but in service of the scientific method as practiced in the social sciences. They should become more comfortable recognizing hypotheses stated in texts and examining the evidence presented to support hypotheses, have exposure to theories and the process of theory building in the social sciences, become adept at identifying different sources of information, and perhaps most important, be able to distinguish the credibility of sources generally and of those on the Internet in particular. Research in the social sciences requires students to be able to recognize biases, their own and those present in materials they read. In the process of developing these skills, students gain some experience with various research methodologies.

5

What Does a High School That Prepares Its Students for College Success Look Like?

Steps Faculty Can Take in Social Sciences

These characteristics of the social sciences suggest that schools can certainly continue with a four-year course sequence, if it is focused on developing the capabilities and skills described here. However, this does not preclude seminar-like opportunities for students to develop more integrated understandings of social science concepts and methods as they approach graduation. Some might even choose to take two social science courses during their senior year: a required civics course and an integrative seminar to develop analytic skills for college success.

In a coherent program of study, such seminars would be designed to draw on content knowledge gained previously in the social sciences to comprehend current issues and topics through the lens of a social scientist. The seminar format allows students to collect, analyze, and present data on a social problem or issue. Such data are now more available on the Internet and easier to analyze with existing software. Students can make data-based presentations and suggest solutions derived from analysis and not just opinion. These products can then be put to the test of public review and comment, an excellent way for students to learn to accept criticism of their work while also coming to understand that others may have very different viewpoints than they do. This broader perspective on civic engagement would help students learn how to get more out of a college-level social science course.

Second Languages

Second language programs in high school face a particular challenge. The amount of time students have to study and practice another language is rarely sufficient to result in mastery after four years. Class sizes generally limit the quality of feedback teachers can provide individual students. A further challenge is the relatively rudimentary understanding of English grammar that most students bring to the study of a second language. As a result, as much time must often be devoted to English grammar instruction as to second language instruction.

On the positive side, the study of second languages benefits from having a relatively clear set of mastery criteria. It is readily apparent if a student knows the vocabulary and grammar. Still, language mastery involves speaking, comprehending, reading, and writing. Achieving mastery in all four of these areas is truly challenging. Accomplishing this based on fifty minutes of interaction daily in a group with perhaps twenty-five or thirty others is even more challenging.

5

What Does a High
School That Prepares
Its Students for College
Success Look Like?

Second language instruction has some advantages over other disciplines when it comes to facilitating a smooth transition to postsecondary learning. This discipline benefits from a clear set of standards that define language proficiency and are in the process of being accepted broadly in the language teaching community. The standards are those proposed under the American Council on the Teaching of Foreign Languages (ACTFL) proficiency guidelines. The competence level required of high school students is generally accepted to correspond to the ACTFL intermediate-low proficiency level. Students at this level can use a second language to express themselves in simple, full sentences and have pronunciation that is comprehensible, but they are not expected to approach the quality or accuracy of a native language speaker.

In a coherent program, study of a second language would extend beyond mechanical mastery of vocabulary and grammar to understanding the culture the language represents. For this, students would need awareness of geography to ascertain where the language is spoken and of history to be aware of why it is spoken in those places. Cultural understanding also requires study of family structures, customs, holidays, religious traditions, and regional or national differences among those who speak the language. Holidays are an important way to begin to understand another culture. High school students are more prepared for postsecondary studies when they do not automatically think of the behaviors of people in other cultures as "weird" or aberrant because they are different from their own.

> **Study of a second language would extend beyond mechanical mastery of vocabulary and grammar to understanding the culture the language represents.**

Second language study also opens the door for native speakers to view their own language in perspective, to understand their own culture from another point of view. This enhanced perspective allows a greater appreciation not only of English vocabulary and language usage but of the American cultural tradition and its values.

One other important set of skills that can be developed through the study of second languages is learning strategies. Students can be encouraged to add to their repertoire of methods for mastering material. Second language study can introduce new ways to memorize material and employ mnemonics to recall rules and relationships. Learning to translate involves understanding that not all words have a one-to-one correspondence with another word in the language being studied.

Coping with exceptions and striving to understand the culturally constructed meaning of a word are more sophisticated learning skills that benefit students in the study of second languages and other disciplines.

Steps Faculty Can Take in Second Languages

A high school program of instruction in second languages designed to prepare students for college success would attend to this array of skill and attitude development. It would also take advantage of the natural connections between second language instruction and information from some of the other disciplines described. Coordination between grammar instruction in English and the second language helps students strengthen connections between first and second language, for native English speakers. Similarly, geography classes may study the countries where a particular language is spoken in concert with lessons in the second language class that emphasize these countries and their geographical characteristics. Numerous opportunities exist for this sort of coordination throughout all four years of high school study.

Cultural understanding can also deepen from simple to more complex over four years of language study. As students achieve some mastery, opportunities can be created for them to interact with native speakers; for example, volunteers from a local college or the community can come to class or students can find other opportunities, such as foreign newspapers on the Internet, where the language is actually used in a practical manner. These controlled interactions with a language in a cultural context are powerful motivators for students to improve their mastery of the language and their understanding of the culture. Such interactions are often the only way to encourage some students to attempt to speak a language or give any serious attention to their pronunciation.

In a coherent program, the capstone high school experience in second language would have an application and interaction component, where the goal would be to interact with native speakers or text. With such a program, students would not leave high school without some interaction with native speakers or some use of the language in a genuine context. Such experiences provide the best real-world feedback to students on how well they know a language. Such experiences also create connections that over time can develop into relationships with communities in which the second language is used. In addition to the human value, such relationships also can yield projects and experiences that can be included in a college application packet to demonstrate a student's maturity and ability to handle adult responsibilities and to interact with and appreciate people from other backgrounds.

The Arts

Arts programs in high school are quite different depending on the art involved. Music, drama, painting, ceramics, and dance are very different from one another in many ways. They also have certain commonalities. They may be designed to develop in students certain dispositions toward learning, and they require a degree of knowledge of self in addition to any technical skills that must be mastered. For many students, they are the reason to go to school. They are the center of their social lives and the place where students can demonstrate competence and be judged on that competence.

Most of all, art studies require significant time, focus, and concentration if students are to become competent in the discipline. Students can learn to achieve a state of mind known as *flow,* where concentration blocks out distractions and great creativity is achieved. Few other areas of study offer this opportunity so naturally. Successful arts programs at the high school level help students develop these skills and become more self-aware in exercising them.

One of the defining characteristics of college-level study in the arts that is often lacking in high school is the critiquing process. As we have already seen, high school students often view any less-than-positive feedback as an attack or a personal criticism. Learning to accept feedback on one's performance or artistic product, and then using it to improve, is an important capability for students who wish to continue in the arts. The more ubiquitous use of video cameras presents new opportunities for critiques in high school performing arts programs. In the visual arts, traditional critiques are still very useful in helping artists reflect on the technical and aesthetic properties of their work. High school students need to be introduced to the critique process gradually and with some sensitivity.

Arts programs can also seek to help students learn not to become discouraged when they are asked to do complex, time-consuming tasks, or tasks that they do not easily master. Many students who are outstanding in the arts in high school enter college only to be surrounded by others who were equally outstanding in their high schools. This increased competition can be threatening or devastating. To rise to this new challenge requires a certain amount of resilience and confidence that can be developed only when students have prior experience in being confronted by challenges that appear

> **High school students often view any less-than-positive feedback as an attack or a personal criticism.**

5

What Does a High
School That Prepares
Its Students for College
Success Look Like?

insurmountable but turn out to be manageable. If students are challenged at a level that causes them to be forced out of their comfort zone, and if they succeed in meeting the challenges, they will be ready for programs that take them to an entirely new level of challenge. They will view the expertise, talent, and creativity expectations they encounter in college as an exhilarating opportunity to grow and develop, rather than a discouraging threat to a carefully preserved image of competence in rigid boundaries.

Regardless of the specific art being taught, high school arts programs in a coherent program of study would help students develop competence along three distinct dimensions: technical knowledge and skills, cultural and historical knowledge and skills, and aesthetic and arts criticism knowledge and skills. Technical knowledge and skills are particular to the discipline being taught and are clearly developmental in nature. Students proceed naturally through a hierarchy of progressively more complex technical requirements in the discipline with each succeeding year of high school study. The arts lend themselves very naturally to this type of coherent skill development. Cultural and historical skills help the student understand how and where the discipline is situated in a historical context. This is important for understanding the styles, trends, and standards of the discipline and recognizing the main reference points of the discipline. Finally, students must master both aesthetic and arts criticism in order to receive constructive comments from peers and instructors and offer useful critiques to others.

Although performance is certainly one of the most powerful and useful formats in which to develop almost all of these skills, performance should not be an end in itself. The arts exist to be experienced by others, so performance or demonstration is central to their meaning. But a high school program of instruction has to develop all students who participate, not just those who excel in presentation. Attention to the development of all students in the context of the arts experience is key to involving a wide range of students in the arts.

Steps Faculty Can Take in the Arts

It is important to create avenues for participation in the arts that do not require performance or technical skills. Art history, music appreciation, and aesthetics courses are some examples. If it is impractical to create entire courses in these areas, it may be feasible to build units into other courses that touch on or expose students to aesthetic concepts and traditions. English and history courses are two obvious places where students can have at least minimal interaction with the arts in ways that contribute to the study of the primary discipline being taught.

Humanities courses specifically designed to achieve integration across English, history, and the arts can also accomplish this goal and in the process help students prepare for college-level humanities courses, which may be among the most stimulating that entering students take because they bring together so many different points of view and help students to make sense of them.

A Note About Senior Seminars

The senior-level seminar strategy that has been suggested throughout this chapter deserves a much more detailed exposition than space allows in this book. Developing these seminars is a challenging process for most schools, requiring, at a minimum, a careful curriculum mapping process in which the objectives and content of the prerequisite courses are articulated to lead to the seminar as a place where higher-level knowledge and skill integration can take place. Defining the relationship between the seminars and existing AP courses can also be daunting for many schools, as can finding the teachers who have the content knowledge and pedagogical skills necessary to make these exciting and valuable to students. Finally, the seminar is also dependent to some degree on close relations between the high school and postsecondary institutions, which can be the source of much advice and coaching on seminar content and assessment standards. For best results, the seminars should be designed jointly by high school and postsecondary education faculty and referenced against clear standards for college success.

The Center for Educational Policy Research (CEPR) is currently undertaking a project under the sponsorship of the Fund for the Improvement of Postsecondary Education (FIPSE) of the U.S. Department of Education to develop templates for seminars of this nature. The development process engages high school and postsecondary faculty as equals and also incorporates the Knowledge and Skills for University Success standards as the reference point for development work. The seminars will be field tested, and the final versions of templates will be posted on the CEPR Web site (http://cepr.uoregon.edu) as they are completed.

Given the challenges that exist in keeping students engaged in a meaningful fashion throughout the senior year, the risk of creating seminars specifically designed to treat twelfth-grade high school students more like college students in anticipation of their imminent transition may not be unacceptably high. Ideally, these seminars will create a reason for students who are taking less than a full schedule to remain more fully engaged in academics through graduation. If the seminars are valued by local colleges, student (and perhaps parent) motivation will grow as well.

5

What Does a High School That Prepares Its Students for College Success Look Like?

Increasing College Success: What We Can Do

What a school can do first to transform itself into one that prepares its students for college success is to examine carefully the goals, structure, and sequencing of its curriculum to determine if it develops students' intellect over the course of four years and demands more of them as they become more intellectually capable and cognitively competent. Schools can begin the process by answering the following questions.

Questions

- What frame of reference does the school use for developing its instructional program?
- What is the current explicit or implicit definition of a well-educated graduate?

Actions

These daunting questions can be answered by constituting a task force that is designed to determine the knowledge and skills around which the school's instructional program is organized currently. Although it is never easy to put together a task force, the key to doing so here is to keep the focus clearly on creating an inventory of current practices.

External standards can be useful in creating an analytic framework against which to gauge current practice. The task force should map these external standards against the school's curriculum to determine areas of strength and deficiency. The Knowledge and Skills for University Success standards can serve as a logical reference point for such discussions. As already noted, state standards now exist (although few explicitly identify knowledge and skills desired of all students by the end of twelfth grade), and these too can help frame the process. A number of resources now exist to help cross-reference state standards with college success standards. Mid-continent Research for Education and Learning (McREL; http://www.mcrel.org/standards-benchmarks) is one place to begin the search for such resources; Standards for Success is another (http://www.s4s.org).

Although the process is complex, it need not be exact. The goal at this point is to get a good, general idea of how to align a program, but not yet to consider remedies. The next chapter specifies the steps to take to redesign the program so that it is intellectually coherent.

Designing High Schools for Intellectual Coherence

Programs of study like the ones described in the previous chapter require attitudes toward learning that support student engagement and intellectual development throughout high school. Creating a structure focused on student intellectual growth will be a challenging task for many high schools. This chapter outlines some first steps a school can take in what will be a continuing journey toward enhanced intellectual coherence and better alignment with postsecondary success.

Creating Intentionality and a Clear Vision

The idea of an intellectually coherent, developmentally oriented program of study is a challenging one for most American high schools, in part because few are designed to ready the majority of their students for challenging postsecondary study. However, during the past fifteen years, student desires and state policies have nudged the educational system more in the direction of universal participation in postsecondary education. Simultaneously, many economic opportunities for those with high school diplomas alone have disappeared. The high school is thus challenged to create a program that prepares most of its students for postsecondary success. Yet most high schools are designed implicitly around the idea that students should be allowed to choose among several possible futures, with postsecondary education being only one of them.

A high school program of instruction that prepares students for college success requires intentionality and a certain commonality of purpose. The program must be geared toward a clear goal: a level of intellectual and skill development that connects seamlessly with what will be expected of students in college. Therefore, the faculty must have a vision of what a well-educated student looks like after four years of study at their school. This vision of a well-educated student can serve to guide the structure of the academic program and ensure that educational experiences over the four years are intentional and additive from the student's perspective. A good test of the degree to which a school has such a vision framing its instructional program is the number of students who can articulate the vision and describe how their current, previous, and future classes are contributing to achieving it. Few schools have attempted to create this sort of integrated, coherent, intellectually definable and defensible articulation of how a successful student would think, act, and learn after completing the school's program of instruction.

High schools may be hindered by their departmental structure and consequent compartmentalization of knowledge. Seldom do high school teachers engage in cross-disciplinary discussions about how students should mature intellectually over four years of instruction at their school. Few schools have agreements on how to make the curriculum progressively more challenging intellectually, or even on the precise material to be covered collectively in a series of courses.

> "High schools may be hindered by their departmental structure and consequent compartmentalization of knowledge."

Let us think for the moment about a vision that articulates what well-educated, intellectually mature students know and can do. Here is an example. These individuals can present and support a point of view convincingly and catch the potential flaws in an argument or in a text. They may even be able to make connections across different disciplines, drawing on principles learned in science to analyze policy proposals intended to remedy a complex social problem. These students might occasionally read something challenging simply because it catches their interest and then want to discuss it. This is not to imply that these students are not still vibrant adolescents. They are full of unanswered questions, are passionate about many things, and are still coming to an understanding of their full potential.

What is remarkable about these young people is how different they are now from when they entered the high school four years earlier. What is even more remarkable is how the high school they have attended has consciously and deliberately brought about this transformation in them. They can now construct a well-reasoned argument, and research a topic by locating appropriate source material and distinguishing the credibility of sources. They can express themselves in writing in formats ranging from short essays to extended papers. They ask interesting questions, understand complex concepts that are foundational to a line of thinking, apply high standards to the quality of the work they produce, and comprehend the general structure of the disciplines they study. They may even challenge teachers who put forth poorly reasoned arguments or unsubstantiated assertions or opinions.

Of course, some students at every high school already fit this description, and it is tempting to conclude that the others could as well if they simply took advantage of what was being offered to them. Would that it were so simple! Unfortunately, the majority of adolescents in contemporary American culture ride on the surface of their education, drawing their cues from its industrial roots to view themselves as widgets in an assembly line that requires little of them beyond showing up and doing as they are told. The high school must figuratively grab them, demand that they become engaged, develop their minds, stretch them, and make it clear that they are expected to become full members of a learning community whose goals are intellectual maturity and college success.

Creating Clear Expectations and Progress Markers

One of the first places to begin the curriculum transformation is with the orientation program for incoming students, particularly new ninth-graders. Most often, such orientations consist of a review of the student conduct manual and a cursory advising process focused on getting students to fill out a planned program of study. What is needed instead is a process that foreshadows for students the intellectual journey on which they are about to embark. They need a clear sense of the distance they will be expected to travel intellectually. They should adopt the perspective that they are about to enter into an extended period of growth.

> *They need a clear sense of the distance they will be expected to travel intellectually.*

To create this frame of mind requires the use of examples of culminating high school work samples, scoring guides, and course outlines. Some examples of college-level work samples are also presented in Chapter Seventeen. (More can be downloaded from the Standards for Success Web site: http://www.s4s.org.) High school faculty will want to create their own work sample collections over time, with special emphasis on the exit-level papers students about to graduate from the high school have produced. Basic versions of work samples with scoring guides can be published for parents as well. Internet-based communication allows more extended commentary and explanation of these examples as well as access by parents and students alike to the complete set of work samples.

Incoming students need to get a good idea of the type of work they will be doing and the products they will be expected to create. There is nothing wrong with them hearing from upper-class members about what they have experienced, but nothing can substitute for actual reviews of student writing, projects, assignments, tests, and readings. A number of state assessment systems require students to complete prescribed writing tasks while in high school, which are then scored by trained scorers outside the high school. Those states commonly make samples of student writing and scoring guides available, although such samples are almost never at a level consistent with college expectations. The College Board has added a writing requirement to the SAT, and the scoring criteria for that test can be viewed at the College Board Web site: http://www.collegeboard.com/student/testing/newsat/writing/essay_scoring.html. The College Board's college-readiness program, SpringBoard, which was described in Chapter Four, has an extensive set of exemplars in writing and mathematics at each of six performance levels spanning eighth through twelfth grade. ACT has similar examples for its optional writing test. Many college faculty are willing to share examples of student work if they are given enough time to secure student permissions.

Students should have the broad view of the intellectual arc of the program of study laid out before them to see where they will be going. They need to know how they will be judged and what the final target looks like. Becoming familiar with scoring guides is a useful process, even scoring sample work themselves. However, the most important feedback students receive over four years comes directly from teachers. The quality of the teachers' feedback determines whether students

> "They need to know how they will be judged and what the final target looks like."

understand what is expected of them in postsecondary education and how they are doing relative to those expectations.

All feedback should help students understand the key skills they need to be developing, not just what they get right or wrong. The feedback should be complex and detailed. Feedback on writing, for example, should critique overall organization, quality of argumentation, originality of thought, and accuracy of assertions, in addition to conventions and use of language. Feedback in science labs should focus on the degree to which students demonstrate understanding of scientific principles or the quality of their explanations of observed phenomena, in addition to how well they conduct an experiment. Feedback in math should focus on methods of problem solving, nontraditional solutions to problems, and student understanding of underlying mathematical concepts, in addition to number of correct answers. This is not to say that correct answers should not be valued, but only that the underlying cognitive processes necessary to construct them should be considered equally important.

When students are given this type of detailed, in-depth feedback over four years, they come to understand the thought processes they are expected to develop, and for the most part then strive to gain mastery of these thought processes. Absent appropriate feedback, they do not understand which skills they are supposed to be mastering, other than to provide correct answers or complete assignments as directed.

Portfolios are an idea that bears closer scrutiny now that electronic storage media make it easier to collect student work efficiently. As more student work is produced electronically and scanners and digital cameras become widely available in schools, student work can be collected and housed on a server. Students can use rewritable CDs and DVDs to retain their own copies of their portfolios, which they can share with their parents and use as a focus for parent-teacher conferences.

What the portfolio should contain can be determined by the KSUS standards, which may also serve as a checklist or rating system to determine the college success standards that each piece of work in the portfolio should meet. In other words, students can make a systematic effort to collect work and score each piece of work against the KSUS standards. This evidence can demonstrate college readiness as well as help diagnose areas in need of development. Although few admissions offices are set up to process portfolios today, as the movement toward comprehensive review of student applications continues, it is increasingly likely that at least some universities will learn how to assess carefully structured electronic portfolios rich in actual student work against university success standards. But even if portfolios cannot be incorporated into the admissions process anytime soon, they are nevertheless a powerful means of documenting intellectual development. For example, having each incoming ninth-grade student include in his or her portfolio a "baseline" writing sample, to be compared against writing produced at the end of each succeeding academic term, helps create "bookends" within which students' development over four years can be gauged.

Using the Alignment and Challenge Audit

Just as students should collect information that provides an overall perspective on their intellectual growth and development, so too should the school create a repository for all the information about the current state of its program of study and its evolution over time. Such a database would allow both students and teachers to determine how the pieces of the school's curriculum fit together into a cohesive whole. The Alignment and Challenge Audit, described in Chapter Four, creates exactly this type of database, which can be used to store information on each course so that quick and easy comparisons in and across courses and departments can be made.

The product of the audit is a profile that indicates which aspects of the instructional program are well aligned with university success standards and which are not. Curriculum design teams can then examine what is occurring cumulatively in like-named courses and throughout a sequence of courses—for example, from freshman through senior English. Thus, it becomes possible to build a more coherent program of study in which particular intellectual skills are developed systematically and progressively. Instead of having one English class emphasize writing while the next includes little writing at all, a well-sequenced curriculum develops writing capabilities systematically, along with a host of other key cognitive skills. Much room remains for teachers to choose specific instructional materials and activities, but the school has a commitment to a common focus and curriculum progression that is apparent to students and is cumulative in an intellectual sense as well.

The audit can also result in a report that highlights the areas of strong and weak alignment between the high school's instructional program and college readiness standards. Based on this information, the school can create better connections between and across courses, calibrate the challenge level expected of students as they progress, spot redundancies and omissions, and clarify the overarching goals and purposes of the school's instructional program. Staff can then work together, accessing the source data themselves, to revise and fine-tune their course content and teaching methodologies to create greater consistency and ensure proper challenge levels over four years of study.

Ensuring Students Do Not Make Bad Decisions

A properly structured high school is one in which it is virtually impossible for students to make a bad decision about which courses to take, because all courses have been designed and articulated in a framework of common goals and expectations. When a school has such a carefully designed and connected program of study, students can plan their course of study very differently from how they do it today. Rather than being focused on checking off requirements to achieve the required total of credits, they would plan a course of study that is intellectually coherent and developmentally appropriate. Different students may find different paths through the program, but all would be headed in the same general direction—toward intellectual growth consistent with success in postsecondary education.

> "A properly structured high school is one in which it is virtually impossible for students to make a bad decision."

It is true that students would have fewer choices, but they also would have more common experiences. With greater clarity on what is required for success, they would be able to support each other's success. A common vocabulary would develop, and students would gear their efforts toward the core concepts, knowledge, and skills that such a vocabulary portrays. Each successive graduating class would offer guidance to those that follow it. Because experiences would be similar and well defined, older children would help prepare their younger siblings or friends for what lies ahead. Everyone would know that each person will face similar experiences and expectations. Rather than seeking to avoid such experiences, students would learn how to succeed at them. The curriculum and the high school experience overall would be clearer and more meaningful. The commitment to engage positively would be greater.

The common courses would be designed to include hands-on experiences and opportunities for students to create products, the goal being to accommodate a range of learning styles. Not all learning would be abstract or book-based. Mastery of requisite knowledge could be demonstrated in various ways in a variety of course types, including many now considered electives by colleges. The KSUS standards value interdisciplinary understanding, inquisitiveness, and the excitement about knowledge that can arise only with application and experimentation. Thus, students could work on video development projects, solar car models, computer assisted design, robotics, and a host of hands-on learning experiences that would augment, supplement, or even replace, where appropriate, text-based instruction and learning.

Increasing College Success: What We Can Do

To achieve this goal—an intellectually coherent instructional program that eases the transition to postsecondary education—requires an examination of current practices in relation to external standards, specifically the Knowledge and Skills for University Success standards. A comprehensive external set of standards is a crucial component in a systematic process of examination and redesign to create the kind of coherent program described here. Some of these strategies overlap and extend ideas presented in the previous chapter.

Question
- What does the profile of a well-educated graduate look like, one who is prepared to succeed in postsecondary education?

Actions
This profile can be built on the work done by the task force that Chapter Five suggested creating. This task force is charged with analyzing the strengths and weaknesses of the curriculum and program of instruction in relation to external standards. From this analysis and discussion, the task force can proceed to develop a profile of a well-educated graduating senior. It should describe what this person knows, how this person thinks, and how well this person has mastered the key knowledge, skills, and strategies necessary for college success.

This profile can be used to gauge discrepancies between the results of the current instructional program and the desired results. After discrepancies are identified, the task force can determine the proportion of each graduating class for which discrepancies exist. This analysis helps determine which changes in the curriculum are necessary to increase the proportion of students who achieve the level of intellectual competence specified in the profile.

Question

- How well do graduates from the high school fare during their freshman year in college?

Actions

In combination with measures of how many students enroll in postsecondary education directly from high school, one of the best gauges of the success of the high school instructional program is college freshman-year performance. Many colleges provide this information, but few high schools use it systematically.

To do so, the high school can begin by gathering information on the GPA of college freshmen but also seek more detailed information on performance in individual college courses, particularly the first math and writing courses that students from the high school take at local colleges. The goal is to examine the trends over time to ascertain if more students are increasingly successful. This is not likely to occur if no changes are being made in the high school program of preparation. However, if the types of changes outlined in this book are undertaken, improvement in college success should be seen over time. Success in entry-level courses is the "gold standard" against which the quality and suitability of the high school program of instruction should be judged.

Questions

- How do local postsecondary institutions place incoming students into entry-level math, English, writing, and second language courses?
- What can students do, particularly during their senior year, to prepare to perform well on these measures in order to place into the appropriate entry-level college courses?

Actions

Many students are placed improperly when they reach college, in part because they have no idea what the placement policies are and in part because the placement instrument does not match up well with what they were taught in high school. The first step high schools can take is to research the content of the placement tests used at the colleges to which most of their students apply. Once this information is known, it can be shared with juniors and particularly seniors in the high school. The seniors who are not taking math classes are most at risk. They should participate in workshops to help them prepare for the placement tests. Ideally, the high school math curriculum, and particularly the course most students take last in high school, should be adjusted so that it addresses in a more deliberate fashion the content of placement tests.

Question

• How can the content of the high school and college curricula be better aligned?

Actions

As noted throughout this book, the alignment between high school and college is loose, inconsistent, or even coincidental. Achieving intentional curriculum alignment should be a key goal for high schools and colleges.

One way to begin this process is to convene teams of high school teachers and local postsecondary faculty to study student work from high school and college and set mutual expectations for quality work, both in content and in cognitive challenge.

A more sophisticated and demanding strategy is to construct high school and college courses that are systematically aligned. As mentioned in Chapter Five, work is ongoing to develop templates for courses in the core academic areas that schools and colleges could then adapt locally. In addition to the course templates mentioned previously, this research will document the process that high schools and colleges should follow if they seek to work together to develop such courses. Current plans are to post descriptions of a process for collaborative course development on the CEPR Web site in early 2006 (http://cepr.uoregon.edu).

The senior seminar was discussed at length in the previous chapter. This is another way to link high school and college. As a result of joint development efforts and closer collaborative relationships, the colleges could be expected to agree to accept these seminars as meeting course requirements for the discipline in which they are offered as well as to use data from them in lieu of placement test results. This would provide greater motivation for students to participate in the seminars.

As we have seen, these seminars would focus on several key issues from the discipline and investigate them in depth. In order to succeed in the seminars, students would already need to have well-developed content knowledge. Without such a foundation, the seminars could easily become intellectually empty exercises in process. However, when they demand that students draw on and extend their content knowledge in order to deepen their understanding, such seminars can foster deep thinking about what has already been learned and what will be learned in college.

PART TWO

The First-Year Experience and Beyond

The chapters in Part Two go on to present greater insight into the first-year college experience. Chapter Seven examines the attitudes and behaviors associated with success in college, followed by a glimpse of what goes on in freshman college classrooms as gleaned from research. Also in Chapter Seven we get a last look "Through the Students' Eyes," rejoining our students Alicia, Derrick, and Teresa, who have now begun college. Chapter Eight provides a discussion of the general education curriculum with examples of the types of programs offered at a range of universities, a discussion of placement tests, and examples of typical schedules for students during their freshman year. Chapter Nine concludes Part Two with a discussion of the policy trends that may lead to greater alignment between high school and college, and outlines what key constituencies must do to create better high school–college alignment, including policymakers, high school and college administrators, and faculty, students, and parents.

Experiencing Success
in the First Year of College

Sadly, the celebration of admission to college is often soon followed by the harsh realization that being in college is a struggle. Many students never make the successful transition from high school to college. There are two main reasons for this lack of success: factors directly related to ability to succeed in the classroom, and more general behaviors. Although general behaviors, and particularly poor time management, cause problems for many students, factors directly related to classroom performance are most germane to this book, which focuses on the knowledge and skills students must master to be ready to succeed in entry-level college courses.

In the process of gathering the data that yielded the KSUS standards, certain themes emerged time after time at every campus meeting. What was surprising was that even at America's best universities, faculty frequently commented on the gaping holes in students' content knowledge. It was not that students did not know anything; they knew quite a lot. However, they were often unable to connect what they knew or see how the pieces fit together. In addition, there were gaps in their knowledge that prevented them from understanding course concepts or caused them to fall behind.

A discussion among faculty members at a leading research university illustrates the problem. Students' knowledge of the general flow of history—not necessarily of specific dates—reflects widely divergent understandings of how events are sequenced. Students might know that there was an event called the Civil War; they might even be able to recite several of its causes. They might know there was something called World War I, and they might be able to identify that it occurred in Europe. Yet they might not know which of the two events came first.

Similarly, even though they may have taken three or four years of high school mathematics and received respectable grades, students often enter college mathematics courses with math phobia. As a result they block out much of their basic knowledge of algebra and mathematical language and symbols. College math teachers find themselves reteaching the direction the arrow points in the "greater than" and "lesser than" symbols, or how to add and subtract exponents. Thus, many students never progress much beyond an entry-level college math course—assuming they are not placed in a remedial course in the first place.

> **Students often enter college mathematics courses with math phobia.**

Lack of experience with statistics makes economics and some life science courses much more difficult for entering students. College instruction in entry-level courses often draws on statistical models and statistical databases as the framework for understanding the subject matter being taught. Quantitative analysis skills are expected in an ever-increasing number of courses. Potential business majors are severely handicapped if they do not have the ability to interpret charts and graphs and other data accurately and insightfully. When students fail an entry-level college course because they lack the prerequisite skill, they often avoid majors in that area of study altogether, closing off entire avenues of the curriculum and career pathways.

This may drive students toward the nontechnical majors, but what they face there is an expectation that they write, reason, conduct research, document their assertions, edit and rewrite a piece of work, and interpret information to reach conclusions or make generalizations. These skills are as demanding in their own way as knowledge of mathematics, statistics, or physics.

And woe to the student whose game plan is based primarily on completing assignments at the last minute or dashing off the first thing that comes to mind.

University instructors expect students to produce well-reasoned, mechanically sound pieces of writing in a wide array of classes. Writing has always been at the heart of a university education and the university culture, and it will only become more important in a society whose economy is based on information exchange.

Second language instruction at the college level is hindered by students' poor grasp of English grammar. Even the concepts of subject and predicate have to be reviewed and relearned. Students also have difficulty understanding the fundamentals of the culture in which a language is spoken because they lack geographical knowledge. They have misconceptions about the location of countries in which the language is spoken and the historical relationships between neighboring countries that influence language and culture. Students are often surprised to realize that Latin influenced the evolution of a whole set of geographically related languages in central and southern Europe. They are shocked at how small Greece is, given its influence on Western culture.

Part of the problem is that not enough students complete a rigorous program of study in high school. According to a 2001 U.S. Department of Education study, approximately one-third (31 percent) completed a core curriculum consisting of four years of English, three years of social studies, three years of mathematics, and three years of science. Half completed a midlevel curriculum with a minimum of one year of foreign language, geometry, and Algebra I and three years of science including two of the three following courses: biology, chemistry, physics. Only 19 percent completed what researchers defined as a "rigorous curriculum," which had at least four years of English, four years of mathematics (including pre-calculus or higher), three years of foreign language, three years of social studies, three years of science (including biology, chemistry, and physics), and at least one advanced placement (AP) class or test taken.

Although much of what has been presented here may seem to paint a picture of university students who are not properly prepared for the expectations and demands of postsecondary education, graduation rates at the best universities actually approach or even exceed 90 percent. At state universities it drops to about 50 percent. State colleges see a lower rate yet, according to figures from the National Center for Education Statistics. Overall, about a third of any entering class can be expected to graduate in four years. If we widen the window to six years, the figure again increases to closer to half. Thus, students are not incompetent but they often

> **"Students must learn or relearn material they should have mastered in high school."**

take more than four years to graduate, in part because they must learn or relearn material they should have mastered in high school.

Students in the United States are noted for changing majors, which is one of the reasons why it takes many of them more than four years to graduate. However, they should not have to change majors because they lack the foundational knowledge and skills necessary to pursue the original field in which they were interested. The university experience works best when students truly can choose among their options rather than be consigned to a default option for lack of particular background knowledge.

It is also worth considering the additional cost incurred when a student must spend more than four years in college. Those costs include money spent on the education itself—tuition, books, room and board, and so on—as well as the opportunity cost, which is the cost of not doing something else during the additional year or two spent in college, such as beginning one's career and earning a salary that year.

Two Key Stumbling Blocks

Besides mastery of core content knowledge, at least two other factors are critically important to student success, particularly at research universities but at all postsecondary institutions to a significant degree. These are intellectual maturity and understanding the purpose of college and the opportunities it presents.

> **"When a student has intellectual maturity, his mind is simultaneously open to new possibilities and disciplined to apply particular tools for thinking and analysis."**

Lack of Intellectual Maturity

When a student has intellectual maturity, his mind is simultaneously open to new possibilities and disciplined to apply particular tools for thinking and analysis. Such "habits of the mind" have been discussed extensively throughout this book. They are ways of thinking about knowledge and learning. They are the basic perspective students bring to the learning task or to any field of study.

The college curriculum at the entry level has many shortcomings, but most college programs of study do expect students to go beyond mere mastery of content knowledge to engage in tasks that require higher-order thinking. Curricular coherence in many colleges has been enhanced with the introduction of strands, pathways, and other vehicles to create conscious connections among courses in ways that develop intellectual skills in addition to conveying content knowledge.

The curriculum at smaller liberal arts colleges is often defined by its strong emphasis on developing these exact skills—basically, to make students better thinkers. They accomplish this through multicourse sequences and classes designed explicitly to develop intellectual maturity. Faculty at these colleges, and to a large extent throughout postsecondary education, share a tacit agreement on the importance of intellectual development generally and the role of general education requirements in preparing students for success in the major of their choice.

Of course, it is in the major that students really develop this intellectual maturity and hone their skills. Majors are generally designed very systematically to ensure not only content knowledge mastery but development of the key ways of knowing and thinking associated with the discipline and area in which the major is situated.

When students enter college without the sense that their intellect is a work in progress, they often become confused and frustrated by the demands made on them to think, reason, critique, analyze, reflect, ponder, posit, and value. College constantly confronts students with the expectation that they do more than the minimal amount of thinking required to complete assignments. Students with little training in this way of approaching learning spend more time complaining about professors or their grading systems than on delving deeply into the challenging intellectual tasks they are given.

Lack of Understanding of the Purpose and Opportunities of College

According to research conducted by Andrea Venezia, Michael Kirst, and Anthony Antonio, close to 90 percent of high school students say they want to go to college or at least think it is a desirable goal. A smaller proportion of them settle on a career direction and see college as a step on the path to that career. The great majority hold the rather unsophisticated view that college is some sort of extension of high school, albeit without the same restrictive rules. They are naturally concerned about roommates, dorm food, and the like, but few have really digested what it is

7

Experiencing
Success in the
First Year of College

Experiencing Success in the First Year of College   **117** that college is going to do to them or expect from them. More important for our discussion is that few students understand the full range of opportunities college offers them or how to take advantage of those potential opportunities.

For example, few students distinguish much between a research university and a similar large institution with the word "university" in its name. Clearly, students are acutely aware of institutional prestige, as are their parents, but far fewer can identify institutional purpose for the colleges on the lists of schools to which they intend to apply. Many factors influence student choice: geographic location, size, perhaps even the presence and quality of a particular major or field of study. Few students select a research university because they are interested in the research in which faculty are engaged. Few select a land-grant university because its mission is to generate research and solutions for agriculture and industry in the state. Perhaps more students select small liberal arts colleges because they understand that such schools put a greater emphasis on the quality of their undergraduate classes.

However, understanding these differences is important to avoid frustration, particularly during the first year of college. Many research universities (and other state schools) have large undergraduate courses with breakout sections taught by graduate students. This is not necessarily a bad model, but if the students' entire freshman year consists of large, impersonal lecture courses and accompanying discussion sections, they may soon wonder what advantage they gain from being at an institution with eight Nobel laureates.

This is where students who have a better sense of their own intellectual growth and development have an advantage. A student need not be the best or the brightest to capture greater faculty attention or gain access to the myriad programs and opportunities that are available in large, complex institutions. What is necessary is some spark, some enthusiasm for the subject being taught, and a willingness to go beyond the minimum to engage in the process of intellectual growth and development that most faculty hope their students will attempt.

> "A student need not be the best or the brightest to capture faculty attention or gain access to the myriad programs and opportunities that are available."

Students who take such an approach can find themselves involved in research projects, seminars, assistantships, summer programs, field studies, internships, or in a mentor relationship. The 2003 National Survey of Student Engagement reported that 72 percent of college seniors had participated in an internship or practicum,

66 percent in community volunteer work, and 27 percent in a learning community. At research universities 29 percent of students engaged in research with a faculty member, a considerable proportion. But at liberal arts colleges nearly 40 percent of students reported working on research with faculty members. Even in large courses, students report engaging in discussion, study, and project groups, which offer opportunities to interact with students who may have very different backgrounds or points of view. According to Richard Light in his book on Harvard freshmen, one of the experiences that students consistently cite as among the most positive aspects of their first year is the interaction they have with others who come from backgrounds different from their own.

College is the place to take advantage of a wide range of opportunities outside the classroom. This is just as true at a community college as at a research university. The key, according to research by Light and others, is to establish a personal relationship with a faculty member. Students who connect with faculty and other students express greater satisfaction with their college education. Connecting with faculty or other program staff generally means doing more than the minimum of attending class. It happens for students who conceive of college as a time to learn who they are and what is possible in their lives.

Many colleges and universities have designed freshman experiences to foster these connections. Incoming students should be certain to take advantage of seminars, interest groups, discussions, lecture series, trips and outings sponsored by the college, and volunteer and internship programs, as well as opportunities to work directly with faculty on research, writing, and teaching. These multidimensional experiences not only connect students more personally with their education but also offer the rare opportunity for self-discovery that occurs only at certain points in a person's life. The freshman year is one of those points. It can be a life-changing experience, and when those experiences lead to greater engagement in college, the effect is to enrich the academic experience for students and enhance their success in college.

Insights into the First-Year College Experience

We do have some insights into how students experience their first year of college. The information comes from the National Survey of Student Engagement, which during its first four years in existence has been administered at over 725 different colleges and universities around the nation. This is a much wider population than the sixty Association of American Universities (AAU) research universities that served as the reference point for the KSUS standards presented later in this book. The results offer a revealing picture of college life as new students experience it across higher education.

First-year students were asked how much time they spent on academic work. This category includes preparing for class, studying, writing, rehearsing, and other activities related to the academic program and is in addition to the ten to twenty hours students are expected to attend class if they are taking a full academic load. On average, the study found that 18 percent of American college students spent between one and five hours on preparation per week, 24 percent spent from six to ten hours per week, 20 percent from eleven to fifteen hours, 16 percent from sixteen to twenty hours, 10 percent from twenty-one to twenty-five hours, and 6 percent from twenty-six to thirty hours. Only 5 percent spent more than thirty hours per week preparing for class. (See Table 7.1.)

The national averages can be contrasted with results for the top 5 percent of students. These students reported a somewhat different pattern in terms of the time they spent preparing for class. Seventeen percent spent twenty-one to twenty-five hours, 13 percent devoted twenty-six to thirty hours per week, and another 13 percent worked more than thirty hours each week preparing for class. In other words, 43 percent of the top students spent more than twenty hours preparing for

Table 7.1. Hours Per Week First-Year Students Spend Preparing for Class

Hours Per Week	Percent of Students Spending This Amount of Time:	
	National Average	Top 5 Percent of Students
1–5	18	5
6–10	24	14
11–15	20	19
16–20	16	19
21–25	10	17
26–30	6	13
More than 30	5	13

Source: National Survey of Student Engagement. (2003). *Converting Data into Action: Expanding the Boundaries of Institutional Improvement,* p. 33.

class in addition to the hours they spent attending class. For these students, college was equivalent to a full-time job.

This information on time spent preparing for class is even more striking when considered against the results of a study Tom Loveless conducted in 2003 on the amount of time high school students spend studying. He found that only a third of seventeen-year-old high school students devoted at least an hour a day to homework. Compare this figure with the hours college freshman report necessary to prepare for class, and the contrast is clear. The change in expectations can be a shock to the system of students accustomed to spending little time on class preparation and homework while still receiving good grades.

When selecting a college, it is important to have a realistic idea of the amount of time required for class preparation. This is particularly true for students who plan to participate in activities that take up significant amounts of out-of-class time or who must work more than about twelve hours per week. They must recognize the need for good time management early on, before they get behind in their studies, which is a harbinger of disaster for most first-year college students.

As for the material that first-year students are expected to read, 49 percent of all college students received eleven or more assigned textbooks or book-length packets of course readings per year. For the top 5 percent of students, 76 percent read eleven or more textbooks or reading packets per year, including 37 percent with twenty or more texts. (See Table 7.2.) This is one of the differences between high school and college—the amount and pace of reading, particularly in literature, history, humanities, and other reading-intensive courses. Students accustomed to reading only a few books each semester are shocked to find out they are expected to read a book per week, and to understand it well at the same time.

Writing is very important in college, and many classes besides composition emphasize it. But how much are incoming students expected to write during their first year in college? Many students would be relieved to hear that 84 percent of the students surveyed said they were not expected to write a paper twenty pages or longer, whereas 13 percent reported being required to write between one and four papers that were longer than twenty pages. When it came to writing papers of five to nineteen pages, though, 48 percent reported writing between one and four of them and 28 percent said they wrote between five and ten of them. For shorter papers—less than five pages long—33 percent wrote between five and ten of these, 26 percent wrote between eleven and twenty, and 16 percent wrote more than twenty. (See Table 7.3.) So when students tally up the number of short and

Table 7.2. Texts or Reading Packets Read During the First Year of College

Texts or Reading Packets Read	Percent of Students Spending This Amount of Time:	
	National Average	Top 5 Percent of Students
1–4	15	4
5–10	34	18
11–20	32	39
More than 20	17	37

Source: National Survey of Student Engagement. (2003). *Converting Data into Action: Expanding the Boundaries of Institutional Improvement,* p. 33.

Table 7.3. Length and Number of Papers Required During the First Year of College

Length of Required Papers (in Pages)	Number of Papers of This Length Required	Percent of Students Completing This Number of Papers: National Average	Percent of Students Completing This Number of Papers: Top 5 Percent of Students
More than 20	1–4	13	20
	5–10	2	2
	11–20	1	1
	More than 20	1	0
From 5–19	1–4	48	35
	5–10	28	40
	11–20	10	19
	More than 20	2	4
Less than 5	1–4	23	17
	5–10	33	33
	11–20	26	28
	More than 20	16	20

Source: National Survey of Student Engagement. (2003). *Converting Data into Action: Expanding the Boundaries of Institutional Improvement,* p. 33.

medium-length papers required, it becomes apparent that they are likely to be writing something every week, and in many cases, two or more papers of moderate length each week.

The emphasis and goals of courses may shift between high school and college. In college, courses are more likely to emphasize analyzing the basic elements of an idea, experience, or theory. High school courses often focus more on memorizing information or interpreting and applying information in a basic fashion, whereas college courses contain more concepts and ideas, theories and principles. Although knowledge of specific content and even the memorization of specific facts can still be an important part of a course, college often requires students to go beyond what is written in the text or said in class to develop a deeper understanding of underlying theories and principles in a discipline or area of study. In fact, 80 percent of students surveyed said they engaged in learning that required "quite a bit" or "very much" analysis of the basic elements of an idea, experience, or theory.

Some 66 percent reported that their coursework emphasized synthesizing and organizing ideas, information, or experiences "quite a bit" or "very much." In the same vein, 64 percent of students reported coursework that emphasized making judgments about the value of information, arguments, or methods "quite a bit" or "very much." Meanwhile, 72 percent were in classes that emphasized applying theories or concepts to practical problems or in new situations regularly. These activities require much more independent action by students and less guessing what instructors want to hear, following textbook directions, or simply completing assignments. In short, they value engagement and motivation over passive learning. Students eager to face an intellectually challenging environment will fare far better in such courses than those who only seek to get a good grade or complete a requirement.

In what ways do students become more actively involved in learning during the first year of college? The majority (58 percent) discussed ideas from their readings often or very often, and 59 percent asked questions in class or contributed to discussions. Just over half, 56 percent, sometimes made a class presentation, and an additional 29 percent made class presentations often or very often. Over a third (38 percent) worked with other students during class time on class projects often or very often. Similarly, 42 percent worked with classmates outside of class on a class project often or very often. (See Table 7.4.) College classes are environments that expect students to engage with one another as a central dimension of the learning process.

Table 7.4. Ways First-Year Students Say They Engage in Learning

Way of Engaging in Learning	Percent of Students
Discuss ideas from readings (often or very often).	58
Ask questions in class or contribute to class discussions (often or very often).	59
Make a class presentation (sometimes or often).	79
Work with other students on projects during class time (sometimes or often).	79
Work with other students outside of class on a class project (sometimes or often).	78

Source: National Survey of Student Engagement. (2003). *Converting Data into Action: Expanding the Boundaries of Institutional Improvement,* p. 35.

The National Survey of Student Engagement data help paint a picture of the experience incoming students actually have in college classrooms. One additional study is also informative of how students experience the freshman year. The *2003 Your First College Year (YFCY) survey,* conducted by the National Resource Center for the First-Year Experience and Students in Transition, provides a "snapshot" of how students experience the first year of college. In terms of students' self-ratings of success during the first year of college, 52 percent rated themselves "somewhat successful" adjusting to the academic demands of college, 61 percent reported they were somewhat successful developing study skills, and 60 percent reported they were somewhat successful managing time effectively. The majority of students, 71 percent, reported attending classes and labs more than eleven hours per week. When it came to hours of homework, students broke into those who said they spent less than six hours per week (37 percent), six to ten hours per week (31 percent), and eleven or more hours per week (32 percent.) Half of all students reported receiving tutoring during their freshman year. When asked about pedagogical practices present in their classes, 83 percent indicated their classes contained lectures "occasionally" or "frequently," 74 percent produced multiple drafts of written work, two-thirds engaged in research projects, 61 percent in group projects, and 58 percent completed weekly assignments. Regarding the personal challenges experienced during their first year, 40 percent said they "frequently" felt overwhelmed by all they had to do. They saw their grade point averages (GPA) decrease from high school to college as well. Although 29 percent of students reported high school GPAs in the 3.75 to 4.0+ range, only 17 percent were that high at the end of their first year in college. Similarly, of the 46 percent of students whose high school GPAs were in the 3.25 to 3.74 range, only 32 percent had equivalent college GPAs at the end of one year.

Once again we see that the college experience can be quite different from the high school experience in expectations and intentions. In what other ways is the college classroom different from high school? The next section explores this question further.

The Evolving College Classroom

Most people have one of several common pictures of a college classroom. The one most often presented in popular culture is of the professor in the tweed sport coat waxing eloquent about the meaning of life while a class of perhaps fifteen sits enthralled. At the other extreme is the image immortalized in the 1973 movie *The Paper Chase,* where the stern, white-haired maestro of the podium calls on students at random, then peers over half-glasses to ask a deceptively simple or impossibly difficult question to an obviously unprepared and clearly flustered student. A third common view is of the lecture hall, filled with at least three hundred students, half of them asleep or listening to their headphones, while some pedant drones on about the bones in the foot of a lizard, never looking up while scribbling on the board or displaying slides on the overhead projector. According to a more recent view, the class that the star professor is listed as teaching is actually being taught by a graduate student, newly arrived in the United States and speaking with such a heavy accent that it is impossible to understand what he or she is saying while the professor makes only cameo appearances throughout the term.

Each of these images probably does represent some college classrooms. However, the reality is far more complex, and thankfully, more positive. College teaching is constantly evolving, as driven by technology, changing student wants and needs, and the most important factor of all, the institutions' need to compete for students with other institutions of higher education.

Colleges and universities in the United States can no longer take for granted that students will tolerate any form of instruction that is served to them. Nor do they need to rely solely on traditional teaching methods, although many most assuredly continue to. However, today's incoming college freshmen are likely to expect and want an array of learning experiences. Although institutional realities ensure that at least one of these will almost certainly be a large lecture class—except at the smaller liberal arts colleges that pride themselves on small classes—even in the large lecture class, many things are changing.

> *Today's incoming college freshmen are likely to expect and want an array of learning experiences.*

Electronic course management systems such as Blackboard have become ubiquitous. In more and more colleges, all courses automatically have an electronic online component created for them. In addition, some faculty have been employing customized Web sites for their classes for some time already. These online augmentations contain notes, supplemental materials and readings, links to useful Web sites, assignments, and a host of other resources that would not have been available to students in the past simply because reproduction costs would have been prohibitive. More instructors are taking advantage of course management options that permit online discussions and easier coordination of group assignments, submission of work electronically, and more frequent interaction with instructors outside of class time and office hours. It is not uncommon for instructors to reply to student e-mail inquiries at odd hours of the day and night or on weekends. This is a real departure from the past, when students were only able to talk with professors during the limited time period devoted to office hours (although most professors still maintain office hours too).

Lectures are being recorded and stored for download via high-speed campus networks or for retrieval on CD or DVD for viewing on a computer. Illustrations, charts, graphs, formulas, and visual aids can all be downloaded. Tests can be taken and grades checked online.

The net effect of this increased reliance on Web-based technology is to make it much more convenient for students to access and review information from lectures, interact more conveniently and meaningfully with fellow students and instructors, and gain some flexibility in how they learn material in these large classes. The flip side is that students are expected to take advantage of these online resources, take the initiative to use them as necessary, and explore them as appropriate. This means that those who routinely did what they were told and only what they were told to do in high school are at a distinct disadvantage. Although some of the better-equipped American high schools have begun to move in the same directions with online learning, most have not, at least not to the degree that colleges and universities have recently done. And even if the gap between the availability of online learning support in high school and college closes, it is likely that college students will still be expected to take much more initiative in using these resources.

Through the Students' Eyes

Let us rejoin our friends Alicia, Derrick, and Teresa one last time as they progress through their first year of college.

Alicia

Alicia's first year of college comes as a surprise to her in many ways. She does not even enroll until two weeks before classes begin. She had intended to, but then she thought she might take off time to travel with her friends. When that fell through, she looked around for a job but found nothing other than minimum-wage positions in which she had little interest. She was still helping out in her parents' business, but she did not have a great deal of interest in making that her career, at least not at this point. She also realized that she really did not have any marketable skills, although the business class she took, an office assistant position in the school's main office, and a brief internship at a local bank had helped her understand what would be expected of her in an office environment. In addition, although the business class and the other experiences were not bad, she found that the prospect of spending all day in an office did not really appeal to her.

She enrolls in person at the local community college because her parents' home does not have the high-speed Internet access necessary for the online enrollment option, and in any event she is not sure what courses she needs to take or how to pay fees online. Although counseling services are available at the community college she does not take advantage of them, in part because she did not become familiar with what a counselor does while she was in high school. She does know that she wants to attend a four-year college eventually, so she enrolls in the transfer curriculum that the college's registration materials outline so clearly.

Another thing Alicia does not realize when she begins the year is that she will have to take a math placement test and receive a placement, because she has not taken math in two years and does not have an ACT or SAT score. This requirement delays her selection of math courses; as a result, the section offered at the most convenient time is no longer available by the time she is ready to register for it. Furthermore, she does not do as well as she had hoped on the test and has to begin with a remedial mathematics course for her first term. Her placement test scores came with a cautionary note: her score suggested she was at risk of having difficulty in the remedial course. She locates the room number and hours of the campus math-tutoring center. She has to take a similar placement test in reading and writing and discovers, much to her surprise, that she performs poorly in writing too and so has to take a remedial writing course as well in order to become eligible for the regular writing course. These two classes will ultimately add a semester to the time it will take her to transfer.

When she begins the math course, she understands why she has gotten the cautionary note. The pace is much faster than in high school, even though the basic concepts and material are not new to her. Because the homework is not collected or graded, she finds it difficult to motivate herself to complete the assignments. But she soon finds out that her preparation for the first test is inadequate, because she does not have the homework as a frame of reference for studying. She finds herself thinking that she does not really need math anyway, and within six weeks has decided never to take another math course, other than what is required to transfer. She now understands that her choice of college major will be limited to those that require little math.

As she has struggled with her remedial writing course, she has wondered what college majors will be open to a student like her, who cannot do math and cannot write well. Such stark thoughts have helped motivate her to concentrate on her writing in a way she never did in high school. She now finds herself actually willing to rewrite an assignment to improve it based on the feedback provided. She pays much closer attention to the conventions of the

English language and can construct grammatically acceptable passages with some effort. She has even picked up a book on vocabulary building and over time has expanded the range of words she employs in her writing. By the end of the first quarter, she completes the remedial course successfully and enrolls in a regular college English course.

She still has no real idea of what she will pursue in college, but she is getting a better idea of what is involved in being successful. Who knows? Maybe she will try another math course next summer when she can concentrate on it fully. This would have been easier, she thinks, if she had known in high school what she knows now about what it takes to succeed in college!

DERRICK

Although it hardly seems fair to his sister, Derrick is doing reasonably well academically during his first year in college. Having been accepted to the smaller liberal arts school to which he applied has turned out to be a blessing. Still, it has been necessary for him to drop college math first semester and he has really struggled in his science lab courses to interpret the results of experiments instead of simply writing them down.

On the brighter side, his winning personality is an asset in this smaller, more personal environment, as his sister predicted. One of his instructors invites him to participate in a seminar for freshmen only in which, much to his surprise, he discovers an interest in political and economic issues. He decides a statistics course is going to be a necessity to progress in these fields, and he adds one to his planned program of study. But the seminar does more than awaken an interest in a new subject. He realizes how much work it takes to formulate a cogent argument, one that can be supported when attacked in a discussion. He also realizes he said almost nothing in high school class discussions when he might have appeared not to know the answer to the question at hand. This, of course, limited his participation dramatically. It occurs to him that this is what speech and debate had probably been about, and that it would have been a good idea to have participated in something like that while in high school. But he does not take much time to ponder what might have been, and anyway, he is late for practice.

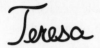

Teresa was pleased to learn that she had been accepted at her top three choices. The more she thought about it, the more inclined she was to accept the offer from what had originally been her number two choice. She found that the more she learned about the specific programs the college had, the more she felt it matched her interests and style. She particularly liked the idea that she would be actively engaged in conducting research even during her freshman year, and that she would have the opportunity to interact with faculty who were engaged in research. She was starting to think she might be more interested in the research end of aerospace sciences than in the astronaut end, which was fine with her parents.

She enters college with enough credits to put her two-thirds of the way through her freshman year. She is also able to begin with courses beyond the introductory level. This enables her to enroll in some smaller courses right from the beginning. The advanced standing her credits give her also allows her to select courses before other freshmen, which helps her get into some of the specialty courses in which she has an interest, including a composition course where she will learn about writing short stories.

What has been particularly nice for her is that she is not intimidated or overwhelmed by the challenge or pace of college work. Although her time management skills certainly come in handy, she is also prepared for the intellectual challenge. She tries to make sure to get the "big picture" for each class, to understand what is really essential and important to the subject being studied. She knows how to utilize the extensive resources that are available on campus to advise students and to inform them about the myriad activities open to them. That is how she has gotten involved in whitewater rafting as well as the poetry discussion group, each of which leads her to meet a new group of people she would not otherwise have gotten to know. Although she often works late into the evening preparing for class, she does so with a sense of satisfaction. She finds herself frequently thinking that college is turning out to be everything she had hoped it would be, and more.

What We Can Learn from "Through the Students' Eyes"

The experiences of Alicia, Derrick, and Teresa offer several lessons that are worth recapping. College success, in the current system, depends on a complex partnership among high school faculty, college admissions officers and faculty, students, and their parents. If any one of these partners does not uphold its responsibilities, the system breaks down to varying degrees. Students in particular shoulder an inordinate responsibility for navigating a complex system with which they have no prior experience, gathering expert knowledge they use only once.

The differences between the experiences of Alicia and Teresa in particular emphasize the knowledge-intensive dimension of the college preparation process and the importance of having good information about what to expect in college and then acting on it. High schools can do a better job of preparing all students for college success by making sure that all of them understand what they need to know and be capable of doing to succeed in college.

As the experiences of these three students illustrate, different people prepare for college in fundamentally different ways. To close the gap between those who understand how to prepare to succeed in college and those who do not, high schools will have to make sustained efforts to redesign their instructional programs and their informational systems. Our three students' journeys from high school to college illustrate and suggest some of the changes that need to be made, all of them outlined in greater detail elsewhere in the book.

7

Experiencing
Success in the
First Year of College

What Really Happens in the First Year of College

For high schools to align their programs of study more closely with first-year college programs, they need more information about these programs. This chapter describes some of the current trends in the general education requirement, discusses issues related to placement tests, and presents some examples of typical first-year schedules in order to help illustrate some important aspects of the first year of college.

Changes in the General Education Requirement

The general education requirement has long been a primary component of degree programs in U.S. colleges and universities. Students must fulfill it before graduating, and they often take most of their general education courses during the first two years of study. This requirement is designed to ensure that all students receive a broad liberal education and do not leave college having only specialized in one thing. The general education requirement is one of the elements that distinguishes the U.S. higher education system from others in the world.

The general education requirements exist to help counteract the tendency in higher education toward specialization and requiring more courses in the major. General education courses help ensure that students are exposed to the essential concepts of the natural sciences, social sciences, other languages and cultures, mathematics, literature, the humanities, and a host of other disciplines. Almost all undergraduates today are expected to meet some set of general education requirements. Usually, fifteen to twenty credits are required in each of a number of designated subject areas in the college of arts and sciences, including classes in natural sciences, social sciences, and humanities.

General education core requirements are fulfilled through a more multifaceted curriculum than is available in high school, but some universities have a set sequence of courses that all students must take as undergraduates. The sequence considers the knowledge that all graduating students should acquire, the skills they should have, and the values they should possess after completing an undergraduate degree. The program helps develop the capacity for exchange of ideas, particularly written communication, as well as critical thinking, quantitative reasoning, and ability to conduct research on a range of topics by employing a variety of modes of inquiry. Besides covering an array of educational material deemed essential to a well-educated person, these courses also lay the groundwork for studies in the major.

Although the general education requirements at colleges and universities across the nation have much in common, there are differences as well. The size of the core requirement, for example, varies considerably by institution, although at most colleges and universities it represents approximately one-third of the undergraduate program. General education in the past usually consisted of a simple set of "distribution requirements"—courses grouped by discipline among which students must take a specified number from each group. Today, the structural design of general education varies from institution to institution.

In the traditional view, general education stressed distribution requirements that students would fulfill by taking introductory courses in a variety of academic disciplines. These courses were seen as critical foundations for the more important specialized knowledge they would encounter in the major. The required course, in this model, was viewed as a service to students majoring in other areas.

> "Today, the structural design of general education varies from institution to institution."

But a new concept of general education has emerged that recognizes that general education is more than exposure to different fields of study. The programs today give students the opportunity to learn specific ways of thinking and communicating. They examine cross-cultural perspectives as well as diversity issues in their own culture, amalgamate thinking and concepts across disciplines, and develop the essential personal qualities and characteristics of college graduates. A coherent course of study that has intrinsic value greater than the sum of its parts is perhaps the most important goal for general education in the contemporary framework. The majority of general education programs continue to utilize the distribution approach with its requirement of several courses from each of a number of disciplines. Other approaches to general education stress greater coherence among the courses taken to meet requirements. These more integrated approaches emphasize the connections between the different subjects through interdisciplinary courses and experiences and other strategies that allow and cause students to connect what they are learning into a more coherent whole.

Improving and reworking general education programs seem to be important issues at most colleges and universities for a variety of reasons. Gaff reports that studies conducted in 2000 indicated that 57 percent of four-year institutions, representing a majority of all colleges in the nation, were carrying out extensive formal reviews of these curricula. Improving general education remains an unfinished task. Pressure from policymakers, influential members of the business community, accrediting agencies, faculty members, and even parents and students has resulted in an increased emphasis on assessment, coherence, and alignment of the curriculum in relation to specific learning goals and cognitive skills. This recent shift in the purpose of distribution requirements toward developing students' capacities and intellectual skills across the curriculum has culminated in numerous new configurations of general education nationally. Models of innovative and effective general education programs are evident at all kinds of institutions: small and large, religious and secular, private and public, research university and community college.

Characteristics of Effective and Innovative General Education Curricula

Effective core curriculum programs (another term for general education requirements) generally integrate skills development with course content, integrate new approaches to scholarship, emphasize assessment, employ small-group learning, and utilize primary texts.

Integration of Skills   When skills development is integrated with course content students improve their communication, reasoning, personal interaction, and quantitative thinking skills. Although some colleges and universities continue to require first-year students to take separate courses to develop particular skills (required writing or composition courses, for example), the trend recently has been to integrate skills development with course content. The Writing Across the Curriculum (WAC) movement is a prominent example of this trend, in which writing is embedded into the general education curriculum in a systematic fashion so that students are expected to improve their writing in a range of general education courses, not just the writing courses. Some institutions that have not adopted the WAC framework nevertheless also favor writing-intensive courses in all departments.

Appreciation of Diversity   Besides focusing on development of skills across the entire curriculum, many U.S. institutions of higher education now mandate study of multicultural issues, gender issues, and other topics new to the undergraduate curriculum. The creation in the 1970s and 1980s of departments in fields such as ethnic studies and women's studies has led to the development of many new courses in these areas and to new approaches that emphasize integration of cultural, gender, and other diversity issues in an interdisciplinary framework across the curriculum. Current trends reflect the institutional motivation to teach diversity across the curriculum in general education with the goal of connecting the study of self and the values of a democratic, pluralistic society.

> "The trend recently has been to integrate skills development with course content."

Standards and Assessments   Another emerging trend is a focus on standards and methods of assessment. An example of a recent effort to define standards for assessment of undergraduate knowledge and skill is Quality in Undergraduate Education (QUE), a national project that accentuates the critical nature of the assessment process in general education. The project is being undertaken at selected four-year public institutions and their partner two-year colleges, which are creating discipline-based standards or student learning outcomes for undergraduate majors.

Faculty members at participating institutions developed standards for assessing student knowledge and skill in biology, chemistry, English, history, physics, and mathematics. By establishing a context in which faculty in particular disciplines can compare their work, the project may be a model that other institutions can use as they design assessment standards. The ultimate goal of the project is to use the developed standards to create a clear, public, transparent system to assess the learning outcomes desired of undergraduates.

California State University, Sacramento, has developed written criteria and expected learning outcomes for its general education programs. For example, according to the critical thinking criterion, students must study and consciously develop knowledge through logical analysis and argument construction and understand logical relationships between premises and conclusions. The desired outcomes for critical thinking are that students will be able to locate the argument in a passage, detect errors of reasoning and explain how the reasoning is in error, evaluate evidence and make appropriate inferences from that evidence, and construct and defend an argument in support of or in opposition to a proposition. Such specific goal statements help instructors develop means to teach and assess the desired skills.

Small Learning Communities and First-Year Interest Groups   More and more large universities are adding small-group learning experiences to the general education curriculum. The institutions with the resources to accommodate such interaction often require all first-year students to participate in some form of seminar-style course, often taught by a senior faculty member. The goal is to expose them early on to the core values of the institution so they understand the purpose of the general education, and by extension, what the goal of a college education should be. In the process, these more personalized learning experiences also create tighter bonds between faculty and students, and this also helps improve student retention beyond the first year. Students learn in more detail what will be expected of them and find out how well prepared they are to meet the challenges of the undergraduate curriculum.

> **These more personalized learning experiences also create tighter bonds between faculty and students.**

The first-year interest groups (FIGs) at the University of Oregon are typical examples. Students take two regular degree-satisfying courses together in groups of twenty-five during the fall term along with students from the larger university population. In addition, they enroll in a one-credit course entitled College Connections, which is taught by one of the faculty teaching the larger course. This provides a forum for more discussion and connections between students and professors. Upper-level undergraduates who have already taken and succeeded in the larger course assist in these courses, serving as mentors and teaching assistants as well as arranging out-of-class experiences that help the first-year students develop social connections and learn more about the university. There are four types of FIGs offered at Oregon: Residential FIGs seek to create greater community among students living on campus, Challenge FIGs encourage highly motivated students to stretch themselves and become fully involved intellectually in classes, Transfer FIGs are for students arriving from other postsecondary environments, and Pathway-Connecting FIGs continue beyond the first quarter to clusters of courses called Pathways.

Examples of General Education Curriculum Designs

As noted, the structure of these programs varies widely. The differences reflect different perspectives on ways of knowing, types of knowledge, and the student's relationship to learning. The following examples illustrate the range of structures for general education programs at U.S. universities.

Designated Core Courses   Colleges and universities with designated core courses require students to select from a limited list of courses or course sequences offered by individual departments and designed specifically for the core program. Harvard, Princeton, and the University of Chicago are prominent examples of institutions with a long tradition of using this approach.

The University of Chicago's Common Core is perhaps the most enduring exemplar of general education curricular distribution requirements in the United States. All Chicago students must complete requirements in the humanities, natural sciences, social sciences, math, and language. Students usually finish these requirements during their first two years.

Students must complete a total of six quarters in the humanities and in civilization studies, with at least two courses from the humanities sequence on the interpretation of historical, literary, and philosophical texts and at least one in the dramatic, musical, or visual arts. Students then select the remaining three required courses from among these areas. At the University of Chicago, learning how to analyze texts intellectually, historically, and aesthetically is an essential part of general education. Examples of sequences in the humanities include Readings in World Literature, Greek Thought and Literature, and Media Aesthetics: Image, Sound, and Text. Examples of sequences offered in civilization studies include Religion in Western Civilization; Science, Culture, and Society in Western Civilization; Introduction to Islamic Civilization; Near Eastern Civilization; and Introduction to Russian Civilization. Courses offered in the arts include Art of the Greek City-States, Playwriting, and

Introduction to World Music. Civilization studies requirements may also be completed by participating in one of the college's study abroad programs; students who travel to Rome, Barcelona, Buenos Aires, Vienna, or Capetown, South Africa, can fulfill the requirement in one quarter.

Students at the University of Chicago are also required to complete six quarters of natural and mathematical sciences. Natural science courses focus on the main features of the natural universe and the process of scientific inquiry. Students must take at least two quarters of biological sciences, at least two quarters of physical science, and at least one quarter of mathematical sciences, including mathematics, computer science, or statistics. They may choose the courses for the final quarter requirement. A University of Chicago student planning to major in the humanities or social sciences could fulfill the general education requirements in the physical and biological sciences by enrolling in a four-quarter natural sciences sequence called Evolution of the Natural World. That student would be able to meet the distribution requirements for mathematics, physical, and biological sciences with the five-quarter Environmental Sciences sequence, then satisfy the three-quarter course requirement for social sciences by choosing from sequences such as Power, Identity, and Resistance; Mind; and Classics of Social and Political Thought.

The University of Chicago also requires students to show competency in a foreign language prior to graduation. Competency examinations are administered on a yearly basis. Students can exhibit competency while still in high school with a score of three or higher on the AP test in designated languages. Over twenty-five languages and corresponding examinations are offered. The study of language is complemented by the study abroad program and a distinctive Language Proficiency Certificate Program.

In the one hundred years of its existence, the specifics of Chicago's general education curriculum content have been consistently discussed and altered, rarely remaining steady ten years in a row, but its structure has not changed appreciably over that period of time. Almost-constant institution-wide debates over the content, structure, and scope of general education at Chicago have helped shaped core general education requirements nationwide. Despite its history of adaptation, Chicago's Common Core program demonstrates a coherent philosophy of general education as a way to counteract specialization and vocationalism and to emphasize universal principles and breadth of knowledge.

Nevertheless, Chicago's designated core approach has been criticized for its potential for leaving bachelor's degree graduates without adequate preparation for particular careers. The university still does not offer preprofessional majors, such as in engineering, journalism, or business. Without preparation for a job after graduation, students who complete Chicago, it is argued, must find the resources to go on for continued training to secure a viable career in the future. Since one of the key purposes of the university is to prepare the next generation of professors for research universities, this is less of an issue than it might be elsewhere.

> **"** **Chicago's Common Core program demonstrates a coherent philosophy of general education as a way to counteract specialization and vocationalism . . . "**

Stanford has approached the core requirements issue in a similar fashion. Programs of courses certified as fulfilling general education requirements are divided into four areas and designed primarily for freshmen and sophomores, the point in the students' college education when many have not yet chosen their major. The four areas are Introduction to the Humanities; Natural Sciences, Applied Science and Technology, and Mathematics; Humanities and the Social Sciences; and World Cultures, American Cultures, and Gender Studies. Stanford's approach focuses on students as nonspecialists. It is designed to enhance their knowledge of concepts, methods, practices, and applications in the areas studied. Other objectives include giving students the opportunity to develop their powers of reasoning and a capacity for rigorous critical analysis, and strengthening their ability to become informed citizens.

Interdisciplinary Courses with a Thematic Focus   In institutions that organize general education requirements and courses around interdisciplinary themes, students select courses in a theme area that entails an array of disciplinary perspectives. Several successful interdisciplinary general education programs illustrate the strengths of this model.

UCLA's "Clusters" Approach   The University of California at Los Angeles has created a clusters-based approach in which first-year students can enlist in a one-year program aimed at addressing one cluster of topics, such as global environmental change or interracial dynamics. The series of classes are collaboratively taught. UCLA's innovative approach to the general education requirement is designed to give students in the first year the opportunity to experience fundamental principles, techniques, and perspectives across the disciplines of life sciences, social sciences, physical sciences, and the humanities.

There are three courses in each yearlong interdisciplinary cluster. The following course titles illustrate the themes that are taught: the Global Environment; Interracial Dynamics in American Literature, Culture, and Society; Perception and Illusion: Cognitive Psychology, Literature, and Art; the History of Modern Thought; and the United States 1963–1974: Politics, Society, and Culture. Titles of potential clusters from which students can choose include these: Understanding Violence; Computing the Future: The Social Entailments of Computation; and Africa in the New Millennium: Roots and Prospects.

The fall and winter quarter courses are lecture-based and include smaller labs and discussion sections with fewer than twenty students. In the spring, students choose from several smaller seminar courses connected to the cluster subject matter. The overarching goal of the program is to give students the opportunity to experience a broad collection of perspectives and instructional methods, which should have a positive impact on their critical thinking and writing proficiency. The experience of teaching an interdisciplinary course also has the positive outcome of giving faculty the opportunity to collaborate and innovate. Approximately 25 percent of the incoming class, or nearly nine hundred students, participate in one or more clusters each year.

The University of Michigan's Interdisciplinary Option   At the University of Michigan discussions with experienced academic advisers and faculty revealed that first-year students were frequently dissuaded from majoring in the sciences because they were uncertain about which field of science to concentrate on; instead, they labeled themselves as pre-med or pre-engineering. In response to this tendency, the university developed a groundbreaking, three-semester interdisciplinary course sequence titled Introduction to Global Change. In addition to this three-quarter course, two corresponding but independent courses in the program offer natural science credit and social science credit. The intent is to expose students who may be taking the sequence because it is a distribution requirement to the research and new developments in the sciences that they likely would not encounter on a preprofessional path. The global change sequence involves instructors from four different schools at the university: the College of Literature, the College of Engineering, the School of Natural Resources and Environment, and the School of Public Health.

> **First-year students were frequently dissuaded from majoring in the sciences.**

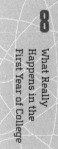

The University of Texas at Austin's ConneXus Program   The University of Texas at Austin developed Connections in Undergraduate Education, a series of programs referred to collectively as ConneXus, through which students can fulfill distribution (that is, general education) and major requirements simultaneously. The primary programs in ConneXus are Forum Seminars and Bridging Disciplines Programs (BDPs). The BDPs are organized around six wide-ranging interdisciplinary topics: Children and Society; Cultures and Identities; Environment; Ethics and Leadership; Population and Public Policy; and Technology and Society. These allow students to build a program of study around an interdisciplinary theme. Students can choose courses that meet area requirements, electives, and courses for the major. When students complete the eighteen to twenty-four hours in a specialization required by the different BDPs, they receive a certificate.

The BDPs incorporate general education in the major by structuring internships, research opportunities, major requirements, area requirements, and electives to correspond with particular interdisciplinary themes. A typical BDP consists of four to six classes from an array of disciplines on a topic accompanied by two or three research opportunities or internships that link the topical theme to the major. A student majoring in government, for example, might enroll in the Children and Society BDP after having first enrolled in a ConneXus cluster that ties a Forum Seminar on children and society with a sociology class on juvenile deviance. The same student could then take courses on issues related to children while participating in research projects carried out on campus. In subsequent semesters the student might seek an internship with a children's advocacy group. Students starting their freshman or sophomore years are encouraged to participate in a BDP. Students may participate in BDPs no later than their junior year. Completion of a BDP is recognized at graduation.

The Forum Seminars present freshmen and sophomores with access to university resources by engaging in weekly discourse with faculty from a range of departments and research facilities. The forums are structured as one-hour classes highlighting salient issues; they have titles such as Technology and the Global Community or the Science of Environmental Change. The discussion courses are scheduled twice weekly for the first half of the semester. After completing a Forum Seminar, students may pursue more extensive interdisciplinary coursework through the BDPs.

> "The forums are structured as one-hour classes highlighting salient issues."

Fairleigh Dickinson University's Core Program   The University Core program at Fairleigh Dickinson University (FDU) has been recognized by the American Association of Colleges and Universities as one of nine model programs in the United States. In the four courses that constitute the University Core, students are exposed to fundamental issues that the human community confronts in contemporary society. Each of the four courses in the sequence—Perspectives on the Individual, the American Experience, Cross-Cultural Perspectives, and Global Issues—consists of input from a variety of disciplines spanning the humanities, science, and social science divisions. Each of the courses is designed to build on the previous course in the series, and evaluation strategies and assignment designs are coordinated across the sequence. The University Core program is a requirement for all students at FDU.

Western Michigan University's Lee Honors College   The framework espoused by the Lee Honors College (LHC) at Western Michigan University stresses the goal of moving beyond learning as rote memorization to intellectual growth through the rigorous exchange of ideas and divergent perspectives. Students in the LHC choose a major at one of the six undergraduate colleges and proceed through the cluster process to deepen their knowledge of an array of topics that are pertinent, innovative, socially significant, and intellectually rigorous. Courses in the cluster are designed to fulfill general education requirements, curricular requirements, and key classes for the major or minor. The clusters in LHC also expose students to imaginative and challenging curricula in small, integrative courses in a community of other honors students.

The LHC offers a cluster of courses in English, anthropology, and geography around the theme of Peoples of the World. The program consists of two designated clusters or one cluster plus additional LHC classes to total six classes. The cluster courses center on interrelated themes such as these: Medical Career Foundations, Business Environment, the World and Its People, Children's Literature, and Science and Technology.

Two single courses at the junior or senior level and a capstone thesis project are also required. During the junior and senior years, students choose a single course or seminar from a range of options. These classes are intended to engage students actively in the learning process. The upper-level offerings are diverse, with class titles such as Epidemics and Ethics, the Religious Quest, Shakespeare's Women, the Holocaust, and Twenty-First Century Challenges in Health and Human Services.

The honors thesis project, which culminates the LHC experience, is a reflection of the student's particular talents and knowledge and serves as a springboard to future academic endeavors and career goals.

Portland State's Freshman Inquiry Program   Freshman Inquiry (FRINQ) is a yearlong sequence of courses designed to introduce incoming first-time students to Portland State's general education goals and the learning opportunities available at the university. FRINQ courses are all interactive and theme-based. The course sequence employs an interdisciplinary approach to understanding one or more themes from different perspectives. Sequences are titled Chaos and Community; Columbia Basin; the Constructed Self; Cyborg Millennium; Design and Society; Forbidden Knowledge; Meaning and Madness at the Margins; Pathways to Sustainability and Justice; and Sex, Mind, and the Mask.

Faculty members from various disciplines teach courses as a team. Each faculty member pairs with an upper-division student, who is charged with leading the smaller mentor inquiry sessions where students can discuss concepts introduced in lectures. Class formats include lecture and large-group group discussions, student-led discussions, and seminar-like formats designed to create opportunities for students to challenge their preconceptions and expand their thinking.

Placement Tests

The placement test is often a hidden component of the high school–college transition process. Although most people know that placement tests exist, few treat them as something that must be addressed systematically in the college preparation process. Students generally have a fatalistic attitude about them, hoping for the best but not knowing what, if anything, they can do to improve their results. Understanding placement tests is important to enhancing student success in the first year of college.

Placement tests come in two varieties: those developed by commercial test publishers and those that are homegrown. The two most common commercial placement tests are Compass, created by ACT, and Accuplacer, produced by the College Board. Each provides information on student readiness for college based on lessons that each of these organizations has learned through the admissions tests they also develop and market, the ACT and the SAT. The placement tests cover a range of subject areas, including reading comprehension, sentence skills, arithmetic, elementary algebra, college-level mathematics, and writing. Recently, additional tests specifically geared to non-native English speaking students have been developed. Most of these tests are now available online, and students can receive instantaneous results, except on tests such as writing that must be scored manually.

These organizations conduct regular studies of the relationship between high school GPA, courses taken, admissions test score, and freshman college grades. These testing organizations also collect information on the courses students take in high school, the content of those courses, and the corresponding entry-level college courses. Based on all this, they develop tests that seek to gauge student mastery of the knowledge and skills deemed essential to success in the entry-level college courses.

In theory, this process leads to tests that are carefully aligned with high school preparation and college expectations. But in practice these tests may not reflect well what students were taught in high school or what is actually being taught in any given college course. They are useful as general screening mechanisms to help colleges reduce failure rates in their introductory courses, particularly in math and writing. The problem for the test takers is that they rarely take the time to learn what will be on the tests or to prepare for them, because such tests are not necessarily designed to have students prepare for them. Often, a student learns of placement test requirements after arriving on campus, making it even more difficult to prepare in any meaningful fashion.

Placement tests are especially problematic for students who have not taken a math course in their last year or two of high school. For these students, their scores on the placement test often come as a rude shock, particularly when the results bar them from taking courses they planned to take, and in the process, delay their progress toward a degree.

Homegrown placement tests, which are developed by faculty at a college, are even more difficult to prepare for and more subject to the whims and prejudices of the faculty members or committee that developed them. This is not to say these tests are automatically inferior or unfair, but only that they may examine a very specific subset of knowledge and skills that students may not possess. Because the content of these tests rarely changes, they are more closely guarded than the commercial tests, which are prepared in new forms annually. This makes it even more difficult for students to prepare for the homegrown placement tests.

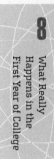

Based on a review of homegrown placement tests from several universities, here is what entering students usually face on the English and math exams.

English placement tests usually contain subtests on English usage, sentence correction, and reading comprehension. They take approximately ninety minutes to complete and contain upwards of 180 items. The English usage and sentence correction subtests assess the ability to distinguish verb, pronoun, diction, modifier, and sentence problems and to identify deviations from standard written American English. Sentence correction items examine a student's ability to distinguish verb, pronoun, diction, modifier, and sentence problems. These items require a student to select the most effective expression from among choices. The reading comprehension subtest requires students to understand and interpret prose passages equivalent to those they will read in college. Key skills assessed include ability to comprehend literal meaning, interpret figurative language, draw inferences from what they read, recognize principles of organization, and identify the function of prominent stylistic features.

The mathematics placement test measures a range of prerequisite skills in operations with whole numbers and fractions; operations with decimals and percents; applications and problem solving including measurement; pre-algebra and elementary algebra, including operations with integers and rational numbers, operations with algebraic expressions, and equations, inequalities, and word problems; geometry; advanced algebra; and pre-calculus.

The best strategy for students to employ to prepare for placement tests is to avoid them altogether by scoring high enough on entrance exams or having a high enough GPA. But many colleges and universities require all incoming freshmen to take placement tests in reading, writing, and mathematics because high school grades are not always true indicators of student knowledge and skill.

High schools cannot prepare students well for multiple placement exams, but they can do some things to help students prepare for a few of them. First, they can research the tests that are being given at the colleges attended most frequently by their students. This information may not be as easy to come by as one might think. Although most community colleges make this information available, it is harder to obtain from

> **The best strategy for students to employ to prepare for placement tests is to avoid them altogether . . .**

four-year institutions. Sometimes it takes a call to the department on campus to learn what type of placement test is given, who is required to take it, and what happens if a student does not pass it. Finding out what is actually on the test can be even more problematic.

Second, if local postsecondary institutions are using one of the two main commercially-available tests, students can be referred to online sites that provide advice on how to prepare for these tests. For the Accuplacer and Compass tests, extensive information on how best to prepare can be purchased from a variety of vendors easily located on the Internet who provide study guides and other material. High school teachers may want to examine such materials to deduce how well prepared for placement tests students will likely be when they complete their exit-level high school courses.

Access to this information and even a practice test, devised by teachers to give their students a general idea of how they might perform on an actual placement test, should be provided to all seniors, with a particular emphasis on those who do not take math that year. The goal is to give these students a wake-up call to remind them that they may be tested on their math knowledge a year hence. For some, this may serve as motivation enough to take a math or composition course instead of leaving school at 12:30 every day.

Typical Freshman Schedules

There is perhaps no better way to get a feel for the first year of college than by looking at some examples of student schedules. What do students actually do during their freshman year of study? What classes do they take? How much time do they spend in class? These examples of typical student schedules at several universities offer some insight into these questions and help provide a more well-rounded picture of the first year of college.

University of Oregon

Table 8.1 shows a first-year student schedule at the University of Oregon. The class descriptions are as follows:

- *Math 111: College Algebra (four credits).* Algebra needed for calculus including graph sketching, algebra of functions, polynomial functions, rational functions, exponential and logarithmic functions, linear and nonlinear functions. Prerequisite: Math 95 or satisfactory placement test score; a programmable calculator capable of displaying function graphs.

- *WR 121: Writing Composition I (four credits)*. Written reasoning as discovery and inquiry. Frequent essays explore the relationship of thesis to structure and audience. Strong focus on the process of revising. Regular work on editing. Waived if student SAT verbal score is above 710 or ACT verbal score is above 32.

- *PHYS 201: General Physics (four credits)*. Introductory sequence. Focus on mechanics and fluids.

- *PEI (Individual Activities) 261: Trampoline (one credit)*.

- *DANC 199: Hip Hop Dance (one credit)*.

Total: sixteen credits.

Table 8.2 shows the courses taken by the same student that winter. This quarter the class descriptions are as follows:

- *WR 122: Writing Composition II (four credits)*. Prerequisite: WR 121. Written reasoning as a process of argument. Developing and supporting theses in response to complex questions. Attention to critical reading in academic setting. Continuing focus on revising and editing.

- *ASTR 121: The Solar System (four credits)*. Naked-eye astronomy, development of astronomical concepts, and the solar system.

- *EDST 111: Educational Issues & Problems (four credits)*. Examines specific issues and problems confronting educators. Compares and contrasts different approaches to the ways in which society defines and deals with educational issues and problems.

- *BA 101: Introduction to Business (four credits)*. Historical, social, political, economic, and legal environments within which business operates. Inter-relationships of the functional areas of management, finance, marketing, accounting, and international studies.

Total: sixteen credits.

Table 8.1. First-Year Student Schedule, University of Oregon, Fall Quarter

	Monday	Tuesday	Wednesday	Thursday	Friday
8:00					
9:00	Math 111	Math 111	Math 111		Math 111
10:00	PEI 261		PEI 261		
11:00					
12:00	WR 121		WR 121		WR 121
1:00					
2:00	PHYS 201		PHYS 201		PHYS 201
3:00	DANC 199		DANC 199		
4:00					
5:00					
6:00					

Table 8.2. Example of First-Year Schedule at the University of Oregon: Winter Quarter

	Monday	Tuesday	Wednesday	Thursday	Friday
8:00	WR 122		WR 122		WR 122
9:00	ASTR 121	EDST 111 (discussion)	ASTR 121		ASTR 121
10:00		EDST 111		EDST 111	
11:00					
12:00					
1:00					
2:00	BA 101		BA 101		
3:00	BA 101		BA 101		
4:00					
5:00					
6:00					

Table 8.3 follows this student in the spring. The class descriptions are as follows:

- *AAD 252: Art & Gender (four credits)*. Addresses sociocultural factors influencing the role of women and men in arts disciplines; examines underlying social structures that affect how art and artists are defined.

- *ASTR 122: Birth & Death of Stars (four credits)*. The structure and evolution of stars.

- *ENG 207: Shakespeare (four credits)*. Examines the major plays in chronological order with emphasis on the early and middle plays through *Hamlet* and on the later plays beginning with *Twelfth Night*.

- *EC 101: Contemporary Economic Issues (four credits)*. Examines contemporary public policy using economic principles. Topics include balanced budgets and tax reform, unemployment, health care, poverty and income redistribution, environmental policy, and international trade policy.

- *PEAE (Aerobics) 231: Step Aerobics I (one credit)*.

Total: seventeen credits.

Table 8.3. Example of First-Year Schedule at the University of Oregon: Spring Quarter

	Monday	Tuesday	Wednesday	Thursday	Friday
8:00					
9:00					
10:00	EC 101		EC 101		EC 101
11:00	ENG 207		ENG 207		ENG 207
12:00		AAD 252		AAD 252	EC 101 (discussion)
1:00					
2:00	ASTR 122		ASTR 122		ASTR 122
3:00	PEAE 231		PEAE 231		
4:00					
5:00					
6:00					

Other Schools

Here are some examples of first-year schedules at other schools.

Cornell College of Engineering

- *Fall:* Math 191: Calculus for Engineers I *(four credits)*; Chemistry 211: Chemistry for Applied Sciences *(four credits)* (college requirement); Writing 137: An Introduction to Writing in the University *(three credits)* (course outside the major); Computer Science 100: Introduction to Computer Programming *(four credits)* (college requirement). *Total:* fifteen credits.

- *Spring:* Math 192: Calculus for Engineers II *(four credits)* (college requirement); History 151: Introduction to Western Civilization *(four credits)* (course outside the major); English 270: The Reading of Fiction First Year Writing Seminar *(three credits)* (course outside the major); Information Science 230: Intermediate Design and Programming for the Web *(three credits)* (elective course). *Total:* fourteen credits.

University of Colorado, Boulder, Computer Science Department

- *Fall:* Computer Science 1: Programming *(four credits)*; Calculus 1 *(four credits)*; Introductory Astronomy *(four credits)*; Introduction to Western Philosophy *(three credits)*. *Total:* fifteen credits.

- *Spring:* Computer Science 2: Data Structures *(four credits)*; Calculus 2 *(four credits)*; Introductory Chemistry *(four credits)*; Responding to Social Problems *(four credits)*. *Total:* sixteen credits.

University of Michigan

- *Fall:* English 124 or 125 Introductory Composition *(four credits)*; Math 115: Analytic Geometry and Calculus 1 *(four credits)*; Studio-Based Pre-Architecture/Art *(three credits)*; electives *(four credits)*. *Total:* fifteen credits.

- *Winter:* Studio-Based Pre-Architecture/Art *(three credits)*; Architecture 212: Understanding Architecture *(three credits)*; electives *(nine credits)*. *Total:* fifteen credits.

University of Nebraska, Lincoln

- Management 198D *(one credit)*; English 150 *(three credits)*; Math 104 *(four credits)*; History 100 *(three credits)*; Philosophy 106 *(three credits)*. *Total:* fourteen credits.

- Sociology 101 *(three credits)*; Math 106 *(five credits)*; Computer Science 155 *(three credits)*; Chemistry 111 *(four credits)*. *Total:* fifteen credits.

- Library 110 *(one credit)*; Political Science 101 *(three credits)*; English 101 *(three credits)*; Astronomy 103 *(three credits)*; Anthropology 110 *(three credits)*. *Total:* thirteen credits.

- Education 131 *(three credits)*; English 150 *(three credits)*; University Foundations 103 *(three credits)*; Art History 101 *(three credits)*. *Total:* twelve credits.

This chapter has presented a more fine-grained description of the issues involved in making the transition to higher education and the opportunities available to students who are adequately prepared for college study. Postsecondary education in the United States is an incredibly rich environment in which to develop intellectually, socially, and personally. Although students certainly do mature intellectually and otherwise during their first year in college, the experience is much more positive and valuable for those who enter prepared to take advantage of all that college has to offer. Students who come from high school programs that have helped them developed the knowledge and skill and habits of mind outlined in the Knowledge and Skills for University Success will be more capable of taking full advantage of the experience.

What We Must Do to Create a System
That Prepares Students for College Success

This book emphasizes the disconnect between high school and college programs of study and presents strategies to strengthen the connection so that students can succeed in college. The key recommended change is for high schools to gauge the appropriateness of their instructional programs against the Knowledge and Skills for University Success standards or other well-defined college success standards. The result they should seek is an intellectually coherent program of study that imparts to students both the necessary knowledge and skills and the appropriate habits of mind. Each chapter has identified specific issues and offered strategies that high schools can employ to achieve a better alignment with postsecondary education.

Why We Must Create a System That Is Better Aligned

All of these good efforts, of course, exist in a larger system of educational policies and regulations. Although this book alludes to these policies and rules on occasion, it does not directly discuss the policy context of the high school–college articulation. This chapter considers policy issues to provide secondary and postsecondary educators with a more complete picture of how their efforts at improved alignment may be supported by emerging policy trends, or even eventually compelled by them. This broader perspective can also help educators, administrators, school board members, and others to understand why they should be motivated to undertake change in a system that may appear to many to be functioning more or less without significant problems.

Increasing Government Incursion and Regulation

At the heart of this kind of change is a fundamental restructuring of power in and control over education, from kindergarten through college. Several forces are at work here: state and federal control is increasing while local control is decreasing, the link between education and economic success is tightening, and there is a general sense that a college education should become as universal in the twenty-first century as a high school education was in the twentieth.

As education policy falls increasingly under state and federal control, local school districts no longer call the shots to the degree to which they have been accustomed. Similarly, postsecondary institutions find themselves subject to greater government intervention in their operations. Although policies designed to align secondary and postsecondary education have by no means reached tidal wave proportions, they are more prevalent now than they were twenty, ten, or even five years ago. Employers too are increasingly reaching the conclusion that their future will require workers who are not merely competent high school graduates but knowledgeable and skillful in ways best achieved through a college education. The baccalaureate degree remains one of the greatest value-added attributes of a person entering the labor force. The final force, the desire for universal postsecondary participation, is driven by students and parents facing the increasing complexity of life in the information age. The baseline level of education expected of the populace is moving toward the baccalaureate degree. As long as large numbers of parents and students expect a close relationship between high school and college, politicians will be motivated to move policy in that direction. For these reasons and others, high schools and colleges are likely to have to strengthen their connection over the coming decade.

Expanding High School Standards and Exams

State adoption of academic content standards laid the groundwork for high school assessments of student knowledge and skills. By 2004, nineteen states had implemented high school graduation examinations and six others had plans to do so. In addition, the federal No Child Left Behind Act requires all states to adopt statewide tests in English, math, and science to be administered in the tenth, eleventh, or twelfth grade. The net effect is that all states either have or will soon have high school exams linked to academic standards that all students take before graduating from high school.

This assessment structure creates the potential for closer connections between high school and college, but only if the exams are aligned with college success standards. Research conducted by Standards for Success and published in the report *Mixed Messages* found that most state standards–based high school tests were not well aligned with postsecondary learning. The effect of poor alignment is that as high schools prepare students to pass state tests, they are not considering how they are preparing students for college success. As a result, high schools may find themselves organizing themselves into two tracks: one for students preparing for the state exam and another for students preparing for college. States eventually will have to come to grips with this divide and develop second-generation assessment systems in which they seek to connect their tests to outcomes beyond high school.

> **"All states either have or will soon have high school exams linked to academic standards that all students take before graduating from high school."**

Changing Admissions Tests and Processes

The college admissions process is undergoing a metamorphosis; the public gets periodic glimpses of it, but much remains hidden. At the heart of this metamorphosis is the use of increasingly more complex information on a range of student characteristics and additional measures of student knowledge and skill. This is driven by intense competition for admission to the most prestigious institutions and by demand for lower remediation rates, higher graduation rates, and less time to degree completion at public postsecondary institutions.

Admissions testing is shifting from aptitude-based models, which seek to identify those students who have what has been considered the native ability or intelligence to do college-level work, to achievement-oriented tools, which seek to measure knowledge and skill in greater detail. The increase in the number of students taking AP tests is only one indication of this phenomenon. The rise in the use of SAT II subject area tests by universities is another indication of this trend. Even the two largest admissions tests, the SAT and ACT, are emphasizing their connection to state content standards and the high school curriculum and distancing themselves from previous characterizations as measures of student aptitude.

The SAT in particular is in the process of transforming itself so that it better reflects student content knowledge. The test makers went so far as to remove the word "aptitude" from the test's name in the early 1990s. The test now labels the section previously entitled "Verbal" as "Critical Reading" and has added a new section entitled "Writing" that requires those who take the test to write in response to a prompt. The new reading test eliminates analogies and adds short reading passages on which student knowledge of grammar and usage is tested. The purpose is to send the message to students preparing for college that being able to read and write well is more important than being able to identify sometimes obscure relationships between word pairs.

The old quantitative section is now aptly renamed "Mathematics." The math content tested now extends to what the College Board, the maker of the test, describes as "third-year college preparatory math," which, in practice, corresponds roughly to Algebra II. To make room for this additional content, quantitative comparison questions are eliminated. In all cases, the changes emphasize content knowledge and higher-order thinking specific to college success at the expense of items that sought to measure the more abstract notion of aptitude to do college work.

Plans are also in the works for those who take the SAT to be given a diagnostic profile that tells them where they stand in college readiness based on their responses to test questions. Instead of simply getting a score report with a number such as 950 or 1100, they will receive a statement that outlines the areas where they may wish to improve while still in high school in order to increase their college readiness, not just their SAT score. The diagnostic profile concept is a powerful addition to a test notable for generating a number that many remember for the rest of their lives, but that motivates few to do anything different academically. Rather than viewing their SAT score as some sort of life-defining marker, students will be able to act on the information provided in the profile to take more courses or study specific areas where they need to improve their knowledge and skills. Even if their score on subsequent SAT tests does not improve dramatically, or if they do not need to retake the test but simply use the information to strengthen their knowledge and skill

> **"** Rather than viewing their SAT score as some sort of life-defining marker, students will be able to act on the information provided. **"**

foundation, they may be more likely to succeed in postsecondary education as a result of their response to the profile.

The reference point for this feedback is the College Board Standards for College Success. Here, again, is an example of how the culture of admissions testing is changing. The College Board has adopted its own set of content standards defining what students need to know and be able to do to succeed in college. The College Board Standards for College Success in math and English span six levels from middle school through high school, offering a more integrated road map to college readiness. The committees convened to develop these standards in reading, writing, mathematics, and science reviewed a range of nationally recognized standards documents in relevant content areas. The development of these standards was complex, but the Knowledge and Skills for University Success standards were a key resource to ensure that the exit-level standards, level six in the College Board standards, connected with college success.

Availability of Integrated Data Systems

State governments are increasingly viewing education as a continuum from preschool to postsecondary education. The focus is less on each separate entity and more on the movement of students through a unified system. To understand the system as a whole, information on student performance must be transferred seamlessly across institutional boundaries.

The evolution of such large-scale data systems is proceeding rapidly as computer hardware and software become more sophisticated and the Internet matures as the system for inputting and reporting data. The result will be a much tighter connection between elementary, secondary, and postsecondary learning and a drive to standardize reporting on student knowledge and skill. These data systems will not only allow for continuity in reporting but also store and manage much more complex performance data than paper transcripts have allowed.

Lawmakers are encouraging the evolution of these systems because they desire greater educational accountability and efficiency. In an era of limited resources and soaring tuition costs, there is growing pressure to increase the success of students admitted to college and educate them as quickly as possible, without need for remediation or reteaching of content that students have already been taught once. Each segment of the educational system will increasingly be judged based on how well it prepares students for the next step in their education or their transition to life beyond school.

For schools, the implications of this coming revolution are significant. Traditional grading systems will be subject to greater scrutiny as technology enables comparisons between schools and even individual teachers. More data on the relationship between high school preparation and college success will allow an increase in research on this all-important set of practices. In general, academic content standards will start to become more consistent across states. Definitions of mathematical proficiency and adequate writing, for example, will become more universal. Internet-based systems will permit more widespread use of exemplars and student work samples along with grades.

> **There is growing pressure to increase the success of students admitted to college and educate them as quickly as possible . . .**

To achieve this goal, all students will have to be given a common identifier they retain throughout their education so that all their relevant data can move with them. A number of states have already adopted such systems and have instituted procedures that allow information to be entered once, then used for multiple purposes by different systems. The privacy issues here are complex, and at the moment, a greater impediment than the technical challenges.

These connections will be particularly important if states articulate and coordinate their high school assessment systems with postsecondary learning standards. The potential to reduce remediation will be enhanced if data from high school tests can be used by postsecondary institutions for placement and also by high schools for instruction.

Desire to Create a K–16 Educational System

The idea of a K–16 or even P–16 educational system has intrigued policymakers for some time, although educators have been less enthusiastic about it. However, the policymakers seem to be winning as they increasingly blur the line between secondary and postsecondary systems through a range of programs designed to allow students to move from high school to college when they are ready, and not necessarily when they complete a prescribed course of study.

As a result of these kinds of changes, expectations for student learning are likely to become increasingly aligned across institutional levels in the educational system. Although this offers some real advantages to students, it can wreak havoc with curricula that have not been calibrated to connect. American education is not only fragmented between secondary and postsecondary systems but also internally between elementary, middle, and high school programs of instruction and across two-year colleges, four-year colleges, and universities.

At the state and even the national level, there is irresistible pressure on school systems to align the content knowledge and cognitive skills students attain and demonstrate as a result of participation in the public schools. Because results from state assessments are reported publicly to an ever-increasing degree and because federal requirements have upped the ante for many schools, real efforts are being made to ensure that the same material is no longer taught twice while some material is not taught at all. More attention is being paid to student readiness to learn at all levels and to providing additional opportunities for students to master material they failed to learn the first time it was presented to them.

In the final analysis, all of this activity will lead to an environment in which teaching and learning are more systematic, more purposive, and more focused. The challenge for many schools will be to incorporate the college preparatory curriculum into this process. Because the college prep curriculum has been defined in terms of course titles, alignment has been assumed to exist if titles are sequenced properly.

As states begin to align their high school content standards with university entrance requirements and entry-level course expectations, the old model of the high school college prep curriculum will no longer suffice. Getting a B in algebra will not be enough if key content has not been mastered. Passing junior-year English may meet the course requirement for college admission, but if students cannot write well as a result of the course they will be no better off in their ability to undertake postsecondary studies than they were before they took it.

A well-aligned curriculum should help decrease college remediation rates, which are particularly high in two-year and open-enrollment institutions where all applicants are admitted but many lack the skills necessary to enter the course sequence at a college level and must begin by relearning high school material. These courses generally do not bear college credit, and studies by the U.S. Department of Education's National Center on Education Statistics show that students who begin college by taking remedial courses are less than half as likely to graduate within six years as their colleagues who do not. Clearly, states have a vested interest in decreasing the number of students who must be taught the high school curriculum when they are in college. Doing so is costly and inefficient, in part because these students are occupying seats in the postsecondary system and thus preventing other students from attending college.

The complete implications for high schools of a fully aligned K–16 system are not entirely clear at this point, because much depends on exactly how states put such a system into place. However, it seems reasonable to conclude that at the least students will be entering and leaving high school on a more continuous basis than they do under the current cohort-based model. As middle school students become ready for high school instruction, it will need to be provided to them. And perhaps more importantly, as high school students become ready for college instruction, they too will need to move on.

The tool for determining when students are ready to move on will be academic content standards and measures of how well students have mastered specific standards. Here is where the KSUS standards will again be a useful tool. Because they are designed to bridge the gap between high school and college, they can become a yardstick of student readiness for college-level work in an aligned system. When students are ready to learn at the level described in the KSUS standards, they should either start taking college courses or participate in learning experiences at that level on the high school campus. High school teachers rarely want to lose the students who are ready to do college work, but it should not be acceptable to hold onto them simply because they are labeled juniors or seniors. Many schools already provide postsecondary options, but with little guidance on when a student is ready to participate in a college-level course other than the student having completed the high school course sequence in a subject area. Based on the KSUS or a state-mandated set of articulated high school–college standards, it will be possible to make better decisions and offer more closely connected programs that enable students to make successful transitions from high school to college.

> **"It will be possible to make better decisions and offer more closely connected programs."**

Creating a System Where More Students Are Prepared for College Success

What are some of the specific things that need to occur to connect high school preparation and college success more directly? The changes will need to take place at several levels in the educational system, and will require the involvement of many different constituencies.

What Policymakers Can Do

In all likelihood, policymakers will continue to provide the primary impetus to move education toward an aligned K–16 system. Although there has been a great deal of educational reform already at the K–12 level, as noted previously, few reforms have specifically been designed to strengthen the connection between high school and college. Some activities, such as postsecondary options and dual enrollment programs, have created more opportunities for students, but these programs often work only for certain students under specific circumstances. They do not address broader issues of high school–college articulation for all.

Policymakers need to contemplate bold steps that break down the barriers between high school and college. Such policies are likely to displease many in those institutions because each will perceive that it is losing power and control over particular aspects of its programs. This perception may not be entirely inaccurate.

> "Policymakers need to contemplate bold steps that break down the barriers between high school and college."

The key policies that will need to change are in the areas of high school graduation and college admission requirements, both the courses and the tests that students take. Two dozen states either require or will soon require students to pass some form of test in order to graduate. None of these tests was designed to connect in any systematic fashion with postsecondary readiness. The first step states can take is to redesign high school graduation tests so that, at the very least, they provide diagnostic information to students on their college readiness. Because the tests are often given in the tenth grade they are not likely to be very useful as admissions measures, but they can alert students to their readiness for college and to the knowledge and skills they should be working to develop during their remaining time in high school.

Similarly, state policymakers should be prepared to revise or augment their state assessment systems to measure more complex cognitive skills. One way to do this is to add a requirement for classroom-based assessment of student work samples. Term papers, research projects, and other learning products that are representative of higher-order cognitive functioning can be assessed against college success standards.

Finally, policymakers can encourage high schools to emphasize intellectual coherence by identifying the characteristics of a high school graduate and stating these in terms related to postsecondary success standards. High schools could be required, at the least, to describe how their curriculum is sequenced in a fashion that develops the habits of mind so crucial to college success and lifelong learning. State policymakers could encourage pilot projects to develop seminar-like courses for seniors. This work could be further facilitated by mandating that high school and postsecondary faculty meet to agree on the exit and entry knowledge and skills students should have mastered.

Higher education institutions would also benefit from state policy guidance designed to enhance articulation with high schools. Although institutions would retain control over whom they admitted, admissions decisions would have to be made largely on the applicants' demonstrated mastery of the knowledge and skills deemed critical to college success. The Knowledge and Skills for University Success standards contained in this book offer one model, but others have been developed or could be created specifically for a state. With these standards in hand, colleges and universities could articulate different standards of necessary content mastery as a clearer way to distinguish which students should apply to which institutions. This clearer focus would permit each institution to develop support systems for entering students keyed to their assumed knowledge and skills and to gear general education courses more precisely to begin at the point where the knowledge of incoming students is assumed to leave off.

Finally, states can change the placement testing system. Once campuses agree on the knowledge and skills required to be admitted to each of them, a common placement test could be administered statewide. High schools would then be in a better position to help students anticipate the contents and demands of this test as well.

What High School Educators Can Do

Earlier chapters have gone into some detail on how high schools can align better with postsecondary success standards. The heart of the challenge for high schools is simply the willingness to do things differently. Most American high schools are complex cultures committed to continuing in roughly the same fashion as they always have. Schools that are organized into distinct subject-based units or departments that offer roughly the same courses taught in largely the same way year after year, that distinguish curricula between the college-bound and non-college-bound, and that tend to group students by perceived measures of ability are difficult to change so that they focus on student mastery of key knowledge and skills.

The key strategy in an articulated system is to clarify what it takes for students to be ready to move on to college. High schools that embrace this goal will need to make big changes. They will become learning environments in which students are constantly measuring their performance and progress against clear outcomes and standards in order to gauge where they are lacking and where they have succeeded. They will emphasize portfolios of student work, teacher-led student critiques of college readiness, challenging projects and assignments that require students to develop the habits of mind associated with postsecondary success, and an overall intellectual coherence that leads to progressively greater challenges and learner responsibilities to achieve desired performance levels.

Such schools will require strong connections between students and teachers. These schools will function as communities of learners where expectations are clear and high. Students will have to be actively engaged in their learning and pursue the goal of equipping themselves with the necessary tools for college success rather than merely checking required courses off a list.

> "Such schools will require strong connections between students and teachers."

This may sound idealistic, and to some degree it probably is, but it is not impossible. Some schools have already achieved these goals and others are actively pursuing them. Students seem open to being more engaged and challenged when they perceive the tasks as being meaningful and interesting. As technology allows more independent student learning and as ever more students raise their educational sights, high schools can become places where all students understand the critical need for them to gear their learning toward specified performance levels and become involved in learning in ways that lead to the development of the complex cognitive skills associated with college success.

Educators can assist students by identifying content that can be mastered by them semi-independently, expecting them to do so largely outside of class and then focusing class time on the types of value-added learning experiences that help them integrate, consolidate, and build on basic understandings. For example, seminar-like courses, particularly writing seminars where students critique each other's work, put a greater emphasis on projects that have a connection with the real world and require application and integration of content knowledge and investigation of complex problems. Such courses require students to apply content knowledge and discipline-based technical skills as well as develop their understanding of social and political systems. A curriculum geared in this direction will engage students while simultaneously developing the important knowledge and skills for college success.

What Postsecondary Faculty and Administrators Can Do

Some of the changes that colleges and universities have to make are clearly implied in earlier chapters, but they will not be easy for institutions that are accustomed to a high degree of autonomy and believe that secondary education's primary role is to serve the needs of higher education. Although many public colleges in particular have begun to acknowledge that their success is inextricably bound up with the capabilities of secondary schools, the changes required of postsecondary education cannot be made if only a few institutions choose to work with a few high schools.

Postsecondary education will have to make over its admissions requirements so that they are clearer about the knowledge and skills students must master to be successful in college. This will not be an easy change to make; in fact, this may be the most difficult change of all. However, there can be no real progress in improving alignment until colleges move beyond course titles and grade point averages to methods that incorporate evidence of student proficiency. Some states have already pioneered possible models, such as Oregon's Proficiency-based Admission Standards System (PASS). Its goal is to have standards that reflect clear agreement between high schools and colleges about what students must know and be able to do, and how this will be measured at the high school level, in the admissions process, and in entry-level college courses.

Postsecondary faculty will also need to interact more with their high school colleagues. This interaction can take place face-to-face, or more indirectly through the sharing of course materials and student work across institutional levels. High-speed Internet connections, the ubiquitous use of e-mail, and the emergence of the PDF file as a universal standard for document exchange make it much easier for high school and college faculty to trade ideas and materials.

Similarly, colleges must be ready to identify more clearly the content of placement tests, the cut scores being used, and the justification for both. Ultimately, placement tests should derive directly from an identifiable body of knowledge and skill for which compelling evidence exists to demonstrate the relationship between mastery of the knowledge and success in entry-level courses, and high school educators should have some involvement in the development of these tests if for no other reason than to ensure familiarity with their content.

Colleges can use placement test redesign as a tool to define better the purposes of their general education requirements. When the goals of general education are better understood by high school educators, the secondary school curriculum can be carefully crafted to create the strongest foundation possible to enable students to enter general education courses prepared to succeed.

What Students Can Do

Although many of the changes described here will need to occur at the policy and institutional levels, students themselves will also need to behave somewhat differently if they wish to take advantage of an aligned educational system. Ultimately, the goal of aligning the systems is to send more consistent messages to students about what they should be doing to prepare for college success. Students, for their part, need to be ready to respond to these messages.

The single most important change will be for students to focus on developing the necessary knowledge and skills, as identified by standards linking high school and college. Most importantly, they will need to seek courses and educational experiences that provide the knowledge, cognitive skills, and habits of mind essential to postsecondary success and to engage fully in those learning experiences. Thus students will need to seek out classes that ask more of them, rather than less of them, in writing, research, and other key skill areas. Many educators (and parents) may be surprised to discover how many students actually prefer and thrive with a higher challenge level.

> They will need to seek courses and educational experiences that provide the knowledge, cognitive skills, and habits of mind essential to postsecondary success.

Students will be rewarded for their accomplishments with proper placement into entry-level courses and more opportunities to earn college credit while still in high school. Ideally, they will assemble an electronic collection of their greatest accomplishments, including tests, papers, assignments, and projects that demonstrate their capacity to do the thinking and learning that will be required of them in college. Over time, admissions offices will learn how to interpret these collections against established performance standards.

Such a proficiency-based system of college preparation and admission will reward the desired behaviors and vastly simplify the process of college preparation and admission. When students know what is expected of them and high school instructors are supported by college entrance expectations that value intellectual coherence and competence, the culture of the typical American high school will shift dramatically in the direction of focused academic achievement. Students will have real reasons to become much more actively engaged in monitoring their own knowledge and skills.

Tools such as the Checklist for College Readiness, presented in the appendix of this book, help gauge the distance students have to cover to be ready for college-level work. As students learn to self-diagnose, they will be able to focus their energies in areas where they know they need additional preparation. Those who feel well prepared have the option to develop deeper understandings in select areas, primarily to prepare to take full advantage of the college experience. The option to move on to college after demonstrating mastery of requisite knowledge and skills remains as well. An aligned system ultimately allows students more control over their own education and their transition from high school to college.

What Parents Can Do

Parents too will have a somewhat different role and different responsibilities in a more aligned educational system focused on student success in college. For one thing, they will be more likely to understand the knowledge and skills their children should be developing in high school and thus ensure that their children understand these requirements and judge the degree to which the high school's instructional program is equipping them for college success.

Parents will need to communicate to their children the importance of acquiring the key knowledge and skills. For example, they could set quality standards for homework. Those standards should reflect the need for students to understand material, not just complete assignments. Thus there will need to be a parental commitment to reviewing important student homework, particularly research papers and other major projects, so they can ensure that their children are devoting the time and attention required for the activity to be worthwhile and really develop desired skills. Although parents may not always have the content knowledge necessary to tell if their child is doing homework correctly, they can still determine the quality of the work, particularly if the teacher provides quality standards against which they can measure the work.

This sort of communication between a parent and children of high school age can be challenging, particularly when they become juniors and seniors. However, it can also be a means to retain some common reference points as the child prepares for the inevitable separation that accompanies college attendance. Parents can at least emphasize their stake in and commitment to their child's success by reviewing and discussing how the child does on the Checklist for College Readiness.

This communication can be extended to the high school through discussions at parent-teacher nights, where parents focus on the ways in which the high school class addresses college success standards. Is the teacher aware of the Knowledge and Skills for University Success standards and the Checklist for College Readiness, and how does he or she develop the key habits of mind described in this book? Does the teacher use exemplars to point students toward the performance they need to achieve ultimately? Although this sort of questioning could be taken by some teachers as being combative or challenging, parents will be fully justified in asking these questions in a system where alignment is expected. Under the current model, teachers can align as much or as little as they please, and parents have no real way to gauge the appropriateness of the decisions a teacher has made. Parents can be a powerful force to help ensure that high schools are doing all they can to develop the cognitive and intellectual tools students will need in the college environment by encouraging both students and teachers to align their efforts with success standards.

Beginning the Journey

The ultimate goal of all the methods, activities, and strategies laid out in this book is a highly aligned educational system. As was noted in the very beginning, the American educational system was designed intentionally *not* to be well aligned. However, students have spoken by the choices they have made to attend postsecondary education in record numbers. The goal now is to decrease the problems they encounter after being admitted by designing the system so they can make a smooth transition. They want to know what will be expected of them, what they should be doing in high school to be ready to succeed in college. Few high school students approach college preparation with the goal of not succeeding in college. Yet the effect of the current relationship between high school and college is that many who do all they are told to do still enter college only to find that they are unprepared for college-level study. As has been outlined here, many do not proceed beyond the freshman year, up to 40 percent require some form of remediation, and only about a third achieve a degree within six years.

Few people would advocate for the characteristics of the current system. Achieving and managing the necessary changes is a daunting proposition, however. The goal of this book is to offer those interested in improving the relationship between high school and college a starting point for concrete action. Although it does not provide all the answers, it does lay out a path down which those who are interested in improving college success for all students may begin their journey.

PART THREE

Knowledge and Skills for Success

Part Three describes what students will encounter in postsecondary institutions. Chapters Ten through Sixteen present the complete Knowledge and Skills for University Success (KSUS) standards. As explained in earlier chapters, these standards are not about what students must do in high school but rather what will be expected of them when they enter first-year college courses. They provide a blueprint of the cognitive skills, habits of mind, dispositions toward learning, key principles and concepts of the disciplines, important attributes, and key content knowledge that students must possess.

The KSUS standards are organized by discipline, beginning with English. Each discipline has two sections. First, and perhaps most important, is a presentation in narrative format of the foundational skills needed to excel in the study of the discipline. Second is a detailed listing of the content students should master by the time they reach university.

Many readers may feel a natural tendency to skip the narrative foundational skills sections in favor of the more straightforward content standards presentation. However, the university faculty involved in creating these standards were most adamant in their assertion that success at research universities in particular is probably based more on mastery of the foundational skills than the content standards.

Although this is not to imply in any way that content knowledge is not tremendously important, it does mean that content knowledge is necessary but not sufficient for college success.

A university education is largely about learning how to think in particular ways. Content is a means to that end. That end is the ability to think about things differently and in deeper, more systematic and complex ways. For students who think of college strictly in terms of mastering content knowledge, the experience will be less valuable and probably more frustrating. Content is to be understood and mastered in the context of particular ways of thinking about that content. This is what the foundational skills capture and reflect.

The content standards present a comprehensive view of the prerequisite knowledge associated with college success. The more of this knowledge a student possesses on entry into college, the greater the probability that he or she will experience success. Because these standards include all the important knowledge and skills that entry-level college courses build on, they range from basic to complex. As a result, students should expect to have mastered the more basic standards at the automatic level and to have a solid grasp on the more complex standards.

Chapter Seventeen presents work samples from actual college classrooms; these student work samples illustrate how the KSUS standards translate into the work that students do. Finally, the appendix of the book contains a self-assessment that allows students to determine how well they have mastered each standard by rating themselves on tasks relative to the standard. High school teachers can also use the Checklist for College Readiness to gauge the challenge level of their courses. Which of the content standards are students being exposed to in a particular high school class? Which are they mastering? Which are they not encountering at all? Such determinations are useful when planning curriculum coverage and seeking better alignment with postsecondary education.

chapter TEN

Standards for Success

The following chapters present the results of three years of research by twenty top U.S. universities, culminating in the creation of the Knowledge and Skills for University Success (KSUS) standards. The institutions are members of the Association of American Universities (AAU), a one-hundred-year-old organization to which sixty of the nation's leading research universities belong. The KSUS standards represent the first comprehensive statement of what it takes to succeed in entry-level college courses ever produced by a group of U.S. universities.

The research was undertaken at the behest of a group of presidents from these institutions who were concerned about how the changes occurring in high school education affect students as they move to postsecondary education. They wanted to support the efforts states were making to increase the number of core academic courses high schools required and to establish demanding academic standards. They worked to create the standards presented here in order to forge a stronger link between high school and university expectations.

The standards thus reflect the collective wisdom and insights of hundreds of faculty members from coast to coast who actually teach entry-level courses at these institutions. They are well-equipped to describe what it takes to succeed in these all-important courses and where students struggle the most.

High school teachers and students who make use of these materials can improve the preparation and success of students as they move from high school to college. The standards can serve as a framework for producing the definition of a well-educated student to which high school teachers can refer as they design an instructional program united by common expectations of what constitutes a graduate well-prepared for college. A high school that adopts the KSUS standards as a template for its instructional program will have taken an important first step toward creating the kind of program that facilitates success in college.

Over four hundred faculty from twenty AAU universities participated in nine daylong meetings to develop these standards. The meetings were held at the University of Oregon; University of California, Berkeley; University of Iowa; University of Minnesota; University of Missouri; Rutgers University; Massachusetts Institute of Technology; University of Wisconsin; and Indiana University.

The faculty members and officers of administration who participated in the process represented a wide range of academic viewpoints. They came from the institutions mentioned in the preceding paragraph and eleven other AAU universities, including Harvard University, University of Illinois, University of Michigan, University of Nebraska, University of Southern California, New York University, The Pennsylvania State University, and Rice University. In addition, the Knowledge and Skills for University Success standards were endorsed by these AAU institutions: Carnegie Mellon University; Case Western Reserve University; Duke University; Iowa State University; University of California, Irvine; University of California, Los Angeles; University of North Carolina; University of Maryland; Stanford University; University of Virginia; and Washington University in St. Louis.

The participants' input was analyzed to identify key knowledge and skills expected of students by those who teach the entry-level courses they usually take during their freshman year. The research team also collected and analyzed course outlines, assignments, tests, projects, and student work from these classes. This was done to ensure that what faculty members said students needed to do to succeed in their classes was borne out by what actually went on in those classes. Next, the standards generated from the nine faculty meetings and the analysis of course documents were reviewed by an external consulting group with expertise in standards setting, Mid-continent Research for Education and Learning (McREL), and finally by a Content Review Panel consisting of professors from AAU universities with relevant expertise and content knowledge.

The resulting standards and objectives—the Knowledge and Skills for University Success (KSUS)—were mailed in April 2003 to every public high school in the nation, state education departments, major universities, and educational policy organizations. As mentioned in Chapter Nine, these standards have also been licensed to the College Board, which has incorporated them into a range of its programs and tests.

Covering six disciplinary areas—English, mathematics, natural sciences, social sciences, second languages, and the arts—the KSUS standards are the most comprehensive and complete ever developed to answer one question: *What must students know and be able to do in order to succeed in entry-level university courses?* This is a difficult question because admissions requirements only hint at what colleges actually expect of students once they get in.

A dominant theme raised by those who were involved in the standards' creation was the importance of the habits of mind students bring to university studies; these were considered by many faculty to be more important than specific content knowledge.

Some of the most important of these habits of mind are critical thinking, analytic thinking, and problem solving; an inquisitive nature and interest in taking advantage of what a research university has to offer; willingness to accept critical feedback and to adjust based on such feedback; openness to possible failures from time to time; and ability and desire to cope with frustrating and ambiguous learning tasks. Other such skills include ability to express oneself in writing and orally in a clear and convincing fashion, to discern the relative importance and credibility of various sources of information, to draw inferences and reach conclusions independently, and to use technology as a tool to assist the learning process rather than as a crutch.

The specific content requirements enumerated in this document should be considered important not as ends in themselves but as means to develop the aforementioned habits of mind. A student understands and masters the content knowledge specified here in the context of broader cognitive skills. It is not enough simply to know something; learners must be able to do something with that knowledge, whether solve a problem, reach a conclusion, or clearly present a point of view. This plexus of content knowledge and cognitive skills is what an education at a U.S. research university (and many other institutions of higher education) seeks to develop.

The KSUS standards include two criteria for success: (1) doing well enough in entry-level core academic courses to meet general education requirements, and (2) continuing on to major in a particular area. An asterisk next to a standard indicates it is at the second level.

Success at university is different from success in high school in another important way. Specialization is greater in college than in high school. Therefore, some students may find that they are able to succeed even though they have a lesser mastery of some of the KSUS standards than others. Indeed, students do not need to master all of them equally well. However, the more of them a student has mastered, the more options that student will have and the more successful he or she is likely to be during the all-important freshman year.

The standards for the six academic content areas presented here have some distinguishing characteristics. For English, mathematics, and second languages, the standards present a relatively clear and distinct set of attributes associated with each respective discipline. Natural sciences and social sciences standards reflect the complexity of these areas, each of which encompasses a series of distinct academic disciplines. These standards are grouped into the skills that cut across the area along with accompanying listings of the key knowledge attributes for a number of the disciplines in the area. The arts section takes a unique approach, because entry-level arts classes may be taken for the first time by students at any point in their academic career, making it more difficult to identify those associated with first-year students.

The arts are uniquely complex in other ways as well. First, they may be divided into the performing arts, where one performs or creates an artistic product, and arts appreciation, where one learns to enjoy or understand the arts. Second, different arts require distinctly different technical skills. Music, art, dance, and theatre have more distinct skill sets and knowledge than do biology and chemistry or geography and history, for example. Therefore, the arts standards are organized by area based on abilities derived from national arts standards documents and the expressed values of arts faculty.

Finally, it should be noted that the KSUS standards are general statements that require additional detail to illustrate the cognitive complexity associated with them. To help clarify, examples of the work students produce when they meet each standard are presented in Chapter Seventeen, and the Checklist for College Readiness in the Appendix presents more examples of how the standards translate into academic tasks. In combination with these additional resources, the KSUS standards provide a multidimensional road map of the content knowledge and habits of mind that are valued by leading research universities in the United States.

Research universities are complex, diverse environments. Not every faculty member will agree completely with every one of the standards presented here. In fact, spirited debate typifies American higher education. Therefore, the KSUS standards should be considered to be good generalizations about what is expected of entering students, not dogma.

English Knowledge and Skills

English consists of reading, writing, critical thinking, and research skills. These skills are not taught or developed solely in English courses, but they are listed here in one chapter to emphasize the connections among them. Many of these skills are developed throughout one's life and perhaps never mastered fully. However, this chapter offers an overview of the standards against which to judge one's readiness for college in terms of literacy and its associated elements.

English Knowledge and Skills Foundations

Students who perform well and derive the greatest benefit from entry-level university English courses are prepared for thoughtful study, engaged in the material and the process of learning, and curious, persistent, and realistic. The following discussion offers greater detail on the skills and attributes that help make students successful.

Reading, Comprehension, and Literature

Successful students connect reading with writing and thinking skills. Reading is an active process that, if done well, involves asking questions and noticing patterns. Active reading strategies include making notes, summarizing, and critiquing the material. Many students read in a mechanical manner—just following the words on the page—instead of using active reading strategies.

Once students understand what it means to be an active reader, their next step is to think critically about what they read. Successful students recognize an effective thesis and how it is constructed. Reading is interactive and leads to experiential and literary connections. Successful students are prepared to answer questions such as, "How does this text make me feel?" and "What features of the text make me feel this way?"

It is important, too, to be able to take a position about the material and defend that position in a discussion. Students need to realize that one piece of writing can be interpreted in a variety of ways and that subjectivity, including personal experience and opinion, influences possible reactions.

The ability to paraphrase a reading assignment shows whether a student has comprehended the material. To paraphrase, students must pay close attention to and understand both the literal meanings and connotations of words. While they read, successful students decide which pieces of information are important and relevant to the current assignment, noting the specific points that support the argument they plan to present.

Students who are ready for introductory literature courses come to the university familiar with a range of world literature. They are aware of major U.S. and British authors—both men and women—and representative literary works from a variety of cultural traditions. These students have had exposure to nonliterary sources as well: documents such as the Magna Carta and the Declaration of Independence. With that exposure, students have a better understanding of the range of writing from which their literature courses will draw.

Awareness of cultural context is important, but students need to be familiar with literary forms and genres as well. They should be able to recognize the forms—such as novel, poem, play, essay, short story—and be able to identify what distinguishes them, what makes a biography different from a novel or a short story different from an essay. To understand the purposes and possibilities of the various forms, students need to be able to tell the difference between genres: comedy, epic, tragedy, romance, and others.

Writing and Editing

Grammar is the basis for good writing. Good writing demands that writers consistently use proper sentence structure. Students in college are expected to know how to diagram a sentence and recognize how this process helps them understand words and their functions in a sentence. It is also important to understand the specific ways correct grammar makes writing clearer and helps communicate more effectively.

All students can benefit from paying more attention to writing mechanics. A review of work samples from students in entry-level courses reveals a high level of grammatical errors. In order to succeed in and benefit from writing and literature courses, students must have a good grasp of writing conventions.

Good writers use language to express ideas, not simply to describe events. Student writing must be coherent, and students need to think rhetorically when they write, consider the audience, carefully select the evidence they use to support ideas, cogently present the overall argument, and understand the purposes of their writing. Successful students also understand how to support an argument well enough that a strong position emerges, while realizing the consequences of taking a particular position. Defending a position requires good knowledge of the material—which also tends to improve students' ability to think about what they write.

Successful students craft an outline before they start writing the actual piece, then use the outline as a tool to develop a detailed structure and to guide their writing. Furthermore, writing itself is just the beginning. Editing is the most important part of the writing process. Going through several drafts of a particular paper is routine for a college-level assignment. Often, students rely too heavily on the computer spell-checker. Students need to know how to proofread, check for mistakes on their own, and appreciate the value of the revision and rewriting processes. These processes improve writing ability; they help students write better and they improve grades on written assignments.

Information Gathering

Students are expected to take useful notes during the lectures they attend during their first year of college. To be useful, a set of notes should be more than just a transcript of what a professor has said. It is all too common for many new college students simply to fill up pages without sufficiently evaluating the relative quality and importance of the information being delivered by the instructor. Students are expected to pay close attention and engage with presented materials, both written and verbal. This requires taking in information, analyzing it, and recording that which is meaningful and useful.

A huge part of the information gathering process takes place outside of the classroom. Successful students know how to make a research plan and carry it out: What questions need to be asked, who has the knowledge and authority to answer them, and what sources can be used to answer those questions? Also, students should either be able to do the following or learn how to do so quickly:

- *Identify a source.* Students must understand what plagiarism is and understand the ethics of writing. It is essential to know what borrowing ideas from other authors means, how to paraphrase properly, and how to cite sources.

- *Distinguish the quality and reliability of information.* Students often accept unreliable information from the Internet or other unverified sources.

- *Connect information from sources to support an argument.* Students need to know the difference between primary and secondary sources and ask themselves whether the evidence they have found is weak or strong, and how that evidence helps create a cogent argument.

- *Be disciplined in doing research, regardless of what the field may be.* Studies in the humanities rely on good research, just as the sciences do.

Analysis, Critique, and Connections

In addition to being able to read effectively and present a solid written argument, students need to think analytically about the information they collect. Students should be able to do the following:

- *Categorize information thematically.* Doing so allows students to see the larger constructs inherent in the information and the relationships between ideas and attendant concepts and theories. Then, students can identify the main message and avoid becoming overwhelmed by details.

- *Go beyond facts presented in readings or lectures.* Students must allow questions to emerge from the text, identify connections with other concepts they have learned, and imagine alternatives to a text's final content message or conclusion.

- *Be aware of the differences between summary and description, interpretation and analysis.*

- *Move between general and specific ideas when analyzing information.*

- *Think comparatively.* Students need to make connections across texts and points of view; this enriches and expands their understanding of the materials.

Once students have gathered information and begun the analysis process, the most important skill for them to employ is critical reflection. Critical reflection goes beyond "I liked it" or "I didn't like it." When asked to evaluate a piece of writing, students are expected to answer questions that do not necessarily have right or wrong answers. It is crucial that students be able to discuss questions in depth and effectively defend a position based on their analysis of the material.

At the college level, students must also be able to accept constructive criticism of their own work without taking it personally. Many students are unable or unwilling to argue effectively, and they cannot differentiate between criticism and critique. To succeed in discussion classes and written work, they need to understand that criticism is not a form of personal attack.

Successful students are able to integrate personal experiences and knowledge with the material they encounter in their coursework. Information comes from a variety of sources, but whether it comes from a different class or department, is a personal observation, or is public knowledge, students should be able to connect the ideas and concepts. When students can make such connections it helps them understand the interdisciplinary nature of knowledge.

Successful students have opinions. They can assert their opinions and ask bold questions. By thinking out their opinions, students develop a consciousness and a distinct voice. At the same time, students need to understand that "I" statements are rarely acceptable in formal academic writing. Opinions may be a good thing, but they need to be substantiated and supported by empirical evidence.

Orientation Toward Learning

Time management is a key part of research, coursework, and effective participation. College-level study often takes more time than students are prepared to spend. New students must learn how to set aside enough time for reading and study and understand that some assignments take many hours. Being able to start assignments early and budget time effectively are essential skills.

Students who participate in public discourse—by reading newspapers, following world events, and considering how events play out in the United States—are ready to participate in academic discussion. Such discussion requires give-and-take, and students should have ideas and questions to add to the conversation. It is necessary for students to ask questions and to understand why it is necessary to do so. To benefit from material presented in classes, students need to be engaged with their instructors and to ask questions that go beyond what is presented in class.

To be able to discuss a piece of literature, students must have a basic understanding of the work's place in history. Placing a work in its historical context can help students understand where they themselves fit and how societal contexts influence writing and thinking.

The same applies to geography: to understand fully the impact of a piece of literature, students must be able to place it in a geographical context. Students must understand how that geographic setting influenced the content of the work.

Students need to be open-minded and willing to consider a variety of viewpoints, texts, and phenomena that may differ from what they learned before. When they are open-minded they can understand how knowledge is constructed. When they are open-minded their perspectives broaden and they can deal with the novelty and ambiguity of new materials.

As tasks become more challenging, it is often difficult for new college students to maintain acceptable levels of attention and application. It is essential that students approach their work with a willingness to push forward. Students are almost always capable of following through; often, though, they are simply unwilling to try and to keep trying.

Students do well if they appreciate what college is—and what it is not. They must understand academic expectations and the realities of college life, including the need to apply themselves and work hard. College is best experienced as a process, not a series of obligatory hurdles toward a degree. The students who appreciate the need to persevere and think independently are in the best position to succeed.

English Content Standards

Items shown with an asterisk apply to students who plan to major in English, comparative literature, or writing.

I. Reading and Comprehension

A. Successful students employ reading skills and strategies to understand literature. They:

A.1. Engage in an analytic process to enhance comprehension and create personal meaning when reading text. This includes the ability to annotate, question, agree or disagree, summarize, critique, and formulate a personal response.

A.2. Make supported inferences and draw conclusions based on textual features, seeking such evidence in text, format, language use, expository structures, and arguments used.

A.3. Use reading skills and strategies to understand a variety of types of literature, such as epic pieces (for instance, *The Iliad*) and lyric poems, as well as narrative novels and philosophical pieces.

A.4. Understand plot and character development in literature, including character motive, causes for actions, and the credibility of events.

A.5.* Identify basic beliefs, perspectives, and philosophical assumptions underlying an author's work. This includes identifying points of view, attitudes, and the values conveyed by specific use of language.

A.6.* Employ a variety of strategies to understand the origins and meanings of new words, including analysis of word roots and the determination of word derivations.

A.7.* Recognize and comprehend narrative terminology and techniques, such as author versus narrator, stated versus implied author, and historical versus present-day reader.

B. Successful students use reading skills and strategies to understand informational texts. They:

B.1. Understand instructions for software, job descriptions, college applications, historical documents, government publications, newspapers, and textbooks.

B.2. Monitor themselves and correct themselves, as well as read aloud, in order to ensure comprehension.

B.3. Understand vocabulary and content, including subject area terminology, connotative and denotative meanings, and idiomatic meanings.

B.4. Employ a variety of strategies to understand the origins and meanings of new words, including recognition of cognates and contextual clues.

C. Successful students are able to understand the defining characteristics of texts and recognize a variety of literary forms and genres. They:

C.1. Comprehend the salient characteristics of major types and genres of texts, such as novels, short stories, horror stories, science fiction, biographies, autobiographies, poems, and plays.

C.2. Understand the formal constraints of different types of texts and can distinguish between, for example, a Shakespearean sonnet and a poem written in free verse.

C.3. Can discuss with understanding the effects of an author's style and use of literary devices to influence the reader and evoke emotions. This includes devices such as imagery, characterization, choice of narrator, use of sound, formal and informal language, allusions, symbols, irony, voice, flashbacks, foreshadowing, time, sequence, and mood.

C.4. Can identify archetypes, such as universal destruction, journeys and tests, and banishment, which appear in many types of literature, including American literature, world literature, myths, propaganda, and religious texts.

C.5. Can discuss with understanding themes such as initiation, love and duty, heroism, and death and rebirth, which appear in a variety of literary works and genres.

C.6. Can use aesthetic qualities of style, such as diction or mood, as a basis to evaluate literature that contains ambiguities, subtleties, or contradictions.

D. Successful students are familiar with a range of world literature. They:

D.1. Demonstrate familiarity with the major literary periods of English and American literature and their characteristic forms, subjects, and authors.

D.2. Demonstrate familiarity with authors from literary traditions outside the English-speaking world.

D.3. Demonstrate familiarity with major works of literature produced by American and British authors.

E. Successful students are able to discuss with understanding the relationships between literature and its historical and social contexts. They:

E.1. Know major historical events that may be encountered in literature.

E.2. Demonstrate familiarity with the concept that historical, social, and economic contexts influence form, style, and point of view, and that social influences affect an author's descriptions of character, plot, and setting.

E.3. Demonstrate familiarity with the concept of the relativity of all historical perspectives, including their own.

E.4. Can discuss with understanding the relationships between literature and politics, including the political assumptions underlying an author's work and the impact of literature on political movements and events.

F. Successful students are able to read and interpret visual images, including charts and graphs. They:

F.1. Identify the primary elements of the types of charts, graphs, and visual media that occur most commonly in texts.

F.2. Interpret accurately the content of charts, graphs, and visual media that occur in texts.

II. Writing

A. Successful students apply basic grammar conventions in an effort to write clearly. They:

A.1. Identify and use correctly and consistently parts of speech, including nouns, pronouns, verbs, adverbs, conjunctions, prepositions, adjectives, and interjections.

A.2. Use subject-verb agreement and verb tense consistently and correctly.

A.3. Demonstrate consistent, correct, and appropriate pronoun agreement and use of different types of clauses and phrases, including adverb clauses, adjective clauses, and adverb phrases.

B. Successful students know the conventions of punctuation and capitalization. They:

B.1. Use commas with nonrestrictive clauses and contrasting expressions.

B.2. Use ellipses, colons, hyphens, semi-colons, apostrophes, and quotation marks correctly.

B.3. Capitalize sentences and proper nouns correctly.

B.4. Consistently avoid run-on sentences and sentence fragments.

C. Successful students know conventions of spelling. They:

C.1. Use a dictionary and other resources to see how to spell new, unfamiliar, or difficult words.

C.2. Differentiate between commonly confused terms, such as "its" and "it's" or "affect" and "effect."

C.3. Know how to use the spell-check and grammar-check functions in word processing software while understanding the limitations of relying on these tools.

D. Successful students use writing conventions to write clearly and coherently. They:

D.1. Know and use several prewriting strategies, including developing a focus, determining the purpose, planning a sequence of ideas, using structured overviews, and creating outlines.

D.2. Use paragraph structure in writing as manifested by the ability to construct coherent paragraphs and arrange paragraphs in logical order.

D.3. Use a variety of sentence structures appropriately in writing, including compound, complex, compound-complex, parallel, repetitive, and analogous sentence structures.

D.4. Present ideas to achieve overall coherence and logical flow in writing and use appropriate techniques such as transitions and repetition to maximize cohesion.

D.5. Use words correctly, use words that convey the intended meaning, and use a varied vocabulary.

D.6.* Demonstrate development of a controlled yet unique style and voice in writing where appropriate.

D.7.* Use a style manual, such as that of the Modern Language Association (MLA) or the American Psychological Association (APA), to apply writing conventions and create documentation formats in a manner consistent with the manual.

E. Successful students use writing to communicate ideas, concepts, emotions, and descriptions to the reader. They:

E.1. Know the difference between a topic and a thesis.

E.2. Articulate a position through a thesis statement and advance it using evidence, examples, and counterarguments that are relevant to the audience or issue at hand.

E.3. Use a variety of methods to develop arguments, including compare-contrast reasoning, logical arguments (inductive-deductive), and alternation between general and specific (for example, connections between public knowledge and personal observation and experience).

E.4. Write to persuade the reader by anticipating and addressing counterarguments, using rhetorical devices, and developing an accurate and expressive style of communication that moves beyond mechanics to add flair and elegance to writing.

E.5. Use a variety of strategies to adapt writing to different audiences and purposes, such as including appropriate content and using appropriate language, style, tone, and structure.

E.6. Distinguish between formal and informal styles—for example, between academic essays and personal memos.

E.7. Use appropriate strategies and formats to write personal and business correspondence, including appropriate organizational patterns, formal language, and tone.

E.8.* Use appropriate strategies to write expository essays that employ supporting evidence; use information from primary and secondary sources; incorporate charts, graphs, tables, and illustrations where appropriate; anticipate and address readers' biases and expectations; and explain technical terms and notations.

E.9.* Use strategies to write fictional, autobiographical, and biographical narratives that include a well-developed point of view and literary elements, present events in logical sequence, convey a unifying theme or tone, use concrete and sensory language, and pace action.

F. Successful students both use and prioritize a variety of strategies to revise and edit their written work to achieve the greatest improvement in the time available. They:

F.1. Employ basic editing skills proficiently to identify obvious mechanical errors, clarify and improve the structure of the piece, and sharpen language and meaning.

F.2. Review ideas and structure in substantive ways to improve depth of information and logic of organization.

F.3. Reassess appropriateness of writing in light of genre, purpose, and audience.

F.4. Use feedback from others to revise their written work.

III. Research Skills

A. Successful students understand and use research methodologies. They:

A.1. Formulate research questions, refine topics, develop a plan for research, and organize what is known about the topic.

A.2. Use research to support and develop their own opinions, as opposed to simply restating existing information or opinions.

A.3. Identify claims in their writing that require outside support or verification.

A.4.* Identify through research the major concerns and debates in a given community or field of inquiry and address these in their writing.

B. Successful students know how to find a variety of sources and use them properly. They:

B.1. Collect information to develop a topic and support a thesis.

B.2. Understand the difference between primary and secondary sources.

B.3. Use a variety of print and electronic primary and secondary sources, including books, magazines, newspapers, journals, periodicals, and the Internet.

B.4. Understand the concept of plagiarism and how (or why) to avoid it and understand rules for paraphrasing, summarizing, and quoting, as well as conventions for incorporating information from Internet-based sources in particular.

B.5. Evaluate sources of information located on the Internet in particular to ascertain their credibility, origin, potential bias, and overall quality.

B.6. Select relevant sources when writing research papers and appropriately include information from such sources, logically introduce and incorporate quotations, synthesize information in a logical sequence, identify different perspectives, identify complexities and discrepancies in information, and offer support for conclusions.

B.7.* Evaluate sources critically, discerning the quality of the materials and qualifying the strength of the evidence and arguments, as well as determining credibility, identifying author bias and perspective, and using prior knowledge of the source.

IV. Critical Thinking Skills

A. Successful students demonstrate connective intelligence. They:

A.1. Can discuss with understanding how personal experiences and values affect reading comprehension and interpretation.

A.2.* Demonstrate an ability to make connections between the component parts of a text and the larger theoretical structures, including presupposition, audience, purpose, writer's credibility or ethos, types of evidence or material being used, and style.

B. Successful students demonstrate the ability to think independently. They:

B.1. Are comfortable formulating and expressing their own ideas.

B.2. Support their arguments with logic and evidence relevant to their audience and explicate their position as fully as possible.

B.3. Understand fully the scope of their arguments and the claims underlying them.

B.4. Reflect on and assess the strengths and weaknesses of their ideas and the expression of those ideas.

Mathematics Knowledge and Skills

Mathematics is one of the "gateway" skills; it is necessary for entry into a vast array of college majors. Expectations for entry-level math courses contain some natural overlap with high school math courses, but the pace in college courses is often much more rapid, the emphasis on conceptual understanding much greater. Mathematical reasoning can be as important as specific content knowledge once students reach college math.

Mathematics Knowledge and Skills Foundations

As in many other disciplines, incoming students in mathematics are expected to bring a combination of hands-on skills and conceptual understanding. Entering students need to know basic mathematical concepts—computation, algebra, trigonometry, geometry—so that they have the tools to work with increasingly complex conceptual mathematical and quantitative procedures and analyses in their college courses.

Understanding Mathematics

Successful students approach mathematical problems as they would an investigation. They ask questions, reflect, and revisit their solutions with one idea in mind, that both how one reaches a solution and why the solution works are important. Problem solving involves analytical processes and sets of skills. These students do the following:

- *Think conceptually, not just procedurally, about mathematics.* Successful students understand the relationships between mathematical concepts and know that formulas do not function in a vacuum. They perceive mathematics as a way of understanding, a thinking process, rather than a collection of detached procedures to be learned and applied separately.

- *Use logical reasoning and common sense to find mathematical solutions.* Successful students are able to provide supporting evidence to construct compelling arguments to explain processes and solutions. They check their solutions through visualization, so they can see whether their findings make sense or not.

- *Think experimentally; exhibit inquisitiveness and a willingness to investigate the steps used to reach a solution.* Successful students understand there can be multiple approaches to solving a problem.

- *Take risks and accept failure as part of the learning process.* When students do not find the correct answer to a problem, it is an opportunity to revisit the procedures they used, try new ones, and ask further questions. Finding a solution may be only vaguely logical; verifying a solution should be rigorously logical.

- *Be able to use formulas and algorithms of computation.* A lack of facility with computation and formulas encumbers the analytical process.

Problem Solving, Technology, and Communication

Problem solving is central to the teaching and learning of mathematics. The step-by-step approach is the best way to solve math problems and draw parallels and connections among various problems. Mathematical problem solving involves logical reasoning; it is important to explore the reasons why Step 2 follows Step 1. Successful students understand the process of modifying, adapting, and combining mathematical tools to find new ways to reach a solution. They also question results until they can explain their answers and defend them. Technology is important and relevant to the understanding of mathematics. However, students need to be aware of its limitations and recognize that calculators are tools that assist but do not replace the thinking process. A graphing calculator can be a tool to deepen understanding of functions and represent them visually. At the same time, successful students can identify whether the calculator's answers are reasonable in light of their own calculations.

Mathematics is the language of the sciences, and thus fluency in this language is a basic skill. Students prepared for college-level study are comfortable with mathematical terminology and use it appropriately. It is crucial to understand that formulas and symbols provide precise statements of often vaguely posed problems. Different interpretations of a problem may lead to different mathematical models and analyses. Students must pay attention to the wording of problems and move with ease between symbolic and verbal representations of them.

Mathematics is a language, and the study of math also requires solid verbal skills. In mathematics, students are expected to write with clarity and cohesiveness. A poorly written solution is often an indication of confused thinking. Although clear writing is the best way to convey information to others, it is also an important indication that one understands a problem.

Orientation Toward Learning

Relating mathematical abstractions to life outside of math class is a highly useful skill. Students who do well in math classes are prepared to translate real situations into mathematical representation, and conversely, extract meaning from mathematical expression. They understand when mathematics generalizes and when it is specific, and recognize the importance of abstraction and generalization as they learn and do mathematics.

Often, college-level mathematics courses require that students work in groups. Although it is important to be able to work effectively with peers, students must also develop the skills necessary to approach mathematical problems on their own, independent of classes, group projects, and work environments. Both situations are valuable—as are the skills needed for each of them.

Students often experience anxiety when confronted with a mathematical problem, even when encountering mathematical terminology. Persistence is invaluable in the quest for correct answers to a problem, and it is vital to tolerate ambiguity on the road to the solution. Interestingly, some of the faculty who participated in developing the KSUS standards expressed a concern about students being too confident in their perceived knowledge and skills. Students are sometimes naively confident, which prevents them from engaging in the mathematical process, finding other solutions, and estimating or questioning the viability of their results.

Mathematical problems rarely have instant or quick solutions and it often takes a long time to find a solution. Sustained inquiry—engaging in the process for more than a short time—is an important part of the process when solving a problem or taking an exam. Successful students understand that math is an academic activity that requires time, sustained engagement, patience, and persistence.

Mathematics Content Standards

Items shown with an asterisk apply to students who plan to major in mathematics, computer science, statistics, and related fields.

I. Computation

A. Successful students know basic mathematical operations. They:

A.1. Apply arithmetic operations with fractions and integers (for example, add and subtract by finding a common denominator, multiply and divide, reduce and perform long division without a calculator).

A.2. Use exponents and scientific notation.

A.3. Use radicals correctly.

A.4. Understand relative magnitude.

A.5. Calculate using absolute value.

A.6. Use the correct order of arithmetic operations, particularly demonstrating facility with the distributive law.

A.7.* Know terminology for integers, rational numbers, irrational numbers, and complex numbers.

B. Successful students know and carefully record symbolic manipulations. They:

B.1. Understand the uses of mathematical symbols as well as the limitations on their appropriate uses (for example, equal signs, parentheses, superscripts, subscripts).

C. Successful students know and demonstrate fluency with mathematical notation and computation. They:

C.1. Correctly perform addition, subtraction, multiplication, and division that includes variables.

C.2. Perform appropriate basic operations on sets (for example, union, intersection, elements of subsets, and complement).

C.3. Use alternative symbolic expressions, particularly alternatives to x (for example, letters of the Greek alphabet that do not already have specific scientific or mathematical meanings).

II. Algebra

A. Successful students know and apply basic algebraic concepts. They:

A.1. Use the distributive property to multiply polynomials.

A.2. Know how to compose and decompose functions and how to find inverses of basic functions.

A.3. Simplify and perform basic operations on rational expressions, including finding common denominators (for example, add, subtract, multiply, divide).

A.4. Understand exponents, roots, and their properties, such as $(x2)$, $(x3) = x5$, and $(\sqrt{x})3 = x3/2$).

A.5. Know basic theorems of exponents and roots.

A.6.* Understand logarithms (to bases 2, 10, and e) and their properties.

A.7.* Divide low degree polynomials (long division).

A.8.* Know basic theorems of logarithms.

A.9.* Factor polynomials (difference of squares, perfect square trinomials, difference of two cubes, and trinomials such as $x2 + 3x + 2$).

B. Successful students use various appropriate techniques to solve basic equations and inequalities. They:

B.1. Solve linear equations and absolute value equations.

B.2. Solve linear inequalities and absolute value inequalities.

B.3. Solve systems of linear equations and inequalities using algebraic and graphical methods (for example, substitution, elimination, addition, and graphing).

B.4. Solve quadratic equations using various appropriate methods while recognizing real solutions, including:

B.4a. Factoring

B.4b. Completing the square

B.4c. The quadratic formula

C. Successful students distinguish between and among expressions, formulas, equations, and functions. They:

C.1. Know when it is possible to simplify, solve, substitute, or evaluate equations and expressions and when it is not possible. For example, they can expand, but do not solve, the expression $(x + 3)(x + 1)$; substitute $a = 3$, $b = 4$ into the formula $a2 + b2 = c2$; solve the equation $0 = (x + 3)(x + 1)$; and evaluate the function $f(x) = (x + 3)(x + 1)$ at $x = -1$.

C.2. Understand that the concept of a function has a specific definition beyond being a type of algebraic expression.

C.3. Represent functions, patterns, and relationships in different ways (for example, statements, formulas, and graphs).

C.4. Understand the algebraic language and notation for functions (for example, domain and range).

C.5. Understand a variety of functions (for example, polynomial, rational, exponential, logarithmic, and trigonometric) and properties of each.

D. Successful students understand the relationship between equations and graphs. They:

D.1. Understand basic forms of the equation of a straight line and how to graph the line without the aid of a calculator.

D.2. Understand the basic shape of a quadratic function and the relationships between the roots of the quadratic and zeroes of the function.

D.3. Know the basic shape of the graph of exponential and log functions, including exponential decay.

E. Successful students understand algebra well enough to apply it procedurally and conceptually to a range of common problems. They:

E.1. Recognize which type of expression best fits the context of a basic application (for example, linear equation to solve distance-time problems, quadratic equation to explain the motion of a falling object, or compound interest as an exponential function).

F. Successful students demonstrate the ability to work with formulas and symbols algebraically. They:

F.1.* Know formal notation (for example, sigma notation and factorial notation).

F.2.* Know arithmetic and geometric progressions and series.

III. Trigonometry

A. Successful students know and understand basic trigonometric principles. They:

    A.1. Know the definitions of sine, cosine, and tangent using right triangle geometry and similarity relations.

    A.2. Understand the relationship between a trigonometric function in standard form and its corresponding graph (for example, domain, range, amplitude, period, phase shift, and vertical shift).

    A.3. Understand periodicity and recognize graphs of periodic functions, especially the trigonometric functions.

    A.4.* Know and use identities for sum and difference of angles, such as sin $(x \pm y)$, cos $(x \pm y)$, and use double and half angle formulas.

IV. Geometry

A. Successful students understand and use both basic plane and solid geometry. They:

    A.1. Know properties of similarity, congruence, and parallel lines cut by a transversal.

    A.2. Know how to figure area and perimeter of basic figures.

    A.3. Understand the ideas behind simple geometric proofs and are able to develop and write simple geometric proofs (for example, the Pythagorean theorem, that there are 180 degrees in a triangle, that the area of a triangle is half the base times the height).

    A.4. Solve problems involving proofs through the use of geometric constructions.

    A.5. Use similar triangles to find unknown angle measurements and lengths of sides.

    A.6. Visualize solids and surfaces in three-dimensional space (they recognize the shape of a box based on a two-dimensional representation of its surfaces; recognize the shape of a cone based on a two-dimensional representation of its surface).

    A.7. Know basic formulas for volume and surface area for three-dimensional objects.

B. Successful students know analytic (that is, coordinate) geometry. They:

B.1. Know geometric properties of lines (slope and midpoint of a line segment).

B.2. Know the formula for the distance between two points.

B.3. Solve mathematical and real-world problems (for example, ladders, shadows, and poles) that involve the properties of special right triangles with the Pythagorean theorem and its converse.

B.4.* Recognize geometric translations and transformations algebraically.

C. Successful students understand basic relationships between geometry and algebra. They:

C.1. Know that geometric objects and figures can also be described algebraically (for example, $ax + by = c$ is the standard form of a line).

C.2. Know the algebra and geometry of circles.

C.3.* Know the algebra and geometry of parabolas and ellipses as a prerequisite to the study of calculus.

C.4.* Use trigonometry for examples of the algebraic-geometric relationship, including law of sines-cosines.

V. Mathematical Reasoning

A. Successful students know important definitions and why definitions are necessary and are able to use mathematical reasoning to solve problems. They:

A.1. Use inductive reasoning in basic arguments.

A.2. Use deductive reasoning in basic arguments.

A.3. Use geometric and visual reasoning.

A.4. Use multiple representations (for example, analytic, numerical, and geometric) to solve problems.

A.5. Learn to solve multistep problems.

A.6. Use a variety of strategies to revise solution processes.

A.7. Understand the uses of both proof and counterexample in problem solutions and are able to conduct simple proofs.

A.8. Are familiar with the process of abstracting mathematical models from word problems, geometric problems, and applications and are able to interpret solutions in the context of these source problems.

B. Successful students are able to work with mathematical notation to solve problems and communicate solutions. They:

B.1.   Translate simple statements into equations (for example, "Bill is twice as old as John" is expressed by the equation $b = 2j$).

B.2.   Understand the role of written symbols in representing mathematical ideas and the precise use of special symbols of mathematics.

C. Successful students know a select list of mathematical facts and know how to build on those facts (for example, the Pythagorean theorem; formulas for perimeter, area, volume; the quadratic formula).

D. Successful students know how to estimate. They:

D.1.   Can convert between decimal approximations and fractions.

D.2.   Know when to use an estimation or approximation in place of an exact answer.

D.3.   Recognize the accuracy of an estimation.

D.4.   Know how to make and use estimations.

E. Successful students understand the appropriate use as well as the limitation of calculators. They:

E.1.   Recognize when the results produced are unreasonable or represent misinformation.

E.2.* Use calculators for systematic trial-and-error problem solving.

E.3.* Plot useful graphs.

F. Successful students are able to generalize and to go from specific to abstract and back again. They:

F.1.   Determine the mathematical concept from the context of an external problem, solve the problem, and interpret the mathematical solution in the context of the problem.

F.2.   Know how to use specific instances of general facts, as well as how to look for general results that extend particular results.

G. Successful students demonstrate active participation in the process of learning mathematics. They:

G.1. Are willing to experiment with problems that have multiple solution methods.

G.2. Demonstrate an understanding of the mathematical ideas behind the steps of a solution, as well as the solution.

G.3. Show an understanding of how to modify patterns to obtain different results.

G.4. Show an understanding of how to modify solution strategies to obtain different results.

G.5. Recognize when a proposed solution does not work, analyze why, and use the analysis to seek a valid solution.

H. Successful students recognize the broad range of applications of mathematical reasoning. They:

H.1. Know that mathematical applications are used in other fields (for example, carbon dating, exponential growth, amortization tables, predator-prey models, periodic motion, and the interactions of waves).

H.2. Know that mathematics has played (and continues to play) an important role in the evolution of disciplines as diverse as science, engineering, music, and philosophy.

VI. Statistics

A. Successful students apply concepts of statistics and data analysis in the social sciences and natural sciences. They:

A.1. Represent data in a variety of ways (for example, scatter plot, line graph, and two-way table) and select the most appropriate.

A.2. Understand and use statistical summaries data (for example, standard deviation, range, mode).

A.3.* Understand curve-fitting techniques (for example, median-fit line and regression line) for various applications (for example, making predictions).

It should be noted that most of the faculty who participated in creating the math standards indicated that knowledge of statistics is not a prerequisite for success in most entry-level university mathematics courses. However, participants in other disciplines identified knowledge of statistics as important to success in some entry-level courses in the social sciences (for example, economics) and sciences (biology and ecology). Although statistics is included here for organizational convenience, it should not be considered as a prerequisite to entry-level mathematics success to the same degree as the other five areas of mathematical knowledge and skills. It is referenced again in the standards for the natural and social sciences.

Natural Sciences Knowledge and Skills

The natural sciences comprise a number of scientific disciplines for which students must master specific knowledge. At the same time, the natural sciences have some elements that span all disciplines, the most important of which may be "thinking like a scientist." Students who are well-prepared for the natural sciences not only have mastered vocabulary and concepts but can also exercise and apply thinking strategies associated with the scientific process.

Natural Sciences Knowledge and Skills Foundations

Science presents both technical and psychological challenges for incoming students. A number of subjects come together in this field, including math and statistics. Students who are prepared to study science at the college level are capable of integrating scientific methods and contextual understanding, critical thinking, and hands-on skills.

Basic Knowledge

In the fields of physics, chemistry, and biology, successful students are familiar with fundamental scientific concepts, including the significance of time, the range of light waves, the nature of force, velocity and acceleration, and the principles of evolution.

Entering students who are well prepared for science courses have mathematical skills. They have knowledge of basic mathematical concepts and processes in arithmetic, algebra, trigonometry, and geometry. They can translate and transform fairly simple word problems into mathematical equations and vice versa. In the sciences, as in mathematics, students demonstrate a dependency on calculators. Technology can help them with scientific experiments but does not replace the thinking processes required to estimate, question, and solve problems.

Thinking About Science

Beyond simple memorization of definitions or theories, successful students understand how scientific processes operate and how those processes relate to one another. Science is a process, and it requires certain skills.

First, students who are ready to get the most out of science courses have a measure of scientific common sense, an overall understanding of how scientific concepts, definitions, and applications fit together. Second, they are capable of experimental thinking. They have an understanding that experimentation is an inherent part of the scientific process. Incoming students benefit greatly from an understanding of the interrelationships among scientific concepts and across the sciences. For instance, a biology student would do well to know about physics and chemistry, and the ways that those disciplines inform the study of biology.

Successful students use mathematical reasoning as they work with chemical formulas and try to solve and explain problems. Once they reach a solution, they can also defend why they have chosen each math process. Evaluating scientific issues in daily life and understanding the origins of scientific knowledge are important as well. As they study, successful students address questions along the way, such as "Do I know for sure?" and "How do I know?"

The relationship between a chemical formula and its real-world application is worth thinking about too. There is a formula behind the process of photosynthesis, and it is applied in plant life all around us. This type of conceptualization helps students realize the position of humans in a global context and appreciate everyday existence. Students who succeed in the sciences employ critical thinking skills as they learn scientific concepts. Beyond mere curiosity, they inquire about their place in the universe and question their own scientific knowledge and beliefs.

Science, like any field of study, has a historical and a social context. Incoming students need not be historians, but they benefit greatly from knowing about the central historical traditions and contemporary events that relate to and influence the development of scientific inquiry.

Solving Problems, Asking Questions

Incoming students are ready to benefit from science courses when they are prepared to solve scientific problems using the step-by-step approach known as the scientific method. Examples of scientific problem-solving skills include these:

- Drawing a picture to represent a situation described in a physics problem
- Identifying and organizing what is known and not known in a problem
- Identifying assumptions and relevant equations
- Testing equations for unknowns
- Checking units
- Checking that answers are physically reasonable

Successful students know how to design a testable scientific question, refine that question, and conduct an experiment to find solutions. They can think creatively as they develop hypotheses and estimate potential results. They also show a willingness to question existing results, and then to generate and weigh new options and questions as a product of the inquiry they undertake.

Reading, Writing, and Communication

In the sciences as in other disciplines, successful students write with clarity, cohesiveness, and meaning. Good science writers have knowledge of scientific writing and the terminology used in scientific texts and know how to translate this knowledge into nonscientific language. As students write scientific analyses, they need to construct logical and coherent arguments that demonstrate an understanding of causation and the various levels of abstraction involved. These are important tools that enable students to communicate understanding of a scientific process, particularly when they present and defend experiments to teachers and peers.

Two specific reading skills are particularly necessary for success. First, successful students comprehend what they read. Second, they are familiar with publications that carry articles on scientific findings (for example, *Discover* magazine and the *New York Times*) and understand both the scientific terminology used and the experiments described in such articles. This comprehension of scientific literature with some technical language, content, or concepts is useful when students try to explain processes used to test a scientific hypothesis. Also, as students read scientific literature they exercise scientific common sense, or a healthy skepticism. This helps them assess the likely validity of the content of articles and continue to build independent judgment about the validity of scientific reports in general.

Orientation Toward Learning

Entry-level students often feel anxiety as they tackle a scientific experiment or try to explain a scientific concept. Persistence is vital in the quest for solutions, as is acceptance of failure and ambiguity as part of the experimentation process. Some scientifically well-prepared students have such a fear of failure that they are unwilling to approach new things. They often have trouble investigating alternative solutions to a problem, offering an estimate rather than a precise answer, or questioning the credibility of their results. To develop a scientific knowledge base, successful students act on their curiosity and take risks to understand the intricacies and mysteries of science.

In addition to the willingness to try, successful students have the ability to conduct honest and sustained inquiry and to engage in the scientific process for long periods of time as they test hypotheses over and over. They understand that scientific learning is ongoing. It is a scholarly activity that requires time, sustained engagement, reflective study skills, patience, and persistence.

In addition to having good study skills, successful entry-level students take responsibility for their own education. They structure and manage time according to course expectations. They know how and when to ask for help. Study in any field of science requires hard work, a focused curiosity, and a willingness to dedicate the time necessary to follow through on a scientific inquiry.

Natural Sciences Content Standards

Items shown with an asterisk apply to students who plan to major in natural sciences fields such as environmental sciences, biology, chemistry, and physics.

I. General Foundation Skills

A. Successful students understand the steps that make up the scientific method. These students are able to observe, hypothesize, test, and revise, and they know the difference between a hypothesis and a theory. They:

A.1. Design and conduct scientific investigations during which they formulate and test hypotheses (formulate and clarify the method; identify the controls and variables; collect, organize, display, and analyze data; make revisions of hypotheses, methods, and explanations; present the results; and seek critiques from others).

B. Successful students know basic mathematics conventions. They:

B.1. Understand the real number system and its properties.

B.2. Use exponents and scientific notation.

B.3. Understand ratios, proportions, and percents and how all are related to the others.

B.4. Use proportional reasoning to solve problems (for example, equivalent fractions, equal ratios, constant rate of change, proportions, and percents).

B.5. Add, subtract, multiply, and divide with a high and consistent degree of accuracy.

B.6. Simplify rational expressions.

C. Successful students are able to recognize and use basic algebraic forms. They:

C.1. Know ways that variables can be used (for example, as a placeholder for an unknown, such as $x + 2 = 9$, or to represent a range of values, such as $-3m-8$).

C.2. Know when it is possible to simplify, solve, evaluate, or substitute in, equations and expressions and when it is not—for example, expand, but not solve, the expression $(x + 1)(x + 4)$; substitute $a = 2$, $b = 4$ into the formula $a2 + b2 = c2$; solve the equation $0 = (x + 3)(x + 1)$; and evaluate the function $f(x) = (x + 1)(x + 4)$ at $x = -1$.

C.3. Represent functions, patterns, and mathematical relationships using a variety of models (for example, statements, formulas, and graphs).

C.4.* Understand various types of functions (for example, direct and inverse variation, polynomial, radical, step, and sinusoidal) and have a deep understanding of exponential and logarithmic functions.

D. Successful students demonstrate the ability to work algebraically with formulas and symbols. They:

D.1.   Are familiar with the concept of continuity.

D.2.* Use formal notation to describe applications of sequences and series.

E. Successful students know and understand basic trigonometric principles. They:

E.1.   Know the definitions of sine, cosine, and tangent in relation to right triangle geometry and similarity relations.

F. Successful students understand the relationships between geometry and algebra. They:

F.1.   Understand that a curve drawn in a certain location is fully equivalent to a set of algebraic equations.

F.2.* Possess the ability to represent a geometrical figure (for example, a triangle or a circle) on a plane using a set of equations, as in descriptive geometry.

F.3.* Understand vectors and how they can be used (representing velocity and force).

F.4.* Use operations on vectors (vector addition and scalar multiplication).

G. Successful students demonstrate an ability to solve problems. They:

G.1.   Use various strategies to approach problem-solving situations and to revise solution processes.

H. Successful students understand that mathematics is a symbolic language, that fluency requires practice, and that mathematics is the language of all scientific pursuit. They:

H.1.   Know the definition of a mathematical expression (a statement using numbers and symbols to represent mathematical ideas and real-world situations).

H.2.   Understand the use of written symbols and the limitations on appropriate uses of such symbols (equal signs, parentheses, superscript).

I. Successful students understand and apply concepts of probability and statistics. They:

I.1. Understand and use data represented in various ways (for example, charts, tables, plots, and graphs).

I.2. Understand descriptive statistics (for example, mean, median, mode, and standard deviation).

I.3. Understand that predictions based on sample data are inferential.

J. Successful students understand and apply concepts of measurement. They:

J.1. Select and use appropriate units to express measurements for real-world problems.

J.2. Know how to make estimates and approximations and when to use those approaches to solve problems.

J.3. Use unit analysis in problem solving.

J.4. Understand the differences between the metric and the traditional U.S. measurement system and are able to perform simple conversions between the two.

J.5.* Know the difference between accuracy and precision, as well as how to use significant digits appropriately.

II. Science and Society

A. Successful students understand the scientific enterprise. They:

A.1. Understand that science and the theories of science are not absolute and should be questioned and challenged, as follows:

- New theories will continue to replace current or older ones.
- Scientific theories must stand up to the scrutiny of the entire scientific community.
- Acceptable validation includes reproduction and internal consistency.

A.2. Know ways in which science and society influence each other. For example:

- Scientific methods and the knowledge they produce may influence how people think about themselves and their world.

- Technology can contribute to the solution of an individual or community problem.

- Social and economic forces strongly influence which science and technology programs are pursued, invested in, and used.

A.3. Understand that science involves different types of work in many different disciplines. For example:

- Different disciplines of science approach investigations in different ways, using different questions, methods, and evidence.

A.4. Know that scientists throughout history have had many difficulties convincing their contemporaries to acknowledge what are now generally accepted scientific ideas.

A.5. Understand that a host of perplexing new problems is generated by our society's new powers (for example, population management, environmental protection, and regulation of weapons of mass destruction).

A.6. Know that technology is the systematic use of materials, energy, and information to design, build, maintain, and operate devices, processes, and systems with a goal of serving individual and societal human needs.

A.7. Understand that interactions between science and technology have led to refined tools (precision instruments, measuring techniques, data processors, and so on) and the means for a safer, more comfortable life for more people (electricity, transportation, medical advances, and so on).

A.8.* Know that investigations and public communication among scientists must meet certain criteria in order to result in new understanding and methods. For example:

- Arguments must be logical and demonstrate consistency between natural phenomena revealed by investigations and the historical body of scientific evidence.

- Methods and procedures used to obtain evidence must be clearly reported and reproducible to enhance opportunities for further investigation.

III. Environmental Science

A. Successful students understand concepts related to environmental science. They:

A.1.   Know that the earth is a body in space whose environmental system (the atmosphere, lithosphere, cryosphere, hydrosphere, biosphere) depends largely on the sun for light and heat and that the current environment (for example, geography and climate) is subject to change.

A.2.* Are familiar with environmental processes (for example, the carbon and nitrogen cycles) and their role in processing matter crucial for sustaining life.

A.3.* Understand that relationships exist among the earth (geology and soil science), the water (hydrology and oceanography), and the atmosphere (meteorology and atmospherics), and that the relationship is best exemplified by the water cycle.

B. Successful students understand concepts related to geology. They:

B.1.   Are familiar with the history of the earth.

B.2.   Are familiar with the history of the solar system.

B.3.   Understand the processes of volcanism and erosion.

C. Successful students understand the interaction of the environment and biota (including humans) and some of the consequences of that interaction. They:

C.1.   Understand the notion of habitats and their role in evolution.

IV. Biology

A. Successful students know the general structure and function of cells. They:

A.1.   Know that all living systems are composed of cells, which are the fundamental units of life, and that organisms may be unicellular or multicellular.

A.2.   Know the importance of both water and the element carbon to cells, and further understand that cells have four important types of macromolecules (carbohydrates, lipids, proteins, and nucleic acids) that are each different in chemical properties and have specific functions in cells.

A.3.   Understand that both unity and diversity exist among cells.

A.4. Know that although all cells share basic features (for example, a plasma membrane and genetic material in the form of DNA), there are different types of cells (prokaryotic and eukaryotic).

A.5. Know that within multicellular organisms there are different types of cells and that these cells perform different functions for the organism.

A.6. Know that different types of organisms (plants versus animals) have different cellular specializations suited for the organism's lifestyle.

A.7. Understand the processes of cell division (mitosis and meiosis), particularly as those processes relate to production of new cells and to passing on genetic information between generations.

A.8. Know that in eukaryotic cells, the organization of DNA into chromosomes is key to both duplication and distribution of the genetic information to new cells or organisms.

A.9. Know that in order to be alive, cells must exchange materials with their environment or with other cells.

A.10. Know that cells transform energy (ultimately obtained from the sun) from one form to another through the processes of photosynthesis and respiration.

A.11.* Know that these processes lead to the production of ATP, which all cells absolutely require for cell work.

A.12.* Understand the chemical reactions involved in cell functions (for example, food molecules taken into cells are broken down to provide the energy and chemical constituents needed to synthesize other molecules, and enzymes facilitate the breakdown and synthesis of molecules).

A.13.* Know that such exchanges involve a variety of mechanisms for transporting materials across a membrane, including diffusion, osmosis, and transport involving specialized membrane proteins.

B. Successful students understand genetic principles that guide the inheritance of biological traits. They:

B.1. Understand Mendel's laws of heredity (genes and alleles, genotype versus phenotype, segregation and independent assortment, and dominant versus recessive traits), how Mendel's laws relate to the movement of chromosomes to gametes during meiosis, and the chromosomal basis of sex determination.

B.2.* Know the chemical and structural properties of DNA in heredity and protein synthesis (for example, DNA synthesis, transcription, translation, mRNA and the genetic code, effects of mutations).

B.3.* Understand how recombinant DNA technology allows scientists to analyze the structure and function of genes.

C. Successful students understand the organization and classification of living systems. They:

C.1. Know that multicellular organisms have a variety of specialized cells, tissues, organs, and organ systems that perform specialized functions (for example, digestion, respiration, circulation, excretion, movement, control and coordination, protection from disease, and reproduction), and understand that the different organ systems are integrated to make a functional organism.

C.2. Know ways in which living things can be classified based on each organism's internal and external structure, its development, and relatedness of DNA sequence.

D. Successful students understand concepts of biological change and the evolution of species. They:

D.1. Know how DNA and protein sequences are used to infer evolutionary relationships among organisms.

D.2. Understand the concept of natural selection (differential survival and reproduction of chance inherited variants, depending on environmental conditions).

D.3. Understand the theory of evolution (for example, the earth's present-day life forms evolved from earlier, distinctly different species), and know that genetic change among individuals is the raw material of evolution of new forms.

V. Chemistry

A. Successful students understand the nature of the physical and chemical properties of matter (for example, classifications of matter such as compounds, mixtures, and solutions, as well as composition of matter such as atoms and molecules). They:

A.1. Understand that atoms, molecules, and ions have a set of physical and chemical properties that control their behaviors in a range of states.

A.2. Know that states of matter depend on molecular arrangement and freedom of motion. For example:

- In the solid state, molecules are packed tightly together with their motion restricted to vibrations.

- In the liquid state, molecules have higher energy and are more loosely packed, sliding freely past each other.

- In the gaseous state, molecules are less restricted and move freely.

A.3. Understand the structure of the periodic table. For example:

- Elements are arranged in sequence by increasing atomic number.

- Similar properties that arise periodically in this arrangement motivate the grouping of elements into columns that share common properties.

- This arrangement is useful for predicting the properties of elements and compounds.

A.4.* Understand acid and base chemistry.

A.5.* Understand principles of ideal gas behavior.

B. Successful students know principles of atomic structure and bonding. They:

B.1. Know the structure of an atom. For example:

- Negative electrons occupy most of the space in the atom.

- Neutrons and positive protons make up the nucleus of the atom.

- Protons and neutrons are almost two thousand times heavier than an electron.

- The electric force between the nucleus and electrons holds the atom together.

B.2. Understand that molecules are composed of atoms in unique and consistent arrangements, and that atoms or molecules may form solids by building up repeating patterns (for example, crystal structures or polymers).

B.3. Understand how the electronic configuration of atoms governs the chemical properties of an element. For example:

- Elements with similar electronic configurations have similar properties.

- Elements interact with one another on the atomic level by transferring or sharing the outermost electrons to form covalent, ionic, or metallic bonds.

C. Successful students understand and apply principles that explain chemical reactions. They:

C.1. Know that substances react chemically in characteristic ways with other substances to form new substances (compounds) with different characteristics and properties.

C.2.* Understand the meaning and uses of chemical equations and employ such equations to quantify relationships between products and reactants. Examples of the meaning and use of a chemical equation include these:

- Mass balance

- Molar or molecular quantities

- Conservation of mass and atoms

C.3.* Understand the mole concept and its applications. For example:

- Moles in chemical equations and formulas

- Molar mass, relative mass, molar volume, and Avogadro's number.

VI. Physics

A. Successful students understand concepts of energy. They:

A.1. Understand the relationship between heat and temperature. For example:

- Heat energy consists of the random motion and vibrations of atoms, molecules, and ions.

- The higher the temperature, the greater the atomic or molecular motion.

A.2. Understand the conservation of energy and the first law of thermodynamics (that is, energy cannot be created or destroyed but only changed from one form to another) and understand that energy must be transferred via work or heat.

A.3. Understand the concept of entropy and the second law of thermodynamics (that is, why engines and refrigerators are not 100 percent efficient, as well as the concept that disorder, in general, increases because some energy is always lost into nonusable forms).

A.4. Understand the distinction between kinetic (thermal, translational, and vibrational) and potential (gravitational and electrostatic) energy.

A.5. Understand how energy can be transferred from one form to another.

A.6. Understand basic principles of optics.

A.7. Understand basic principles of electricity and magnetism.

A.8. Understand series and parallel circuits.

B. Successful students understand motion and the principles that explain motion. They:

B.1. Understand Newton's laws as a classical description of motion. For example:

- A force is required to alter an object's motion.
- In the absence of force, or when forces are balanced, no change in motion is observed.
- Forces are additive and the motion of an object is determined by the cumulative effect.

B.2. Know the characteristic properties of sound and electromagnetic waves, that these waves have energy, and that such waves can transfer energy when they interact with matter, and know that characteristic properties include these:

- Wavelength, frequency, amplitude, speed, absorption, reflection, and refraction

B.3. Know the range of the electromagnetic spectrum. For example:

- Radio waves, microwaves, infrared radiation, visible light, ultraviolet radiation, X rays, and gamma rays

B.4. Know that electromagnetic waves result when a charged object is accelerated and that the energy of electromagnetic waves is carried in wave packets whose energy is inversely proportional to the wavelength.

C. Successful students know the kinds of forces that exist between objects. They:

C.1. Understand general concepts related to gravitational force (for example, every object exerts gravitational force on every other object, and this force depends on the mass of the objects and their distance from one another).

C.2. Know that materials that contain equal amounts of positive and negative charges are electrically neutral but that a very small excess or deficit of negative charges in a material produces noticeable electrical forces.

C.3.* Understand magnetic and electric fields and the relationship between those fields, and that these fields can be thought of as different aspects of a single electromagnetic field (moving electric charges produce magnetic fields and moving magnets produce electric fields).

D. Successful students understand concepts related to modern physics. They:

D.1. Understand the general concepts related to the theory of special relativity. For example:

- In contrast to moving objects, the speed of light is the same for all observers, no matter how they or the light source happen to be moving.

- Nothing can travel faster than the speed of light.

D.2. Know the constituent particles of atoms (that is, protons, neutrons, and electrons) and have a general understanding of physical locations of each (that is, protons and neutrons are in the core nucleus and electrons are in a cloud "far" away from the nucleus).

E. Successful students understand concepts related to matter and its properties. They:

E.1. Know what mass is and how it differs from weight and inertia.

E.2. Know the meaning of density.

E.3. Know that the physical properties of matter and waves are scalar or vector quantities.

E.4.* Understand specific heat, thermal, and electrical conductivity.

F. Successful students understand basic laws. They:

F.1 Know conservation laws of energy (and the conversion of energy from one form to another), mass, and momentum.

F.2 Understand the laws governing electrical and magnetic forces.

F.3 Understand the relationship between electrical currents and magnetic fields.

chapter FOURTEEN

Social Sciences Knowledge and Skills

The social sciences are similar to the natural sciences in that they comprise more than one discipline and each discipline has its own distinct knowledge base, often with its own ways of conducting research. Students who take social science courses in college should be ready to think analytically and critically and to apply skills from other disciplines, particularly the writing and research skills as outlined previously in English, and statistics presented in math.

Social Sciences Knowledge and Skills Foundations

Incoming students succeed when they are armed with specific knowledge and skills in the social sciences—but above all when they are ready to think analytically.

Students who are ready for entry-level courses are familiar with the fundamental concepts of social sciences, such as history, economics, geography, political science, and sociology.

In geography, well-prepared students know how to read, interpret, and locate places on a global map. They are familiar with worldwide immigration and migration patterns.

In economics courses, successful students come prepared with foundational mathematics skills and an understanding of basic concepts such as demand, supply, scarcity, opportunity, and trade-offs.

In political science, a basic civic knowledge is necessary. Such basic knowledge includes a sense of how the U.S. government works, the system of legislative, executive, and judiciary checks and balances, and how a Constitutional amendment is ratified. In addition, successful students have a basic knowledge of, and can distinguish between, economic and political systems. They can describe the differences between capitalism and socialism and between democracy and oligarchy.

In history, students who are ready for college-level study know important events and documents that have shaped the course of U.S. history: the U.S. Constitution, federal Indian policy, and the civil rights movement, to name a few. A clear knowledge of significant periods in world history, both Western and non-Western, is crucial, including, for example, the origins of Judaism, the rise and fall of ancient Greece, the influence of Christianity and the Crusades on European culture and society, the Aztec civilization, the French and Russian Revolutions, and the rise to independence in the postcolonial period of countries in South America, Africa, and Asia, in particular.

In sociology, successful students understand and are able to discuss the implications of changes in U.S. demographics leading to increasing diversity. They understand the significant issues in gender equity and are aware of contemporary social, political, and cultural movements in U.S. society and around the world, and the major theories that underlie such movements.

Besides the basic facts, students entering social science courses need certain skills. Just as in the natural sciences, second languages, mathematics, and English, successful students in the social sciences know the mechanics of writing and basic grammar and communicate their ideas with clarity and coherence. They are familiar with the terminologies and definitions that pertain to each discipline. Basic mathematical and statistical knowledge (arithmetic and algebra, means and correlations) helps students read and understand graphs in economics and analyze and interpret statistical data in sociological, historical, and geographical reports.

General Sense of History and Geography

Besides memorizing dates and events that have marked and shaped the world in general (and the United States in particular) successful students have a sense of history. It is vital that they understand chronological sequence and causation across time. They should possess factual knowledge, be accurate when discussing historical dates, and understand how historical sequencing and events influence one another. They should be able to describe how our current place in time is influenced by the past and informs our future.

Successful students are aware of the diversity and relativity of historical perspectives and interpretations. As they learn about world events, memorize dates, and understand various historical periods, they realize how people in different regions of the world have experienced similar events in different ways. Local experience adds to comprehension of a historical phenomenon. Students who have the ability to make interdisciplinary connections have a broader and deeper sense of history. When students see the relevance of economics, culture, geography, and politics in the shaping and unfolding of historical events, they gain more from college-level social science courses.

Social science students also benefit greatly from a sense of place. Those who are successful know how to read maps. They approach geography from cultural, economic, and political perspectives. Armed with these skills, they better realize how geographical contexts often contribute to the development of a society. They recognize how contexts influence the ways in which people see the world; it is more useful, for example, to know how water use affects society than to memorize the exact borders of all the countries in Africa.

Reading, Research, and Analysis

Reading—and reading well—is a very important part of the learning process. Successful college-level students comprehend assigned reading material and read closely, with attention to nuance. Close reading leads students to infer and extend meaning by identifying main points and distinguishing supportive statements from illustrative details. Successful students can gauge their own comprehension of the material and know what to do when they encounter reading that is difficult. Social sciences are related; to understand these relationships, successful students are familiar with the scientific method. They ask questions such as, "What do we know?" and "How do we know it?" Comprehension of the scientific method in the context of the social sciences is demonstrated by a number of skills and abilities:

- *Capacity to recognize hypotheses in texts and understand when evidence is being presented.* This is a critical reading skill that helps a student evaluate the quality and relevance of materials used to build and support an argument.

- *Familiarity with theory building, with what a theory is, how a theory is developed, and how a theory can be tested, debated, and applied.* Successful students can differentiate theory from opinion in a text.

- *Ability to find information from a variety of sources, including the library and Internet.* Part of this skill is the ability to assess the quality and reliability of information, especially if the source is found online. Successful students ask themselves questions such as these: "Where does this information come from?" "Is it well supported?" "Is this information relevant or irrelevant to the support of my thesis?"

- *Ability to generalize while at the same time to recognize their own biases and identify fallacies in materials they read.* Faculty members expect students to voice opinions, speculate, and relate personal experiences in their assignments, but only if they also generalize to principles discussed in class or connect personal knowledge to the material covered.

- *Awareness of various research methodologies, including quantitative and qualitative traditions of data analysis.*

In addition to reading and doing research, taking notes is an important part of college-level study. Entry-level courses are often lectures, where students are expected to take notes diligently, identify key components of the lecture, and appreciate how notes are essential to understanding the content of a course. Students thus need to know that taking notes is a learning process in itself. Successful students decide whether a piece of information is important or relevant before they write it down. They think about how they will use the information after the lecture is over. They know how to prepare an outline with coherent sections and subsections and understand how this exercise relates to organizing the information they collect, whether from lectures or other sources.

Orientation Toward Learning

In many ways, learning is demonstrated by the communication of facts, concepts, and ideas. Successful students use a variety of communication skills to show that they understand class material. Writing is one such skill, but clear oral and visual communication is important as well. Good communication includes engagement with an audience, whether it is one reader or hundreds. When presenting information, good communicators are attentive listeners to the questions and concerns of others. Good academic communication also means accepting criticism from others and answering questions with an attentive, positive attitude.

Making the connection between ideas and facts is vital to the learning process. Successful students make connections between public knowledge and personal observations and experiences. They make connections across disciplines. How do the ideas in economics classes relate to everyday life? How do the concepts learned in sociology apply to the study of geography? Connective intelligence enables students to integrate and use knowledge from different disciplines both in social sciences and in other areas.

Just as college students are encouraged to make connections between disciplines, they are also encouraged to anchor historical, geographical, or sociological materials to a sense of self. Successful students are engaged intellectually with the material they encounter in their studies. Rather than focusing entirely on outcomes and grades, they engage in the learning process and accept a challenge to do something new. They are comfortable with ambiguity. Students often come into classes in a quest for answers alone. Some questions and problems have no obvious solutions, whereas others have more than one solution.

Social science faculty members, much like their peers in other disciplines, expect students to demonstrate a variety of study skills that will help them succeed in college, including taking personal responsibility for their work, showing up for class, doing homework and reading assignments, completing written assignments on time, and managing their time well.

Social Sciences Content Standards

Items shown with an asterisk apply to students who plan to major in a social science.

I. General Knowledge and Skills

A. Successful students have a basic understanding of the social sciences (history, economics, geography, political science, sociology). They:

A.1. Know the defining characteristics of disciplines in the social sciences.

A.2. Understand the diversity of human beings and human cultures (for example, cultural, biological, emotional, and intellectual diversity).

A.3. Know that each social science discipline is subject to certain criticisms and limitations, and are aware of the primary criticisms and limitations of at least one discipline in the social sciences.

A.4. Are aware of major current world events, issues, and problems and know how concepts and theories in the social sciences can be applied to understand them.

A.5. Perceive events and circumstances from the viewpoint of others, including people in racial and cultural groups different from their own, the other gender, other age groups, and people who live under different political and economic systems.

A.6.* Integrate concepts learned from at least two different social science disciplines.

A.7.* Understand the significant generalizations, principles, and theories of each discipline.

II. History

A. Successful students know significant periods and events in United States history. They:

A.1. Understand important events, social movements, and political processes that have shaped U.S. history, and are aware of the important historical figures who influenced history, such as these:

- European exploration and colonization, fifteenth and sixteenth centuries
- Interaction of Native Americans and European settlers
- Development of American colonial government
- Causes and consequences of slavery
- Revolutionary War
- Creation of the U.S. Constitution
- Bill of Rights
- Development of political parties
- Westward expansion
- Mexican-American War
- Antebellum sectionalism and polarization
- Civil War
- Reconstruction
- Industrialization and the rise of big business
- Federal Indian policy of the late nineteenth century

- Spanish-American War

- Progressive movement

- Social and cultural movements of the 1920s

- Great Depression

- New Deal

- U.S. role in World War II

- Cold war

- Civil Rights movement

- Vietnam War

- Immigration and migration patterns in the contemporary United States

- Influence of religion on U.S. history

B. Successful students know significant periods and events in world history. They:

B.1. Understand important events and social, religious, and political movements that have shaped world history as well as the significant historical
figures who influenced history, such as these:

- Early civilizations in India and the Middle East

- Development of Judaism

- Ancient Greece

- Rise and fall of ancient Rome

- Emergence of Christianity

- Development of Buddhism

- Byzantine Empire

- Emergence of Islam

- Mayan civilization

- Feudalism-manorialism in medieval Europe

- Influence of Christianity in Europe and the Crusades

- Aztecs

- Exchange of flora, fauna, pathogens known as the "Columbian
exchange"

- Renaissance

- Scientific revolution

- Reformation and Counter-Reformation

- French Revolution

- Industrial Revolution

- European nationalist movements of the nineteenth century

- World War I

- Russian Revolution

- World War II

- Cold war

- African and Asian history

C. Successful students understand historical perspective and historical analysis. They:

C.1. Understand their own position in history and how history has influenced their kinship group and family ancestors.

C.2. Know the effects that specific human decisions have had on history.

C.3. Understand the contingency of history—that is, events depend on human ideas and actions and things might have been different in the absence of the ideas and actions that have occurred.

C.4. Demonstrate the ability to perceive past events with historical empathy.

C.5. Know the influences that specific ideas and beliefs had on a period of history and how events may have been different in the absence of those ideas and beliefs.

C.6.* Know how to evaluate the credibility and authenticity of historical sources.

C.7.* Know how to evaluate different historical interpretations.

C.8.* Understand the social, economic, and political climate of significant periods in history and how a particular climate shaped those who lived at that time.

III. Economics

A. Successful students understand basic concepts of economics. They:

A.1. Understand the basic economic concepts of scarcity, opportunity cost, trade-offs, markets, and supply and demand.

A.2. Understand the difference between a market economy (capitalism) and a centrally planned or command economy.

A.3. Understand the role that government plays in the U.S. economy.

A.4. Understand the concepts of exchange and trade and the impacts of a global economy, including implications for individuals, the United States, and other nations.

A.5. Understand the conflict among the social goals of an economic system (for example, security, freedom, equity, efficiency, stability, and growth).

A.6.* Understand and know how to use economic analysis tools, including functions and basic statistics.

IV. Geography

A. Successful students have a basic understanding of the tools and concepts of geography. They:

A.1. Use maps and atlases to find locations and other geographical information.

A.2. Understand the nature, distribution, and migration patterns of human populations on earth's surface.

A.3. Understand the role of geography in explaining processes of environmental and human change.

A.4.* Realize the advantages and disadvantages of maps, globes, and other geographic tools used to illustrate data sets.

V. Political Science (Civics)

A. Successful students have a basic understanding of types of governments. They:

A.1. Understand the nature and source of various types of political authority (for example, the differences between democracy and oligarchy).

A.2.* Know the various types of governments throughout the world (for example, the differences between limited and unlimited governments).

B. Successful students have a basic understanding of the U.S. political system and its history. They:

B.1. Know basic facts about the U.S. political system and constitutional government (federalism, checks and balances, and legislative, executive, and judiciary branches of power).

B.2. Understand the content and context of documents that established the United States, especially the Declaration of Independence and the U.S. Constitution.

B.3. Understand the content and context of documents important for the protection of individual rights in the United States, especially the U.S. Constitution and the Bill of Rights.

B.4. Know the methods citizens can use to participate in the political process at local, state, and national levels, and how political participation can influence public policy.

VI. Sociology

A. Successful students have an understanding of social problems, social structure, institutions, class, groups, and interaction. They:

A.1. Understand that social problems are larger than the individual.

A.2. Understand that social inequalities based on a variety of factors—including gender, race, and age—exist and have a range of effects on society.

A.3. Understand the global diversity of various family forms, as well as kinship in different societies.

A.4. Understand that group and cultural influences contribute to human development.

A.5. Understand that group and cultural influences contribute to human identity.

A.6. Understand that group and cultural influences contribute to human behavior.

A.7.* Understand various meanings of the social group, the general implications of group membership, and the different ways that groups function.

A.8.* Understand the theory and methods of mediation, cooperation, and conflict resolution.

VII. Inquiry, Research, and Analysis

A. Successful students understand the scientific method of inquiry and investigation. They:

A.1. Understand how hypotheses are formulated to examine social behavior.

A.2. Understand that hypotheses are contingent—that they can be disproved by additional evidence.

A.3. Understand that well-tested hypotheses may be integrated into a theory predicting social behavior.

A.4. Know how to apply a theory to new evidence.

A.5. Understand how to write and test a hypothesis using additional evidence.

A.6. Know the ethics associated with data collection and human subjects.

A.7. Understand the limits of scientific investigation.

B. Successful students are able to read and interpret data. They:

B.1. Know how to interpret data presented in tables and graphs.

B.2.* Know the basics of probability theory and the concept of a sample.

B.3.* Know the difference between statistical and substantive significance.

C. Successful students know how to find a variety of sources of information, and how to analyze, evaluate, and use them properly. They:

C.1. Locate information from a variety of sources appropriate to the task at hand.

C.2. Determine main and supporting ideas, then draw inferences from them.

C.3. Critically evaluate information by discerning the quality of the materials.

C.4. Critically evaluate information by qualifying the strength of the evidence and arguments.

C.5. Critically evaluate information by determining its credibility.

C.6. Critically evaluate information by identifying any bias or perspective of the authors.

C.7. Critically evaluate information by using prior knowledge.

C.8.* Demonstrate familiarity with a data analysis software program.

D. Successful students are able to identify and analyze problems appropriate to the social science discipline being studied. They:

D.1. Identify and define a problem.

D.2. Use deductive and inductive problem-solving skills as appropriate to the problem being studied.

D.3. Use multiple perspectives and resources to analyze a problem.

VIII. Communication

A. Successful students are able to communicate clearly and coherently. They:

A.1. Present a coherent thesis when making an argument.

A.2. Support the thesis with appropriate evidence when making an argument.

A.3. Anticipate and answer possible objections when making an argument.

A.4. Present a concise, clear closing when making an argument.

A.5. Organize ideas to achieve coherence in communication.

A.6. Write research papers that incorporate processes appropriate to the topic being researched, including:

- Integrating information from a range of appropriate sources
- Logically introducing and incorporating quotations
- Synthesizing information into a logical sequence
- Identifying different perspectives
- Identifying complexities and discrepancies in information
- Offering support for conclusions

A.7. Understand the concept of plagiarism and how to avoid it through the use of paraphrasing, summarizing, quoting, and citing.

A.8. Identify and use parts of speech correctly and consistently (verbs, conjunctions, interjections, and so on).

A.9. Use a variety of sentence structures in writing (for example, compound-complex, analogous).

Second Languages Knowledge and Skills

Knowledge of second languages combines speaking, reading, and writing with the cultural and historical understanding necessary to communicate fully and accurately in those languages. Students in entry-level college language courses are expected to master the various elements of communication that collectively represent the ability to speak another language. Here, as in the other areas, students are expected to be able to apply knowledge and skills from other disciplines, particularly knowledge of English grammar but also understanding of the history and geography of the non-English-speaking world.

Second Languages Knowledge and Skills Foundations

The goal of second language study is to communicate effectively with speakers of another language in authentic cultural contexts. Learning another language involves much more than memorizing grammatical rules. It requires learners to understand the cultures from which the language arises and in which it resides, use the language to communicate accurately, and use their first language and culture as a model for comparison with the language and culture being learned. Second language proficiency can improve learning in other disciplines, such as English, history, and art and expand professional, personal, and social opportunities.

The Basics

Successful students know the basics of grammar and vocabulary in both their first language and the second language they choose to study. They are able to recognize verb tenses and parts of speech, understand the linguistic functions these elements perform, and compare them to their equivalents in their first language. This formal knowledge helps students learn and use a second language while giving them a deeper understanding of their first language.

Students in entry-level courses should have emerging competence in four areas: communication, culture, comparisons, and learning strategies.

Communication

Successful students are able to read, write, and converse at the intermediate-low proficiency level as defined by the American Council on the Teaching of Foreign Languages Proficiency Guidelines (see ACTFL at www.actfl.org). Essentially, this means that students can use the second language to express themselves in simple, full sentences. Students who are ready for entry-level courses have pronunciation that is comprehensible, but they are not expected to approach the quality or accuracy of a native language speaker.

Culture

Language is inseparable from culture. In order to communicate effectively in an authentic cultural context, students must be aware of the practices and perspectives of the culture. This involves knowledge of geography, holidays, lifestyles, and material resources of the countries where the second language is customarily spoken and the people who speak it. A student of Japanese might be expected to know that Japanese people bow when greeting each other and understand the value of humility in the culture that underlies this routine practice. The student should also be able to know what language is appropriate to particular cultural situations.

Comparisons

The ability to view facts from multiple perspectives is an important critical thinking skill developed through second language study. A solid knowledge of a first language and culture is a starting point for making comparisons and drawing contrasts with the second language and culture. For a native English speaker, a comparison of English to another language will deepen his or her understanding of English, of the second language, and of the nature of languages in general. Similarly, a comparison of American cultural products, practices, and perspectives to those of another culture will lead students to a more profound understanding of what it means to be an American, what it means to be part of another culture, and the nature of social roles, values, and customs.

Learning Strategies

Critical thinking is not only a by-product of second language learning but also a powerful tool for enhancing language acquisition. Metacognitive and metalinguistic knowledge, mnemonic devices, inference, critical reading, process writing, and other strategies should be evident by the time a student begins an entry-level course at a university.

The degree to which a student employs these strategies is a critical factor in determining college success, regardless of second language proficiency level upon entrance. A student who knows how to enhance comprehension by effectively negotiating meaning, for example, may be more successful than a student with superior knowledge of the language itself who relies solely on studying the textbook.

Orientation Toward Learning

It is important that a student tolerate both linguistic and cultural ambiguity. Successful students accept the linguistically ambiguous aspects they confront in a language, such as grammatical exceptions or words that have no exact translation in English. In studying culture, they understand that meaning is culturally constructed—few absolute rules of behavior exist in any society, and context determines both meaning and appropriate behavior. The particular strategies each individual student uses will vary, but common to all successful students are emotional engagement with the language and culture and openness to thinking about other ways of acting and communicating.

Second Languages Content Standards

Items shown with an asterisk apply to students who plan to major in a second language.

I. Communication Skills

A. Successful second-language students can use a language other than their first to exchange information and interact with others in realistic contexts. This is known as the *interpersonal mode.* They:

A.1. Can communicate in an on-demand interview at the intermediate-low level for European languages, or novice-high level for non-European languages (see again the ACTFL Web site).

A.2. Can use the target language to participate in classroom activities and discussions with peers and teachers.

B. Successful students are able to express personal meaning in a language other than their first language in a variety of genre and formats. This is known as the *presentational mode.* They:

B.1. Use writing processes such as brainstorming, drafting, revising, and proofing to produce short texts in the target language.

B.2. Use some basic cohesive devices in discourses in the target language.

B.3. Demonstrate a developing awareness of audience, context, and genre throughout a prepared composition or speech in the target language.

B.4.* Can defend an opinion, argument, or point of view about other cultures, academic disciplines, or international topics in a prepared, edited text in the target language.

C. Successful students construct meaning from authentic spoken and written sources that are in a language other than their first language. This is known as the *interpretive mode.* They:

C.1. Can identify the genre of authentic texts written in the target language—for example, poems, news articles, and essays.

C.2. Can ascertain meaning from context when they confront unfamiliar words and phrases in the target language.

C.3. Can distinguish main ideas from supporting details in a text written in the target language.

C.4.* Can identify literary devices such as point of view, narrative voice, and others in texts written in the target language.

C.5.* Begin to analyze an author's use of language and literary devices in text written in the target language.

II. Culture

A. Successful students are aware of products, practices, and perspectives in the target culture and are able to apply that knowledge in communicative contexts. They:

A.1. Can locate on a map and identify by name countries, continents, and geophysical landmarks relevant to the target language.

A.2. Know basic historical facts and cultural traits of the target language country or countries, including the range of languages spoken.

A.3. Show knowledge of current events in the target language culture or cultures.

A.4. Can identify and articulate in their first language, if necessary, perspectives embodied in the culture that uses the target language.

A.5.* Can identify important physical artifacts and cultural practices of the target language culture or cultures expressed in the form of monuments, icons, and customs, and how cultural practices influence daily life.

III. Structure

A. Successful students have a basic knowledge of English syntax, semantics, and discourse structures and are able to compare these with analogous forms in the target language. They:

A.1. Recognize most common parts of speech, including nouns, verbs, adjectives, articles, and adverbs in English and the target language.

A.2. Understand the role of grammar and context in various linguistic functions in English and the target language.

A.3. Understand and compare how simple clauses are formed in English and the target language.

A.4. Can identify and compare the coding of tense and aspect in English and the target language.

A.5. Apply writing conventions accurately in English and the target language.

A.6. Know that a second language cannot be thought of as a simple word-for-word translation of English.

IV. Learning Behaviors

A. Successful students demonstrate awareness of the process of learning a second language and are able to apply a variety of strategies to that learning process. They:

A.1. Apply personal discipline to the language-learning enterprise.

A.2. Work effectively in a group to help enhance language learning for themselves and for group members.

A.3. Are willing to speak in the target language in front of teachers, peers, and those who are fluent in the language.

A.4. Are willing to take risks with the target language as they practice new grammatical structures and vocabulary.

A.5. Know how to use the dictionary and other reference materials in English and the target language as tools to enhance their understanding of the language.

A.6. Have an interest in other cultures, possess curiosity and a willingness to learn about those cultures.

A.7. Use questions and other strategies to elicit responses from classmates as well as from fluent speakers of the target language.

A.8. Use mnemonic and memorization strategies to enhance the learning of the target language.

A.9. Employ knowledge of their first language to help form and test hypotheses about the target language.

A.10.* Recognize and cope with ambiguity and accept that more than one answer is possible, particularly when trying to understand the perspective of a different culture.

A.11.* Use metacognitive and metalinguistic strategies to advance language learning and cultural awareness.

Arts Knowledge and Skills

The arts present an interesting contrast to the other areas. When we think about knowledge and skills in the arts, we must consider them along more than one dimension. A student in the arts can potentially perform, create, or appreciate the art being studied. Art is experienced and understood personally and emotionally as well as being learned. Although each art has a set of technical skills and knowledge associated with it, simply mastering them is not where study of the arts ends or how competency is judged.

Arts Knowledge and Skills Foundations

Students who are successful in the range of creative endeavors known collectively as the arts display a wide range of behaviors, some that can be learned and some that are reflections of personality traits and personal attributes. Successful students in the arts are self-aware individuals who use their time at the university to continue and intensify a process of skill development and personal growth designed to prepare them to be lifelong learners and participants in the arts.

Faculty members describe successful students as those who can think independently, logically, and then maturely. Successful students understand themselves as instruments of communication and expression who demonstrate mastery of basic oral and physical expression through sound, movement, and visual representations. They embrace a diversity of academic interests from world cultures and political history to scientific research, sociology, psychology, and the study of religion.

They view the arts as an instrument of social and political expression. They formulate and present difficult questions through their personal artistic visions. They are able to justify their aesthetic decisions when creating or performing a piece of work and know how to make decisions about the proper venue for performing or exhibiting any creative product.

One of the things that differentiates college from high school is the longer periods of time spent improving, revising, and perfecting work. Successful students know how to practice in a sustained, focused fashion without external supervision, how to manage their time, and how to discipline themselves to remain focused for extended periods of time while mastering the technical aspects of their area of endeavor. Artists, like athletes, sometimes describe this hard work as *flow:* a state of mind characterized by high concentration and blocking out of distractions, thus enabling advanced levels of creativity. Time management and patience are essential. Starting a project when it is assigned without procrastination, learning to work in stages, and planning so that the project can be completed in the amount of time given are critical skills for all arts students. At the same time, successful students do not lose touch with the larger campus community, and in fact, participate in a wide range of campus activities and interact with a cross section of the student body.

Students prepared for study in the arts demonstrate intellectual curiosity and a willingness to experiment with media. They strive to develop creativity and ingenuity by struggling with a concept, an object, a space, or a sound. Rather than solely fixating on proper form, they seek to employ knowledge of form to facilitate and support personal creative development. They are aware of and curious about genres they do not know well and are eager to experiment with them. They are willing to learn about a diverse range of historical eras and practices related to the arts.

Many arts courses at the college level require research skills in part because the creative process of producing one's own work usually raises questions about issues that are external to the piece, particularly knowledge of what influences the piece. This process requires research that incorporates cultural criticism. The presentation of the research is often in the form of a clearly written essay. Successful students also know about the moral and legal issues involved in plagiarism and can see the difference between being influenced by other artists and stealing from them.

Students must be able to think critically. Students who are ready for college-level study in the arts must be capable of making independent judgments about a work of art and not be afraid to ask questions. Curiosity and a willingness to explore many layers of meaning are also important to success. Successful students reflect on and assess the strengths and weaknesses of others' ideas and ways of expressing them. In addition, they are comfortable formulating and expressing their own ideas.

Successful students are able to accept criticism about their own artwork or performance as well as critique the work of others. One cannot create art or perform without considering at some point the opinions of others. Students learn through formal critiques how to distinguish between constructive criticism and unfounded criticism and how to use constructive criticism to become more self-analytical. The underlying point of critique and feedback is not just to improve one's work but also to foster self-reliance and build a peer network simultaneously. Different methods of critique are used at the college level. Sometimes the emphasis is on listening to classmates' comments, at other times the student is expected to present the class with a rationale for the work or performance.

University-level arts classes help students learn not to get discouraged when they are asked to do things that are complex or time-consuming. Rising to the substantial challenges students face in university-level arts courses is an integral component of the learning experience. Many students who have been accustomed to being outstanding find themselves in a community where everyone is similarly gifted. The shock of not being the best or the most accomplished is often great for students in entry-level courses. The challenge is to embrace this new role and status and learn from the diversity of expertise, talent, and creativity that now surrounds them.

Arts Content Standards

The KSUS standards for students in the arts are presented in a somewhat different fashion than they are for the other disciplines. This chapter takes a unique approach because arts classes are not necessarily taken during the freshman year. Students not majoring in the arts are more likely to take an arts course at any point in their academic career. Thus, it is more difficult to identify arts classes associated with first-year students, the criterion used to identify knowledge and skills in the other five academic areas addressed in the preceding chapters. In addition, the arts are unique in a number of other ways. First, they include both the performing and creative arts and art appreciation. Second, they comprise a number of distinctly different areas of emphasis. Music, art, dance, and theatre require more distinctly different skills and knowledge than do biology and chemistry or geography and history, for example.

The arts standards presented here represent a set of general skills and abilities derived from national arts standards documents and the expressed values of arts faculty. This section includes knowledge and skills for art history, dance, music, theatre, and the visual arts. For each of these subareas, knowledge and skills are grouped under three headings: technical knowledge and skills, cultural and historical knowledge and skills, and aesthetic and art criticism knowledge and skills. Although grouped under these headings for organizational convenience, the knowledge and skills are understood best when viewed as being integrated under each heading and across headings in a subarea.

I. Art History

Technical Knowledge and Skills

Students in introductory art history courses are successful when they:

1. Know a range of subject matter, symbols, and ideas in the visual arts.

2. Know how characteristics of the arts vary in a particular historical period or style and how these characteristics relate to ideas, issues, or themes in other artistic disciplines. For example, paintings often were made for specific architectural contexts, such as a mural made for a room in a palace or a temple.

3. Understand the connections between various artistic genres and media, such as the relationships between music and art during a given period.

4. Know that characteristics of the arts vary in a particular historical period or genre.

5. Connect characteristics of visual arts in a particular historical period or style with ideas, issues, or themes in the humanities, social sciences, or natural sciences.

Cultural and Historical Knowledge and Skills

Students in introductory art history courses do well when they:

1. Recognize that artworks are created in relation to major cultural, sociopolitical, and historical periods.

2. Reflect on how artworks differ visually, spatially, temporally, and functionally and according to geographical place.

3. Analyze common characteristics of visual arts evident across time and among cultural-ethnic groups to formulate analyses, evaluations, and interpretations of meaning.

Aesthetic and Art Criticism Knowledge and Skills

Students in introductory art history courses do well when they:

1. Write clearly and cogently, formulate logical arguments, and demonstrate intellectual curiosity.

2. Are skilled in visual literacy; can interpret artwork as a visual text.

3. Understand the link between the artist and society, and understand that artists are generally professionals who are successful in their time because they produce what their audiences want to see.

II. Dance

Technical Knowledge and Skills

Students in entry-level dance courses do well when they:

1. Possess technical skills in proper body part articulation, strength, flexibility, agility, and coordination in locomotor and nonlocomotor-axial movements.

2. Display an awareness of proper breathing techniques, and understand choreographic principles, processes, and structures.

3. Use improvisation to generate movement for choreography.

4. Understand various complex time elements, such as duple and triple meters and tempi varied in relation to a basic pulse.

5. Create and perform combinations and variations in a broad range of dance styles.

6. Can memorize and reproduce extended movement sequences and rhythmic patterns.

7. Understand that dance is a way to create and communicate meaning.

8. Use movement choices to communicate abstract ideas and social themes in dance.

9. Understand and demonstrate how dance interpretation can be influenced by personal experience.

Cultural and Historical Knowledge and Skills

Students in entry-level dance courses do well when they:

1. Understand dance in various cultures and historical periods.

2. Compare and contrast the role and significance of dance in different social, historical, cultural, and political contexts.

3. Place significant dance events of the twentieth century in their proper social, historical, cultural, and political contexts.

4. Perform and describe similarities and differences between two contemporary theatrical forms of dance, and know the traditions and techniques of classical dance forms.

Aesthetic and Art Criticism Knowledge and Skills

Students in entry-level dance courses do well when they:

1. Discuss the intentions and effects of dance work in both solo and group dance performances.

2. Analyze and describe the tempo, bodily precision, intention, musicality, costumes, lighting, space, rhythm, body position, and synchronicity between elements in their critiques.

3. Describe how a choreographer manipulated and developed basic movement content in a dance.

III. Music

Technical Knowledge and Skills

Students beginning vocal or instrumental college-level music do well when they:

1. Can use their voice as a performing tool.

2. Can sing a varied repertoire of vocal literature with expression and technical accuracy at a moderate level of difficulty, including some songs performed from memory.

3. Pay attention to phrasing and interpretation, various meters, and rhythms in a variety of keys.

4. Can sing music written in four parts, with and without accompaniment.

5. Know how to play a varied repertoire of music both alone and with others.

6. Can perform with expression using appropriate dynamics, phrasing, rubato, and technical accuracy with attention to interpretation.

7. Perform in various meters and rhythms in a variety of keys.

8. Perform in an ensemble, demonstrating well-developed skills in creating balance, varying intonation, and maintaining rhythmic unity.

9. Read and notate music that contains moderate technical demands.

10. Are familiar with music theory and composition and can demonstrate an ability to use the elements of music for expressive effect, including pitch, rhythm, timbre, texture, and form.

Cultural and Historical Knowledge and Skills

Students in music courses do well when they:

1. Understand how music is related to history and culture.

2. Can classify unfamiliar but representative aural examples of music by genre, style, historical period, and culture and explain the reasoning behind their identification.

3. Can identify and describe music genres or styles that show the influence of one or more cultural traditions.

Aesthetic and Art Criticism Knowledge and Skills

Students who observe or listen to musical performances do well when they:

1. Know and apply appropriate criteria to music and music performances.

2. Understand the technical vocabulary of music—including terms in Italian and markings for form, harmony, and tempo.

3. Understand compositional devices and techniques that are used to provide unity, variety, tension, and release in a musical work.

4. Can listen to, analyze, and describe music and music performances.

5. Describe the elements of music in a given work that make it unique, interesting, and expressive.

16

Arts Knowledge and Skills

6. Evaluate composition, arrangement, or improvisation by comparing it to similar or exemplary models.

7. Compare ways in which musical components are used in a variety of works of the same genre or style.

8. Understand and can describe the relationships between music, other arts, and disciplines outside the arts.

IV. Theatre

Technical Knowledge and Skills

Students in entry-level theatre courses do well when they:

1. Demonstrate evidence of dramatic experience, including the ability to analyze the physical, emotional, and social dimensions of characters found in dramatic texts from various genres and media.

2. Develop, communicate, and sustain characters in rehearsal, in informal or formal productions, and in an ensemble that communicates with audiences in improvisations.

3. Understand what goes on behind the scenes—the design, direction, and production of a theatrical piece.

4. Possess the technical knowledge and skills so they can collaboratively and safely create functional scenery, properties, lighting, sound, costumes, and makeup.

5. Can collaborate with directors to develop unified production concepts that convey the metaphorical nature of the drama for informal and formal theatre, film, television, or electronic media productions.

Cultural and Historical Knowledge and Skills

Students are successful in theatre when they:

1. Are familiar with the social, cultural, and historical contexts in which theatre, film, television, and electronic media are performed today and were performed in the past.

2. Demonstrate knowledge of theatrical heritage.

3. Are aware that theatre can reveal universal concepts across time.

4. Appreciate the ways in which personal and cultural experiences can affect an artist's dramatic work.

5. Understand and can describe how their own cultural experiences influence their work.

6. Understand and appreciate cultural and historical effects influencing theatre.

7. Compare, analyze, and integrate traditional theatre, dance, music, visual arts, and emerging art forms.

Aesthetic and Art Criticism Knowledge and Skills

Students are successful in theatre when they:

1. Know how informal and formal theatre, film, television, and electronic media productions create and communicate meaning.

2. Understand how social meanings, represented by aural, oral, and visual symbols are communicated.

3. Can identify how productions and performances relate to current issues.

4. Understand that the context in which a dramatic performance is set can enhance it or weaken it.

5. Can compare and explain the roles and interrelated responsibilities of people involved in a production.

6. Can describe the influence of drama in film, television, rock concerts, and religious ceremonies and other kinds of ceremonies and performances.

7. Have good observational skills.

8. Articulate and justify their personal aesthetic criteria.

9. Use their knowledge of other aesthetic philosophies, such as Greek drama, Shakespearean forms, Japanese kabuki, and others.

V. Visual Arts

Technical Knowledge and Skills

Students in entry-level visual arts courses do well when they:

1. Know fundamental visual arts techniques and processes in a variety of media, including basic drawing, color theory, and design.

2. Initiate, define, and solve challenging visual arts problems in order to create cohesive artworks.

3. Demonstrate awareness of how emotions expressed in art give new insight and clarity to issues.

4. Differentiate between the applications of various media and understand how media generate different types of expression.

5. Explore ways to integrate and combine various arts media.

Cultural and Historical Knowledge and Skills

Students in college-level visual arts courses do well when they:

1. View and identify examples of artworks from a variety of cultural contexts to understand their function and meaning.

2. Understand how visual, spatial, temporal, and functional values of artworks are tempered by society, culture, and history.

3. Show an understanding of the work of critics, historians, and artists.

4. Investigate the influence of international and national cultural institutions and art policies on art and art making.

5. Develop an appreciation of art as a social agent that contributes to a sense of community in situations such as community forums, events, and festivals.

Aesthetic and Art Criticism Knowledge and Skills

Successful students in entry-level visual arts courses:

1. Are willing to learn from the process of evaluation by peers and faculty.

2. Apply intellectual skills such as analysis, synthesis, and evaluation in visual art critiques.

3. Discuss the implications of an artist's intentions.

4. Demonstrate their own interpretations and synthesize those of peers, professors, and critics.

5. Form and defend judgments about artistic characteristics.

6. Compare two or more perspectives about the use of organizational principles in an artwork, and defend personal evaluations of these perspectives.

7. Reflect on and assess how artworks differ visually, spatially, temporally, and functionally.

8. Balance between the ability to identify and trust their own instincts and the ability to question their preconceived assumptions.

University Work Samples

The Knowledge and Skills for University Success standards presented in Chapters Ten through Sixteen describe well what students need to do to succeed in entry-level university courses. However, the standards by themselves cannot illustrate the level of challenge or the types of work students are expected to produce when they begin their college education. A good way to add the necessary specificity is with actual student work done in entry-level university courses.

This chapter provides representative student work samples that illustrate what is expected in college classrooms. The samples included here have been collected from actual courses at U.S. universities. They were chosen to illustrate the level of challenge set by college instructors, the kind of content students are expected to master, how student work is graded, and the skills students develop in entry-level university courses. These materials serve as a resource for determining the skill level high school students should be attempting to reach by the time they graduate. They suggest the tasks and assignments they should be mastering in high school in order to be ready for college-level work.

Work samples allow students not yet in college to compare their own skills with those that were required to create the sample paper or project. This diagnostic process enables them to identify the discrepancy between the quality of the work they produce currently and what they will be expected to produce when in college. Armed with this knowledge, high school students can focus their efforts on acquiring the necessary skills so that they will be ready for the academic expectations and challenges they will face in college.

A Word About the Format

Work samples take many forms. Student writing is the most common, because writing is what students do most often in college. Writing samples may be reflective essays, research papers, opinion pieces, literary analyses, summaries of readings, or any of a dozen other possibilities. Mathematics and science work samples often capture the results of lab experiments, solutions to complex problems, exam questions, or field notebooks, among many other kinds of work. Art courses can produce drawings, paintings, sketches, color studies, and expressions in a variety of media; similarly, dance, drama, and music work samples may include video representations of presentations or audio recordings of performances. All of these work samples help illustrate in concrete terms what colleges expect from entering students.

Work samples frequently include contextual information on the course, including the syllabus, reading list, and schedule as well as the specific assignment or test to which the work is in response. The contextual information can be very enlightening when viewed in combination with the work sample. For example, the course outline may indicate that the paper in question is only one of five such papers expected during a twelve-week quarter. The grading criteria might indicate that the paper must reference a number of sources, cite them properly, and integrate them appropriately. The course schedule may reveal that students are reading seventy to one hundred pages a week for this class alone and are expected to discuss it all intelligently. A review of these documents helps put it all in context: the standards for the quality of the work, the pace of work, the flow of the quarter or semester, and what it takes to earn an A. This information can make it clearer to most high school students that they will have to manage their time outside of class much more carefully than they may be accustomed to doing.

How to Use the Work Samples

The samples presented here vary in content. All include some contextual information on the course, including the syllabus and the specific assignment or test to which the student work is in response, as well as the KSUS standards addressed by the sample. Sometimes several drafts of the same assignment are required but not included here due to space limitations. Some samples are annotated by the instructor to indicate the specific attributes that are consistent with the expectations for success in entry-level courses and what can be improved.

Generally, the work samples included here contain the following four elements:

- *Syllabus.* A summary of the instructor's expectations, lists of assignments, grading policies, books, and other required reading materials and a list of the topics covered in the course. Its length can vary from one to six pages.

- *Assignment.* One of the assignments listed on the syllabus is presented here. It may be an exam or a description of an essay to be written.

- *Student work sample.* This is a student's response to the presented assignment. Each of those shown here was chosen because it demonstrates the Knowledge and Skills for University Success standard and the level of challenge expected of university freshmen.

- *Faculty comments.* Faculty members from leading universities were asked to comment on some of the work samples. Their comments call attention to the most important elements in the work sample.

College-bound students can review these documents with their advisers, teachers, and parents and discuss what they reveal about college and judge how realistic their expectations are. Some students may understand fully what will be expected of them and actually look forward to the challenge. For others, the process may be an eye-opener.

High school teachers and administrators can refer to these examples to determine how the content of college preparatory courses (and the high school curriculum as a whole) compares with the challenge level these work samples illustrate. They can encourage students in their senior year, in particular, to continue working to prepare themselves for assignments of this nature, instead of viewing the senior year as a time to relax or reduce their commitment to academic growth and college preparation.

These work samples can be useful to parents as well; they too can examine the challenge level of the work samples in relation to what their children are doing in their high school courses. Are the assignments difficult enough to get the students to the point where they can do the type of work contained in the samples by the time they enter college? Is the high school curriculum aligned with the types of university expectations contained in this document?

Readers should note that the KSUS standards and the work samples are periodically updated. To download the most current versions, readers can visit the Standards for Success Web site (http://www.s4s.org).

Accel. Rhetoric *Sec. 23, 9:30–10:20 MTWTh.*	Instructor: Email: Web site: Office: Office hours: Rhetoric dept. phone:	 Tuesday 10:30–12:00, Friday 9:30–11:00, or by appointment (leave a message)

American Dustbin

In and out of this class this semester we will spend our time studying what it is that's wrong with you. Oh, yes! You, student extraordinaire, fresh entering college, cheeks still blushing from mom's tearful goodbye kiss, have been discussed for centuries. Educators of all sorts have lamented how poorly you study, how disinterested you are about your studies, how ignorant you are, and more recently, how your minds are corrupted by sex, drugs, and rock and roll—or as we will read in *The Closing of the American Mind,* how the very philosophies that make sex, drugs, and rock and roll glamorous corrupt your minds even more so than they do. You are the source of controversy in this class; it will be our endeavor to understand why. Our reading will be broad: from a history of rock and roll to the pedagogical nightmare that is the film *Blackboard Jungle* to Allan Bloom's extended critique of you to what you discover in your own research, we will try to discern what motivates so many people to discuss you as passionately as they do, to find what truth, if any, exists in their critiques, and how we can respond to those critiques with sympathy and argument.

Required Texts and Other Materials:

Miller, James. ***Flowers in the Dustbin: The Rise of Rock and Roll, 1947–1977.*** New York: Simon & Schuster, 1999. *Available at the University Bookstore.*
Bloom, Allan. ***The Closing of the American Mind.*** New York: Simon & Schuster, 1987. *Available at the University Bookstore.*
Reserve materials. Course pack available in the reserve room of the main library.
A heavy-duty folder (not *a binder).*
A notebook.
An email account. You can sign up for email on _____. You should also subscribe to the class mailing list, ***American-Dustbin.***
The telephone numbers and/or email addresses of two of your classmates. Please see the *Attendance* policy for details.

Name:	Telephone:	Email:

Other Recommended Texts and Materials:

Lunsford, Andrea, and John Ruszkiewicz. *Everything's an Argument.* 2nd Edition. New York: Bedford/St. Martin's, 2001. *Available at the University Bookstore.*

A dictionary. If you do not own one or have ready access to one online (http://www.m-w.com/dictionary.htm; the Oxford English Dictionary is also available online through the library's Gateway to Online Resources), then now is a good time to buy one. You will find a dictionary useful not only in this class, but also throughout your university career. Of particular note is the *Random House Webster's College Dictionary* or the *American Heritage College Dictionary.* This will be particularly useful for reading *The Closing of the American Mind.*

A style manual. Throughout your university career you will be asked to cite sources when you write. However, different fields of study have different criteria for how a citation should look. The default style for this class is MLA; but if you already know what style you will use through your time at this university, cite your sources accordingly. Some manuals include:

—*Publication Manual of the American Psychological Association (APA)*
—*Style Manual of the Modern Language Association (MLA)*
—*Chicago Manual of Style* (Buy Kate Turabian's style manual as a cheaper alternative.)

Note: The _____ Libraries also provide online links to brief summaries of some of the styles above: http://_____

A stapler. You will find that having a stapler will save you much hassle in this class as well as throughout your time at _____.

A public library card. The _____ City Public Library, located off the _____ downtown, has an extensive film collection that you will find useful in this class. Not only can you borrow videocassettes for several days at a time, you can borrow them for free.

Attendance:

It is important that you be present and on time to class. If you know in advance that you will be gone (for an illness, a school function, or for some other legitimate reason), then inform me in advance, either in person, via email, or via message in order to make arrangements about missed assignments. If you do miss class, it will be *your responsibility* to learn *from your peers* what you missed.

Late or Missing Work:

If you have contacted me prior to an absence (see "Attendance" above), I will accept written work due by 4:00 PM the next day without penalty. Otherwise, all late work accrues a penalty: major assignments drop a letter-grade for every day they are late; other assignments lose half-credit per day. Late penalties begin after 4:00 PM on the assignment's due date. Be aware that speeches are almost impossible to make up.

Guidelines for Written Work:

All written work should be typed, double-spaced, with standard margins conforming to style requirements defined in the newest editions of the common style manuals—in most cases, this means a one-inch margin on all sides. Unless otherwise specified by a style manual, the font should be twelve (12) point Times New Roman. No major written assignments will be accepted electronically. In addition,

> *All written work longer than one page must be stapled.* I will not accept papers tied with string, strapped with tape, glued, folded, bound in a folder, held together by voodoo, or linked in any other fashion than staples; and,
>
> *All formal assignments should be informatively and creatively titled.*

One final guideline to remember with your writing assignments:

> *Do not waste your time with cover sheets.* Type your name, my name, your course and section number, and the date in the upper left-hand corner of the page next to the staple.

Plagiarism:

Please refer to the Department of Rhetoric's gold "Information for Students" sheet for the official policy regarding plagiarism (in the section, "Student Conduct").

I expect that you will make every effort to give credit where credit is due when you use other people's ideas or words. If you have questions about citing sources, then ask me, because the penalties for plagiarism can be severe: not only can I assign you an immediate *F for the course,* but also you may be liable to subsequent penalty by the Dean's office.

Student Conduct:

The University _____ and the Rhetoric Department fully support the nondiscrimination policy outlined in the *Human Rights* section of the gold "Information for Students" sheet. In particular, the Rhetoric Department stresses that we are all accountable for the language we use. In admitting responsibility for the things we say and do, we should try to be sympathetic toward those who do not share our attitudes or beliefs.

However, I must stress that, because this class is discussion-oriented, and because we will study issues that many people have strong opinions about, it is likely that disagreements will occur, and possible that some may be offended by what others say. Please be aware that affirming the human rights policy of the University by no means is to say that faction should not occur; if and when it does, I will not discourage your views. However, I consider it my duty to hold you accountable for what you say; I suggest you consider it your duty to hold yourselves and me likewise accountable. If and when disagreement or even offense occurs, we should make it our goal to discuss the words we say and the reasons we say them, not only to try to understand each other but also how our words and actions have influence on those around us.

The Writing and Speech Centers:

The Department of Rhetoric maintains two labs that provide free personal tutoring in writing and speech. The Writing Center has two programs: one in which you enroll for regular tutoring throughout a semester, and another that provides tutoring on a first-come, first-served basis. If you are interested in signing up for the enrollment program, do so quickly because the waiting list fills in a hurry. Each center is staffed by graduate students who have special expertise in tutoring in their respective centers. These centers are available for all students:

Writing Center: _____
Speaking Center: _____

Students with Disabilities:

If you have a disability that will require modification of seating, class requirements, etc., please see me as soon as possible, either after class the first day or during my office hours, so that we can make the necessary arrangements.

Complaints or Concerns:

If you have complaints or concerns about the course or about me personally, please talk to me. It is my firm belief that most problems can be resolved through discussion. (Note: Email is generally a poor medium with which to voice concerns. If you do email your complaints, I will not reply directly except to request that you speak to me in person.) However, if you think you cannot come to me, contact the Rhetoric Department, Associate Chair, _____, through the Rhetoric Office, _____.

Syllabus

Week		Day
1.	8.28:	Introduction
	8.30:	Library Workshop (Meet in classroom unless otherwise notified.)
2.	9.04:	Miller, 15–21
	9.06:	Miller, 25–94
3.	9.09/10:	Film screening: *Blackboard Jungle*, _____, 8:30 PM
	9.11:	
	9.13:	Miller, 95–126
4.	9.18:	Workshop, ESSAY 1
	9.20:	Miller, 129–63; *Due: ESSAY 1*
5.	9.25:	Miller, 163–231; *Due: GROUP 1, Disc.: Elvis had hips!*
	9.27:	Miller, 233–70
6.	10.02:	Miller, 270–94; *Due: GROUP 2, Disc.: All things "corporate" rule America!*
	10.04:	Miller, 295–336; *Due: GROUP 3, Disc.: The Sex Pistols drop the f-bomb on the BBC!*
7.	10.09:	Miller, 15–21, 337–54
	10.11:	*Due: GROUP 4, Disc.: Rock and roll and the youth of America*
8.	10.16:	Bloom, 19–43; Workshop: ESSAY 2
	10.18:	Bloom, 47–81; *Due: ESSAY 2; Due: Portfolios*
9.	10.23:	Bloom, 82–137; *Due: GROUP 5, Disc.: The state of love in America*
	10.25:	Bloom, 141–84; *Due: GROUP 6, Disc.: Feminists respond!*
10.	10.28/29:	Film Screening: *Zelig*, _____, 8:30 PM
	10.30:	Bloom 185–240; Workshop: ESSAY 2
	11.01:	*Due: ESSAY 2*
11.	11.06:	
	11.08:	Bloom, 243–312
12.	11.13:	Bloom, 313–82; Workshop: SPEECH 1; *Due: GROUP 6, Disc.: University life*
	11.15:	*Due: SPEECH 1*
13.	11.20:	*Due: SPEECH 1 (cont.)*
	11.22:	*Thanksgiving. No Class.*
14.	11.27:	Workshop: ESSAY 3; Montaigne, 151–99*
	11.29:	Jarrell, 313–28*; *Due: ESSAY 3; Group 8, Disc.: Teachers*
15.	12.04:	Workshop: SPEECH 2
	12.06:	Workshop: SPEECH 2
16.	12.11:	*Due: SPEECH 2*
	12.13:	*Due: SPEECH 2 (cont.)* Rhetoric 003, Sec. 23

*On reserve.

ESSAY 2: Mapping the American Dustbin

Workshop:

Essay due:

Directions:

Choose one of the following options:

1. Throughout *Flowers in the Dustbin,* James Miller explores the songs and events that defined and redefined rock and roll during its first thirty years. In the process, Miller suggests that youth culture is central to rock's beginnings and perpetuation, and in fact argues with Malcolm McLaren that rock and roll is "the ultimate adolescent fantasy of adulthood" (343). Similarly in *Closing of the American Mind,* Allan Bloom argues that rock and roll prevents youth from learning how to engage in the totality of adult experience. Consulting at least one other source that discusses at length rock and roll's effect upon youth, write a three-to-five (3–5) page essay that explicates the three arguments and explores the intersections and digressions among them. In light of the arguments you investigate, what conclusions do you reach about rock and roll's ultimate effect upon American youth? *No Internet sources.*

2. Allan Bloom's first chapter in *Closing of the American Mind* is an extended critique of what is generally seen as American openness: while we say we are open-minded, he argues, we are in fact as closed as any fanatical group. Bloom's was hardly the first or final word on the matter. Before and since *Closing's* publication in 1987, scholars and critics have weighed in their own definitions of the term. Write a three-to-five (3–5) page essay that either

   - Consults at least four (4) contemporary reviews of *Closing* and examines their critiques of Bloom's definition. What perspective on the concept of *openness* do the reviewers write from? What assumptions do they share with Bloom, and from what assumptions of his do they distance themselves? How does their embracing of or distancing from Bloom's definition sway their evaluations of his book? Use significant quotations from all sources to help you explain your analysis of the debate. (To find in-depth reviews of *Closing,* consult such resources as the *New York Review of Books,* the *Boston Review,* and the *New York Times Book Review.* These and publications like them are known for their in-depth reviews.)
   - Or look at three (3) other definitions of *openness* not limited to reviews of *Closing.* How is Bloom's definition of the concept sufficient or insufficient in view of these other discussions? In light of these other definitions, determine what you think is the full extent of Bloom's critique, and form your own definition in response to your research. What, after all, does it mean to have an "open" society?

3. Several weeks ago, each of you chose a topic on which to research and lead a group discussion. Continuing your research (or beginning it early), write a three-to-five (3–5) page essay that explores how your topic is discussed as significant to

youth culture. Utilizing at least four (4) sources, explore in your essay how one event or idea can inspire different responses by different people. For example, that companies have made their fortunes by pitching products to the young has been widely discussed in both academic and popular literature (cf. James Miller's various comments to this effect, or arguments against alcohol and tobacco advertising as two of many aspects of this debate). How do others discuss your topic as significant to youth culture? Are reactions positive? Negative? Who falls into those categories? Does the passage of time play a role in how critics interpret the event or idea? What values about youth are in conflict when people discuss that event or idea? What values work in tandem? For this option, I encourage you to expand your research base. Use at least one song or film (narrative or documentary) as part of your analysis.

Note on using sources:

- For this assignment, I want you to spend at least as much time in the library as you do on the Internet. Therefore, you have a limit to the number of pure Internet sources you may use. Consider yourself safe if you keep a 2:1 ratio of print or other media sources to Web sources. In other words, for every two print/other-media sources you use, you can use one Web source. Exceptions can be made; however, to obtain one, you must speak to me first, and you must have a convincing argument why you need that exception. You cannot use Internet sources if writing Option #1, above.
- Be sure to use proper bibliographic citations according to APA, Chicago, or MLA formats.

General note:

- Because this is your second essay, I want you to concentrate on fixing major problems in your writing from the first essay. Whether the problem is grammatical, such as with comma errors, or whether it is a greater problem, such as sentence construction or essay structure, work to improve it. If you have questions, I'll be glad to meet with you to discuss how to work with your particular problem.

Due when you hand in your essay:

- Workshop forms;
- Your rhetorical square for this essay, typed on its own sheet of paper;
- Your essay.

Grading:

I will grade this essay primarily according to how well you utilize your different sources into a cohesive, thesis-driven essay. As an addition to your first essay and as part of your overall writing work in this class, I will also pay attention to the improvement your writing shows. In addition, I will take careful note of the variety of sources you discuss; beware that you don't transgress the 2:1 ratio defined above unless you make arrangements with me! This essay is worth fifteen percent (15%) of your final grade.

And finally, please remember: *I do not accept unstapled essays!*

Accelerated Rhetoric Sec. 383
Date

Essay 2: Mapping the American Dustbin
Openness Closes the Mind?

In *The Closing of the American Mind* the author, Allan Bloom, is critical of shallow thinking that he characterizes as the new "American Openness." He believes that "there are two kinds of openness, the openness of indifference—promoted with the twin purposes of humbling our intellectual pride and letting us be whatever we want to be, just as long as we don't want to be knowers—and the openness that invites us to the quest for knowledge and certitude." (Bloom 1987, 41). Professor Bloom would have us strive for the latter, but he complains that our culture, through our educational institutions, embraces the former.

The new American openness is based on two beliefs, (1) that truth is relative (relativism), i.e., there are no absolute truths, and (2) there must be unquestioned allegiance to the concept that all are equal. (Bloom 1987, 25). Bloom finds that the American student accepts this concept of openness as a moral truth without question. (Bloom 1987, 26). In doing so, Bloom argues that we are creating a culture of non-thinkers. An example would be as follows: If an issue was presented as to whether American culture treated women better than the Taliban, Bloom would have no complaint with the student who took a position pro or con. What Bloom objects to is the student who has the capability of reciting all the traits of both cultures as they apply to women, yet, due to indoctrination in openness, lacks the critical thinking to offer an opinion as to the superiority of either stating, "What right . . . do I or anyone else have to say one is better than the other." (Bloom 1987, 26). That type of openness, according to Bloom, forbids any attempt to discover what is good or bad about other cultures and requires us not to think our way is better." (Bloom 1987, 30, 40).

Bloom thinks that prejudices aren't necessarily bad. In order to hold a prejudice one has to engage in some critical thinking. That thinking might be flawed, but through such thinking certain ideas are accepted, others are rejected, and hopefully through reason progress is made toward fundamental agreement for the common good. "Openness," however, "suffocates reason." (Bloom 1987, 40). Bloom speaks of an incident during his university years when he meets a young Southerner who firmly believes in segregation and the inferiority of blacks. Bloom is horrified at the Southerner's beliefs because Bloom was raised in a culture that opposed such ideas and Bloom felt his culture superior. He implies that openness today would dictate that he accept the Southerner's culture without judgment or criticism. (Bloom 1987, 35). In essence, our instinct and intellect are suppressed by openness, and our natural soul is replaced with an artificial one. (Bloom 1987, 30).

Professor Bloom presents his opinion from the perspective of a humanities professor from the University of Chicago who believes that the old books of philosophy, including the Bible, present the best lessons. After the Soviets launched Sputnik, the first orbiting space capsule, America placed its educational emphasis on science and technology. Science and math, however, were boring and he observed that many of his best students were not satisfied with that course of study. (Bloom 1987, 50). Liberal education began to attract those students who were interested in more, an education that would help them examine themselves and their potential through the old great works of philosophy. (Bloom 1987, 50). Unfortunately, Bloom believes, the universities opted for trendy curriculum and the energy of those good students was wasted. (Bloom 1987, 51). The result was apathy toward critical thinking in favor of the less strenuous belief in openness. Now, those beliefs are passed on to the next generation because the last generation had nothing to give. Bloom states, "Today's select students know so much less . . . are so much slacker intellectually, that they make their predecessors look like prodigies of culture." (Bloom 1987, 51).

Joseph Sobran, writing for the conservative "National Review," supports Bloom's case against the current liberal arts education arguing that today's students might mistake (Bloom's) complaint for an old man's nostalgia for traditional education, instead of seeing it for what it is: the protest of a philosopher against the destruction of philosophy and all the good lessons it teaches. (Sobran 04/24/87, 51–52). "Can anything fresh still be said about sex on campus," Sobran asks? "Yes," agreeing with Bloom, "if you've kept your eyes on the current goings-on and your mind on the ancients." (Sobran 04/24/87, 53). Sobran points out that Bloom is perfectly situated to make his case. He is a philosopher who was where the action was: Cornell University in 1969, when leftist terrorism scared the administration into appeasing their demands by offering a curriculum of what's happening now instead of a traditional curriculum of substance. (Sobran 04/24/87, 52). And, Sobran agrees that higher education hasn't recovered yet. "[Bloom] used to think the purpose of education was to teach people to think critically about their own prejudices, but now they come to college without any prejudices at all, a sign not of the open mind but of the vacant one." (Soban 04/24/87, 53).

Roger Kimball, a critic for "The New York Times Book Review," feels that although Allan Bloom's criticisms of today's liberal education may be severe, he does make interesting arguments that deserve serious attention. "Let me say at the outset that *The Closing of the American Mind* is essential reading for anyone concerned with the state of liberal education in this society." (Kimball 04/05/87, 7). He points out that Bloom's views will make many enemies because of his traditional view of what it means to be an educated person. (Kimball 04/05/87, 7). Kimball as the book critic seems to agree with Bloom that much of today's problem with lack of critical thinking comes from the "lost practice of and taste for reading, forsaking the companionship of books for the more accessible but less sustaining pleasures of movies and rock music." (Kimball 04/05/87, 7). Kimball also likes Bloom's style as it offers questions to consider as opposed to shoving solutions down your throat, and that it "is that rarest of documents, a genuinely profound book, born of a long and patient meditation on questions that may be said to determine who we are, both as individuals and as society." (Kimball 04/05/87, 7).

Martha Nussbaum's review in "The New York Review of Books" is more critical. She, unlike Joseph Sobran, does think that Bloom's complaint is based on nostalgia for the old traditional education that doesn't and can't exist anymore. Ms. Nussbaum points out that the university setting has dramatically changed in the last forty or fifty years. A college education is no longer available to only the social elite who have nothing better to do in life than to ponder philosophical debate regarding good and evil. Student enrollment in college has increased tremendously to include people from all social classes. Even at Harvard, one of Professor Bloom's models, most students work one, two or three jobs just to pay for their education. They are more concerned with taking a curriculum that will provide them with the qualifications leading to a meaningful profession than a curriculum where philosophy leads the way. (Nussbaum

11/05/87, 24). Ms. Nussbaum doesn't find the despair that Professor Bloom finds in the current situation. She believes that today's students can be just as rational as the philosophical elite students that Professor Bloom enjoyed in the past. (Nussbaum 11/05/87, 25). Ms. Nussbaum also takes exception to Professor Bloom's attempts to show how the universities have been corrupted by democratic demands for equality, therefore eroding our intellectual standards. (Nussbaum 11/05/87, 20). Bloom thinks that "only in Western Nations, who were influenced by Greek thinking, is there some willingness to doubt the identification of good with one's own way." Nussbaum would rather see a country in which the citizens flourish each in his/her own setting. ((Nussbaum 11/05/87, 26).

Louis Menand, writing for "The New Republic" even takes a harder stand against Bloom and his opinions. He finds him arrogant. "Allan Bloom is a man who knows his own mind, and who thinks well of what he finds there." (Menand 05/25/87, 38). He believes that Professor Bloom uses relativism as a philosophical scare word. Menand doesn't buy the idea that anyone, least of all college students, believe that on any given subject one opinion is as good as any other opinion. He believes that people, including college students, do think critically and hold strong opinions, but Bloom mistakes respect for the views of others as somehow a sign of a non-thinker. (Menand 05/25/87, 40). Menand also finds ridiculous Bloom's belief that unreasonable speech, generated by openness, is not protected. Menand states, "it is precisely offensive speech that the First Amendment is designed to protect. Who cares about regulating the reasonable?" (Menand 05/25/87, 40). Who decides what is reasonable?

I agree with Professor Bloom that the study of philosophy offers valuable lessons and should be taught for what it is and not as mere literature. I also agree with his opinion that lack of critical thinking in favor of openness is not progressive. But Martha Nussbaum's and Louis Menand's points are well taken that elitism is in the minority at universities now, and there is very little of the type of openness that Bloom describes. Perhaps such openness still prevails among the best students at Professor Bloom's twenty or thirty best universities, but in my limited time as a college student I find that most of my friends have strong and varying opinions on many subjects and I am happy for it. I think we should be open and respectful to all types of cultures and opinions, but that doesn't mean we shouldn't be critical in analyzing the positions of others, as well as our own.

Bibliography

Bloom, Allan. *The Closing of the American Mind.* (City of Publication): Simon and Schuster, 1987.

Kimball, Roger. "The Groves of Ignorance." *New York Times Book Review,* April 5, 1987, sec. 7, page 7.

Menand, Louis. "Mr. Bloom's Planet." *The New Republic,* vol. 196, no. 21, May 25, 1987, pp. 38–41.

Nussbaum, Martha Craven. *The New York Review of Books,* vol. 34, Nov. 5, 1987, pp. 20–26.

Sobran, Joseph. "Sammler's Complaint," *National Review,* vol. 39, no. 7, April 24, 1987, pp. 51–53.

English Work Sample Comments

I chose the essay "Openness Closes the Mind" as a work sample because it is a decent response to our Rhetoric course assignment to "map" or describe a controversy—that is, to compare and contrast positions on a social issue. One of our goals in the mapping assignment is to get students to realize gradations in argumentative positions. We want them to understand that not every stance is pro or con, black or white. Some stances are in the gray areas in between. We stress that students themselves have the option of constructing these more sophisticated and subtle, non-pro, non-con stances, which this student begins to do in his last paragraph. In the case of this assignment, the social issue is more abstract than gun control or abortion. It is the openness of today's American college student—what are its causes and effects and is it good or bad?

The reasons this student's essay won the Rhetoric Department's writing contest are:
1) Such an abstract issue as student "openness" is not easy to grasp; indeed, Bloom's book, although a best-seller, was hard to read and understand, and although many academics started reading it, few finished it. This student does a decent job of grappling with the meaning of Bloom's book and summarizing in the first third of his essay Bloom's position against an "openness" rooted in an uncritical cultural relativism that actually closes down the mind.
2) He did library research and found worthy reviews that he could and then did summarize, not separately, but in relation to one another. He found reviews of scholars as well-known as or more well-known than Bloom—Joseph Sobran, Roger Kimball, Martha Nussbaum, and Louis Menand—and arranged them in order from the most conservative to the most liberal.
3) He compared and contrasted the reviewers' stances on Bloom's opinion of openness, its causes and effects. He managed to capture subtleties—the fact that none of the four reviewers either totally panned or totally bought Bloom's argument. He chose illustrative quotations and integrated them well. The quotations did not overpower his own prose and voice.
4) He located his own position in relation to the five other positions he reviewed. He agrees with Menand that Bloom is confusing openness to other views with respect for them, but he also agrees with Bloom that an uncritical cultural relativism would be undesirable. Agreeing with Nussbaum, he perceives that perhaps because he, unlike Bloom, is not in an elite environment such as Harvard or Cornell, he finds most students respect the views of others, but do indeed have strong views of their own.
5) In sum, the student was able to locate, summarize, compare, and contrast positions clearly and meaningfully.

Syllabus   Math 221   Fall 2001

Professor
Office
Office phone
Home phone
e-mail
Class 11:00–11:50
Office hours M 12–1, W 9:50–10:50, F 1–2
Teaching assistant

The first week will mainly deal with mathematics you have seen before. Based on years of teaching calculus, I know that many of you will have seen most of this before, but need some review before you are comfortable with it. You should do all of the assigned problems and do some more if you think you are still unsure of your knowledge. You will be using almost all of this many times this year, so learn it well.

You should read the assigned sections BEFORE class, and be ready to ask questions about what you do not understand yet. There will be an occasional quiz on the material you should have read before lecture. These will count a little toward your final grade.

Grades will be determined as follows. There will be three exams, each counting 100 points. The final will count 200 points. There will be a grade for your work in discussion section, which, with quiz grades, will count 100 points.

Calculators will not be allowed on exams, nor will formula sheets.
The syllabus below is complete through the first five weeks. I will try to stay as close to this schedule as possible but occasionally we may vary a little.

Day	Date	Read	Problems
T	Sept 4	1.1	Read
		1.2	1,2,9,13,15
W	5	1.3	4,9,11,14
		1.4	13,14,15,16,17,18,19,21,24
F	7	1.5	4,7,9,13,15,17,20,21,25,26
		1.6	1,2,7,10,11,21,22,42,51,53

Write $f(x)=1/(1+x)$ as the sum of an even and an odd function.

———————

Day	Date	Read	Problems
M	10	1.7	1,11,16
		1.8	2,5,6,18
		1.9	1,3,7,8,13–17
W	12	1.9	18,22,23
		1.10	1,2,5,8,9,15,18 (show limit exists and find it), 20,21
		1.11	Read
F	14	2.11	2,3,7
		2.1	Read
		2,2	1,2,3,9,11,13,14

———————

Day	Date	Read	Problems
M	17	2.2	16,17,18,21,23,24,25,26
W	19	2.3	2,3,5,7,8,14,16,19,21
F	21	2.4	2,3,5
		2.5	6,8,9,24,25

———————

Day	Date	Read	Problems
M	24	2.5	Find the point or points on the curve $x^3+y^3=3xy$ where $dy/dx=0$. Find the points on the curve where $dx/dy=0$.
		2.8	1,2,3,4,6,8

Find parametric equations for the curve $x^3+y^3=3xy$ by setting $y=tx$ and solving for x and y as functions of t. Then find dy/dx by first computing dy/dt and dx/dt. Later we will use these parametric equations to help sketch the graph of $x^3+y^3=3xy$, and resolve the strange result you should have discovered when you found when $dy/dx=0$ and when $dx/dy=0$.

Day	Date	Read	Problems
W	26	2.6	3,5,6,9,11

| | 2.12
and 2.13 | but not the trigonometric differentiation formulas. They will be done later.
3,9,19,20,22. The point $x=1.5$, $y=1.5$ satisfies $x^3+y^3=3xy$. Use calculus to find an estimate for the value of y close to 1.5 when $x=1.4$. |
| F | 28 | 3.2 | 1,3,4,6,9,10,13,15 |

| M | Oct 1 | Review—Come to class prepared to ask questions. |

There are many review problems at the end of Chapters 1 and 2. Work as many as you think you need to help reinforce what you have learned. Everything covered up to this point could be on the exam.

W	3		Test—This will be during the regular class period.
R	4	2.9	1,2,6,8,16,18,19,26,27. Find the tangent of the angle between the two lines $2x+3y=1$ and $3x-4y=1$.
F	5	2.10	1,2,3,7,9,10,11,15,18,23

The other two tests will be on Friday, November 2 and Friday, November 30. The last class is on December 14, and the final exam will be on December 21 at 5:05 PM.

Day	Date	Read	Problems
M	Oct 8	3.1	1,3,6,8,9
		3.2	The light in a lighthouse rotates at c radians per minute. The lighthouse is a meters from a path on the shore. When you are b meters down the path from the point closest to the lighthouse, how fast is the light moving along the path when it reaches you?
		3.3	
		3.4	1,4,5,7,8
W	10	3.4	13,20,23,24
		2.7	4,6
F	12	3.5	
		3.6	1,2,3,5,6,10,13,14
M	15	3.6	15,16,18,22,27,28,33
		Page 173 49,53,54	
W	17	3.7	1,4
		3.8	4,5,7a,c,9

F	19	3.9	1,3,7,8,12,13
M	22	3.9	18
		3.10	Use formula (7) when $f(x)=\sin(x)$, $a=0$, $b=x$, $n=6$. Find the value of c which gives a non-zero limit for limit as x goes to zero of $(\sin(x)-x+cx^3)/x^5$. Explain a connection between these two formulas.
		3.11	Pages 171–172 15,19,27,41
W	24	4.1	Read
		4.2	1,3,6,8,12,13,15,17
F	26	4.2	20,24
		4.3	1,4,5,7,12,15,16
M	29	4.4	1,2,3,4,9,13,20,21,23,25
W	31	Review Pages 171–174 8,13,14,29,30,67,68,73,76	
F	Nov 1	Second exam, during class time.	

The next test will be on Friday, November 30. The last class is on December 14, and the final exam will be on December 21 at 5:05 PM.

Day	Date	Read	Problems
M	Nov 19	5.3	1,3,5,7,11,12,15
		5.9	10,11,12,13 Do at least two of these.
W	21	5.4	3,9,13,14
		5.5	9,11,13,17,18,19
——————			
M	26	5.6	
		5.7	1,3,8,10
		5.10	1,3,5
		6.1	1,3,9,13,14,21,22,34,37
W	28	5.8	1,2
F	30	Third exam covering all of the material covered so far.	
——————			
M	Dec 3	6.4	1,8
		6.5	1,3,5, problem 22 on page 329, back to section
		6.5	18,19,21,23,29,31,34
W	5	6.6	1,3,5,10
		6.6	3,4,5
		6.8	1,2,3,5,9,12,21

F   7   6.8   20,22,23,26,27,31,33,35,36

                 6.9   2,3, find the derivative of $f(x)=x^x$

The function $f(x)=[\cos(x)]^{a(x)}$ has a limit as x goes to 0 which is not 1 or 0 from $a(x)=x^p$ for some p. What is p and what is the limit as x goes to 0?

                 6.11   1,3

———————-

M   Dec 10   6.1   1,3,9,10,13,14,21,34,37

                 6.2   1,6,8

        12   6.3   5,6,10,12,16,20,23,24,25

        14   Review

———————-

The final exam will be on December 21 at 5:05 PM.

Math 221—Exam I

1. (a) (5pts) State a formula giving the definition of the derivative of the function $f(x)$.

$$f'(x) = \lim_{h \to 0} \frac{f(x+h) - f(x)}{h}$$

(b) (15pts) Using the definition of a derivative, compute the derivative of $f(x) = 1/2x+1$ with respect to x.

$$f'(x) = \lim_{h \to 0} \frac{f(x+h) - f(x)}{h} = \lim_{h \to 0} \frac{\frac{1}{2(x+h)+1} - \frac{1}{2x+1}}{h} =$$

$$\lim_{h \to 0} \frac{2x + 1 - 2x - 2h - 1}{h(2x+1)(2x+2h+1)} = \lim_{h \to 0} \frac{-2}{(2x+1)(2x+2h+1)} = \boxed{\frac{-2}{(2x+1)^2}}$$

2. (a) (12pts) Graph $r\cos\theta = 3/4$ and $r = 1 + \cos\theta$ on the same graph, labeling the points of intersection.

$$x = \frac{3}{4}$$

$r = 1 + \cos\theta$
symmetric about x-axis

θ	0	$\pi/3$	$\pi/3$	$2\pi/3$	π
r	2	$3/2$	1	$1/2$	0

$$\frac{3}{4\cos\theta} = 1 + \cos\theta$$

$$4\cos^2\theta + 4\cos\theta - 3 = 0$$

$$(2\cos\theta - 1)(2\cos\theta + 3) = 0$$

$$\cos\theta = \frac{1}{2} \quad \text{or} \quad \cos\theta = -\frac{3}{2}$$

$$\theta = \frac{\pi}{3} \quad \text{or} \quad \frac{5\pi}{3}$$

$$\left(\frac{3}{2}, \frac{\pi}{2}\right)$$

$r = 1 + \cos\theta$

$$\left(\frac{3}{2}, \frac{5\pi}{3}\right)$$

$$r\cos\theta = 3/4$$

(b) (8pts) Find the area inside $r = 1 + \cos\theta$ and to the right of $r\cos\theta = 3/4$. (Set up the integral. If you have time after doing the rest of the test, 3 extra points will be given for evaluating the integral.)

$$A = 2 \int^{\frac{\pi}{3}} \frac{1}{2} \left((1 + \cos\theta)^2 - \frac{9}{16\cos^2\theta} \right) d\theta$$

$$= \int_0^{\frac{\pi}{3}} (1 + 2\cos\theta + \cos^2\theta) d\theta - \frac{9}{16} \int_0^{\frac{\pi}{3}} \sec^2\theta \, d\theta$$

$$= [\theta + 2\sin\theta]_0^{\frac{\pi}{3}} + \frac{1}{2} \int_0^{\frac{\pi}{3}} (1 + \cos 2\theta) d\theta - \frac{9}{16} [\tan\theta]_0^{\frac{\pi}{3}}$$

$$= \frac{\pi}{3} + \sqrt{3} + \frac{1}{2} \left[\theta + \frac{1}{2} \sin 2\theta \right]_0^{\frac{\pi}{3}} - \frac{9}{16} \sqrt{3}$$

$$= \frac{\pi}{3} + \frac{7\sqrt{3}}{16} + \frac{1}{2} \left(\frac{\pi}{3} + \frac{\sqrt{3}}{4} \right) = \boxed{\frac{\pi}{2} + \frac{9\sqrt{3}}{16}}$$

3. (a) (15pts) Find the interval of convergence for the series:

$$\sum_{n=1}^{\infty} \frac{(-1)^n x^n}{n}$$

$$\frac{|a_{n+1}|}{|a_n|} = \frac{|x|^{n+1}}{n+1} \Big/ \frac{|x|^n}{n} = |x| \cdot \frac{n}{n+1}$$

$$\lim_{n \to \infty} \left| \frac{a_{n+1}}{a_n} \right| = |x|$$

converges for $|x| < 1$

if $x = 1$

$$\sum_{n=1}^{\infty} \frac{(-1)^n}{n} \quad \text{converges because } \lim_{n \to \infty} \frac{1}{n} = 0, \quad \frac{1}{n+1} < \frac{1}{n},$$

alternating series

if $x = -1$

$$\sum_{n=1}^{\infty} \frac{(-1)^n (-1)^n}{n} = \sum_{n=1}^{\infty} \frac{1}{n} \quad \text{diverges (harmonic series)}$$

$\therefore$ series converges when $-1 < x \leq 1$

Math 221—Exam I (cont.)

(b) (15pts) Find the interval of convergence **and the sum** of the series:

$$\sum_{n=0}^{\infty} 3^n(x-2)^n$$

geometric series converges when

$|a(x-2)| < 1$

$|x-2| < \frac{1}{3}$

$\frac{5}{3} < x < \frac{7}{3}$

if $x = \frac{5}{3}$ $\sum_{n=0}^{\infty} (1)^n$ diverges

if $x = \frac{7}{3}$ $\sum_{n=0}^{\infty} (-1)^n$ diverges

$\therefore$ Series converge when $\frac{5}{3} < x < \frac{7}{3}$

sum of geometric series:

$$\sum_{n=0}^{\infty} (3(x-2))^n = \frac{5}{1-(3x-6)} = \boxed{\frac{1}{-3x+6}}$$

4. A girl flies a kite at a height of 200 ft. the wind carrying the kite horizontally away from her at a rate of 4 ft/sec. At the rate of how many feet per second should she release the string when 250 ft. of string has already been let out (that is, the kite is 250 ft. away from her)?

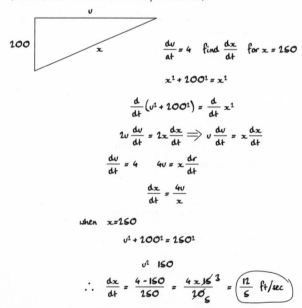

$\frac{dv}{dt} = 4$ find $\frac{dx}{dt}$ for $x = 250$

$x^2 + 200^2 = x^2$

$\frac{d}{dt}(v^2 + 200^2) = \frac{d}{dt} x^2$

$2v\frac{dv}{dt} = 2x\frac{dx}{dt} \Longrightarrow v\frac{dv}{dt} = x\frac{dx}{dt}$

$\frac{dv}{dt} = 4 \qquad 4v = x\frac{dr}{dt}$

$\frac{dx}{dt} = \frac{4v}{x}$

when $x = 250$

$v^2 + 200^2 = 250^2$

$v^2 \quad 150$

$\therefore \frac{dx}{dt} = \frac{4 \cdot 150}{250} = \frac{4 \times \cancel{150}^{3}}{\cancel{250}_{5}} = \boxed{\frac{12}{5} \text{ ft/sec}}$

5. (a). Graph the function $f(x) = x|x|$.

for $x > 0$, $|x| = x$ for $x < 0$, $|x| = -x$

$f(x) = x^2$ $f(x) = -x^2$

at $x = 0$ $f(0) = 0$

(b) Let $g(x) = x + 1/x + 3^5$.

Find for what x is the graph of $g(x)$

   (i) concave up

   (ii) concave down

$g'(x) = 1 + \left(\dfrac{-1}{x^2} \right)$

$= 1 - \dfrac{1}{x^2}$

$g''(x) = -(-2)x^{-3}$

$= \dfrac{2}{x^3}$

1) concave up when $\dfrac{2}{x^3} > 0$, $x^3 > 0$, $\boxed{x > 0}$

2) concave down when $\dfrac{2}{x^3} < 0$, $x^3 < 0$, $\boxed{x < 0}$

6. (15)

(a) (10) Find the sum of the series

$$\sum_{n=0}^{\infty} (-1)^n \, r^{2n}$$

$$\sum_{n=0}^{\infty} (-r^2)^n$$

converges if $|-r^2| < 1, \ r \neq 0$

$$r^2 < 1$$

$$-1 < r < 1$$

if $-1 < r < 1, \ r \neq 0$

$$\sum_{n=0}^{\infty} (-r^2)^n = \frac{1}{1-(-r^2)} = \frac{1}{1+r^2}$$

(geometric series)

(b) (5) Find the sum of the series

$$\sum_{n=1}^{\infty} 1/n(n+1)$$

$$= \sum_{n=0}^{\infty} \left(\frac{1}{n} - \frac{1}{n+1}\right) = \lim_{N \to \infty} \sum_{n=1}^{N} \left(\frac{1}{n} - \frac{1}{n}\right)$$

$$= \lim_{N \to \infty} \left(\left(\frac{1}{1} - \frac{1}{2}\right) + \left(\frac{1}{2} - \frac{1}{3}\right) + \cdots + \right)$$

$$= \lim_{N \to \infty} \left(1 - \frac{1}{N+1} \right) = \boxed{1}$$

Math Work Sample Comments

The first problem requires a knowledge of the definition of a derivative and its use. Some students have not learned how important definitions are, and others just memorize them but are unable to use them correctly. This student knew the definition, (V), knew how to evaluate the expression for the given function, and how to simplify the rational function (IC.1, IIA.3). The second problem required knowledge of graphs (IID) and of trigonometry (IIIA.1,2,3,4), in particular the double angle formula and the connection between cosine and secant. Solving a quadratic equation by factoring was also used (IIB.4a).

Problem 3 requires knowledge of summation notation (IIF1), how to recognize and sum a geometric series (IIA.5, IIF.2), how to solve inequalities involving absolute values (IIB.2) and how to divide rational functions (IIA.3,4). All of the conditions needed to use the alternating convergence theorem are shown to be satisfied (VA7). Problem 4 needs the Pythagorean theorem (IVB.3) and how to deal with the composition of functions (IIA.2) as well as how to set up a mathematical expression from a verbal description, work with the expression, and interpret the result (VA.8).

Problem 5 requires working with functions which have absolute values (IIC.1,3) and (IID.2), and solving inequalities (IIB.2 slightly extended). Problem 6 requires knowledge of summation notation (IIF.1), how to recognize and sum a geometric series (IIF.2), and the ability to work flexibly with rational functions (IIA.3).

These problems come from exams in the first two semesters of calculus, and except for the second part of problem 6 all of the mathematics mentioned should have been learned before starting calculus. The algebra in the second part of problem 6 is taught in calculus, but it is based on a sound knowledge of how to deal with sums and differences of rational functions, which is (IIA.3). Of course there is mathematics which is taught in calculus which is needed to solve these problems, but without the proper background knowledge it will be very hard to do well in calculus. It is appropriate to consider second semester calculus as a beginning course since many students take AP Calculus in high school and start with second semester calculus or higher courses.

The care with which these solutions were written is worth noting. The student does not misuse the equal sign as some do, putting it in between two expressions which are equal and not using it to indicate that a calculation has been done. It is a pleasure to read a well written solution, and a lot of work to try to figure out what a student has done when the calculations are spread out all over the page.

02:021   **HUMAN BIOLOGY**   SPRING 2001

PROFESSORS:
OFFICE: 424 Chemistry Building   125 Biology Building
OFFICE HOURS: Fri. 9:00–11:30 AM or by appt.   Mon., Wed., Fri. 9:30 AM

TEXTBOOK: *Biology* by David Krogh. *LABORATORY MANUAL: Human Biology Laboratory Manual* (edited by Leicht). Both are available at the IMU Bookstore only.

WEBSITE: to be announced in class

LECTURE AND EXAMINATION SCHEDULE:

DATE			LECTURE SUBJECT	TEXT READING
JAN	T	16	What Is Science? What Defines Life?	1–15
	Th	18	Organization of Life: Atoms and Molecules	18–35
	T	23	Water and Carbon-Based Molecules	36–63
	Th	25	From Membranes to Cells	66–99
	T	30	Cell Metabolism: Energy to Enzymes	116–129
FEB	Th	1	Photosynthesis: Sunlight, Redox Reactions, and Making Food	132–133,150–161
	T	6	Cellular Respiration: How Cells Make ATP from Food	130–147
	Th	**8**	**Exam 1**	
	T	13	Genetic Information: Structure and Function of DNA	173–177, 250–262
	Th	15	From DNA to Protein Synthesis	264–277
	T	20	Cell Reproduction: Chromosomes, Mitosis, Meiosis	176–184,186–197
	Th	22	Heredity: Mendel and Meiosis	208–220
	T	27	Mendel's Laws and Human Genetics	220–222, 230–241
MAR	Th	1	Human Genetics (Continued)	230–241
	T	6	Human Genetic Diseases: Detection and Treatment	286–289, 291–297
	Th	**8**	**Exam 2**	
	T	13	No Class—Spring Break	
	Th	15	No Class—Spring Break	
	T	20	Respiration; Circulation	541–557
	Th	22	Digestion; Kidney	551–564
	T	27	Kidney; Movement	492–501
	Th	29	Nerves & Senses	506–516
APR	T	3	Nerves & Senses (Continued)	506–516
	Th	5	Defense Mechanisms and Immunity	523–533

Lecture and Examination Schedule, continued:

	T	10	Immunity and AIDS	Lecture notes
	Th	**12**	**Exam 3**	
	T	17	Systems, Homeostasis, and Hormones	516–521
	Th	19	Hormones; Human Reproduction	584–596
	T	24	Human Reproduction; Development	570–581, 596–603
	Th	26	Evolution, Adaptation, and Natural Selection	326–339
MAY	T	1	Speciation; Ecosystems, Energy, and Materials	346–355, 644–656
	Th	3	Ecosystems: Biostructure, Populations	614–624
MAY	**8**	**T**	**7:00 PM FINAL EXAMINATION**	

NOTE: The final exam will cover all material since Examination 3 as well as comprehensive questions from all previous material.

LABORATORY SCHEDULE:

WEEK OF	TOPIC(S)	MANUAL EXERCISE
Jan 15	Introduction to the Lab	Preface/Foreword to Students
Jan 22	Measurement, Experimentation, and Microscopic Observation	Exercise 1: pp. 1–14
Jan 29	The Cell	Exercise 2: pp. 15–30
Feb 5	Energy Transduction Processes Respiration and Photosynthesis	Exercise 3: pp. 31–40
Feb 12	DNA—The Genetic Material	Exercise 4: pp. 41–50
Feb 19	Mitosis and the Mitotic Cell Cycle	Exercise 5: pp. 51–54
	Chromosomes and Meiosis	Exercise 14, I & II: pp. 137–142
Feb 26	Chromosomes and Meiosis (cont'd)	Exercise 14, III: pp. 142–144
	Genetics Problems	Exercise 15, I–IIC: pp. 145–154
Mar 5	Genetics Problems and Human Inheritance (cont'd) (Omit: Part II,D)	Exercise 15: pp. 145–165
Mar 12	SPRING BREAK—NO LABS	
Mar 19	The Heart and Blood Circulation	Exercise 9: pp. 83–94
	or Enzymes and Digestion	Exercise 7: pp. 65–72
Mar 26	Structure and Function of Skeletal Muscle	Exercise 10: pp. 95–103
Apr 2	Review of Vertebrate Anatomy	Exercise 8: pp. 73–82
Apr 9	Senses and Perception of the Environment	Exercise 11: pp. 105–112
Apr 16	Sexual Reproduction and Its Regulation	Exercise 12: pp. 113–124
Apr 23	Development and Organization of the Animal Embryo	Exercise 12: pp. 117–124
Apr 30	Museum Exercises on Natural History	Exercise 17: pp. 173–175

COURSE GRADES:

Grades for this course will be assigned based on 1) three midterm exams, 2) a final exam, 3) laboratory quizzes and short assignments, and 4) laboratory attendance. The point breakdown is as follows:

Midterm Exam 1:	100 pts.	Lab Quizzes/Assignments:	100 pts.
Midterm Exam 2:	100 pts.	Lab Attendance:	50 pts.
Midterm Exam 3:	100 pts.		
Final Exam:	200 pts.		

IMPORTANT COURSE POLICIES:

1. **Lecture Examinations:** All midterm examinations will be given at the regularly scheduled lecture time. The questions will be in a multiple choice format. Students are expected to take the midterm examinations and final examination on the dates scheduled on this syllabus. Make note of these dates! Vacations should NOT be planned to coincide with exam dates. Make-up exams will be given for absences due to serious illness (with medical excuse), emergencies (with appropriate documentation), and University-sponsored events. **Students should contact one of the professors as soon as possible regarding missed examinations.** The make-up exams will be a different format from the in-class exams; they will consist of short answer and essay questions.

2. **Laboratory Attendance:** The laboratory component of this course is **mandatory**. Attendance points will be deducted for each (unexcused) laboratory that you miss. If you know that you will miss lab, please notify your TA in advance. It may be possible for you to attend another section that week.

   Complete failure to attend the laboratory section will result in failure of the course. If you do not need a course with a laboratory, and do not plan to attend lab, you are advised to take a different course that does not have a laboratory component.

3. **Laboratory Quizzes and Assignments:** Laboratory quizzes and assignments will be made up and given by your own TA. Make-ups for missed lab quizzes/assignments will be at the discretion of each TA. The general policy is that missed work must be **made up within 1 week** of the original due date.

4. **Laboratory Content:** Some of the laboratory exercises are somewhat messy, and you may soil your clothing. We recommend that you **do not wear really nice clothing** to the laboratory. If you must dress up on occasion, bring something to wear over your good clothes. Several laboratory exercises will be **animal dissections**. Participation in the actual dissection is not required, but you will be expected to be familiar with the material.

5. **Accommodations will be made for any persons with disabilities.** We would like to hear from anyone who has a disability that may require modification of seating, testing, or other class requirements so that appropriate arrangements may be made. Please see the instructor after class or make an appointment with her.

Human Biology
Quiz 6 (Take home)

Name:
Section No: _____

INSTRUCTIONS: Because this is a take-home quiz, I expect answers to be thorough and written in complete sentences. Points will be deducted for use of incomplete sentences.

1. Light that enters the eye passes through four separate transparent structures or regions before reaching the retina, where it is absorbed. *Describe, in order, each of the four transparent structures/regions of the eye and what happens to the light at each of these places.* (If it helps you, you can draw a diagram, but remember to describe what you have drawn in complete sentences.) 6 pts.

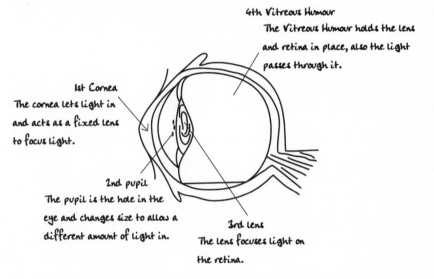

4th Vitreous Humour
The Vitreous Humour holds the lens
and retina in place, also the light
passes through it.

1st Cornea
The cornea lets light in
and acts as a fixed lens
to focus light.

2nd pupil
The pupil is the hole in the
eye and changes size to allow a
different amount of light in.

3rd lens
The lens focuses light on
the retina.

2. Discuss why a reflex (such as the knee-jerk reflex) occurs more rapidly than a conscious decision to move. 2 pts.

A reflex occurs more rapidly than a conscious decision to move
because there is only one synapse needed for a reflex action.
The lower the synapses the faster the reaction. A reflex is
also an automatic nervous response, meaning you wouldn't have
to think to do it. On the other hand, a person has to think
about it to move.

3. Suppose that your TA has handed you a bottle with an "unknown" substance in it. She tells you to determine whether the unknown is starch, sugar, or protein. She also gives you the following chemicals that you can use to test the unknown: Lugol's iodine solution (I_2KI), Clinitest tablets, and 70% $CaCl_2$. Based on what you learned in Exercise 7, *state what you would expect to see with each of the test chemicals* if the "unknown" substance is (a) starch, (b) sugar, or (c) protein. Hint: Each test chemical reacts with just one of the three possible substances and does not react with the other two (gives a negative result). 8 pts.

(A.) Starch

If the "unknown" substance was starch I would add Iodine to see if the substance turned purple or yellow. If the substance turns purple then starch is present but if it turns yellow then no starch is present.

(B.) Sugar

If the "unknown" substance is sugar I would try to use Clinitest tablets to see what color it might turn; orange, green or blue orange means there is lots of sugar, green means there is little sugar, and blue means no sugar.

(C.) Protein

If the "unknown" substance was protein I would use 70% $CaCl_2$ to test it. If there is any sort of white precipitate as a result of adding the $CaCl_2$ then protein is present.

4. Suppose that in a population of monster characters there are three different fur colors: blue, green, and yellow. Monsters with blue fur are the genotype BB, monsters with green fur are the genotype Bb, and monsters with yellow fur are genotype bb. Suppose that there are 100 monsters altogether: 49 with blue fur, 42 with green fur, and 9 with yellow fur. What is the frequency (%) of the B allele in this population? What is the frequency (%) of the b allele in this population? SHOW YOUR WORK. (4 pts.)

General % = $p^2 + 2pq + q^2$

$p + q = 1$

Frequency B = $\dfrac{2(48) + 7(42)}{200}$

= $\dfrac{98 + 42}{200}$

= $\dfrac{140}{200}$

The frequency of B allele s is T.

Frequency B = $\dfrac{2(9) + 7(42)}{200}$

= $\dfrac{18 + 42}{200}$

= $\dfrac{60}{200}$

= .3

100 monsters = total

49 BB
42 Bb
9 bb

0.7 + 0.3 = 1

The frequency of b allele s is 3.

5. Bonus Question: What is the date, time, and place of the Human Biology Final? (1 pt.) (Don't laugh. A few people miss the final every semester because they have written down the wrong thing!)

Thursday, December 20, 2:15

Natural Sciences Work Sample: Biology

This work sample is from a course in biology for non-majors. The course has a 2-hour lab each week and fulfills a general education requirement for a natural science with a laboratory. This course is taken primarily, but not exclusively, by freshman level students. This course covers four aspects of biology (cellular, genetic, physiological, and evolutionary) using mostly human examples. A high level of conceptual rigor is expected, rather than technical detail that typically is expected in an introductory course for biology majors.

The work sample shown is a laboratory quiz given near the end of the semester that covered material on two human organ systems (the nervous system and the digestive system) as well as material on population genetics. Although I would not evaluate the sample shown as "perfect," it is an example of very good work for several reasons: (1) the student followed the instructions (something some students fail to do and needlessly lose points for), (2) the answers were clearly written, with correct usage of specific vocabulary, (3) the student provided a very nice drawing of the eye which illustrated understanding of the biological system that the question addresses, and (4) the answers to each question were concise and addressed the point of the question without superfluous information. In sum, the student demonstrated a solid understanding (albeit not totally complete understanding for Questions 1 and 2) of a variety of concepts by providing clear, concise answers that did not contain irrelevant information. The answer to Question 1 had a small conceptual error in that the pupil is an opening (a hole) rather than a transparent region or structure. The student's description of the pupil was correct, but the second transparent region, the aqueous humor, actually lies in front of the pupil. The answer to Question 2 was missing one important piece of information and would not have been awarded full points. The student failed to explicitly state that reflexes do not involve the brain, but just sensory and motor neurons in the spinal cord.

With respect to the KSUS standards, the questions on this quiz assess the student's ability to apply several general foundational skills as well as their knowledge in several of the Biology categories. Questions 1–3 require that the student have knowledge of cell specialization (IV.A.3) and of the structural and functional specializations of different tissues, organs, and organ systems in a multicellular organism (IV.C.1). In addition, Question 3 requires that the student know how one can experimentally distinguish between different unknown biological molecules, thereby assessing standards I.A.1 as well as the student's knowledge of the different kinds of biological molecules. Question 4, which is a simple problem in population genetics, requires that the student have understanding of principles of inheritance (IV.B.1) as well as several foundational skills (I.C.1–3).

History _____   Issues: Communities in Society

Rural Communities in History

_____ Graduate Instructor

Term: Fall 2001
Class Time: Tuesdays and Thursdays, 8:05–9:20 AM
Place: _____ Hall Room 51
Website: http://www._____.
Email: _____. (I check Monday, Wednesday, Friday at
                   11 AM and 4 PM; Tuesday, Thursday at
                   7:50 AM and 4 PM)
Office: 380 _____ Hall
Office Hours: Tuesdays and Thursdays, 9:30–11:00 AM, and other times by
                   appointment
Office Phone: _____ (Or you may leave a message at _____.)

Objectives: This course examines rural communities in Europe and the United
                   States from the late Middle Ages to the twentieth century. We will be
                   considering how groups in different places and times organized their
                   social lives. Studying their communities will enable us to reflect on the
                   communities we grew up in and are a part of today.
                   By the end of this course, you should be able to: 1) describe dif-
                   ferent types of communities in history and in the world today; 2)
                   give a brief history of rural communities in Europe and the United
                   States from 1500 to the present.

                   The course also provides an introduction to the academic discipline
                   of history, historical literature, and the writing of history.
                   By the end of this course, you should be able to: 1) describe what
                   history is and what historians do; 2) consider texts critically: both
                   what was written in the past and what has been written about the
                   past; 3) construct a persuasive argument based on evidence.
                   All of these skills are of great use after college.

Class Time: Class time will usually be discussion, but from time to time I will
                   lecture briefly to provide background information. We will normally
                   discuss issues brought up by course readings, helping you to develop
                   skills of analysis, critical thinking, and clear speaking. In discussion,
                   you and I work together to meet course objectives.

You should expect to: Come to class, read assignments before class, prepare for class using discussion question handouts (see "Discussion Question" below), and contribute to group discussion (see "Participation" below).

I promise to: Come to class, read and think carefully about the work you hand in, write helpful comments on papers, tests, and other assignments, make discussions as interesting as possible, and answer questions both in and outside class.

Discussion Questions: Questions to assist you in thinking about the reading assignments will be handed out the class session before the reading is due. They are also available on the website (www._____) if you miss class. These will also be used to frame class discussion. You should write down your answers on the sheet and bring them to class. Also write down other questions and comments you may have about the reading—my questions are not necessarily all we will talk about in class.

Texts: The books to be used for the term are:
Strunk and White, *The Elements of Style,* 4th ed.
Natalie Zemon Davis, *The Return of Martin Guerre*
Course Reader—Available at _____. Copies.
Steven Hoch, *Serfdom and Social Control in Russia*
John Mack Faragher, *Sugar Creek: Life on the Illinois Prairie*
All books except the course reader are available at _____ Book and Supply, _____. The course reader is only available at _____. For books used later in the term, you may want to investigate Internet book services, including **half.com** for used books and **dealtime.com** for new books. Each will also be put on reserve at the library.

In addition, there will be some readings available on the Internet. You should probably print these out so that you can mark them up and bring them to class. They are marked (Web) in the course schedule.

Grading: You will be graded on: 1) your knowledge of history from class activities and texts, 2) your ability to think critically, to speak and write clearly, and to construct an argument based on evidence.

Breakdown:

Attendance and Class Participation		20%
Paper 1	(2–3 pages—due Week 3)	10%
Paper 2	(5–6 pages—due Week 5)	15%
Exam 1	(Week 8)	10%
Presentation Preview	(1–2 pages—due Week 12)	10%
Exam 2	(Week 14)	15%
In-Class Participation	(Weeks 15–16)	20%

I grade with pluses and minuses, and I do not grade on a curve.

Participation: Because discussion in class is a cooperative effort among all of us, 20 percent of your grade is based on your participation. Half of this grade is based on attendance, the other half on contributions to class discussions. This includes occasional in-class assignments such as quizzes or other writing assignments.

Attendance: Absences are excused if you notify me **before class** that you will not be in class. This can be done by talking to me, calling me, sending me email (I will check my email shortly before class starts), or leaving me a note in the History Department office. This is a matter of courtesy to me. Absences after class will be excused if I receive a note from the Athletic Department for university sports-related events, or from a physician or nurse for illnesses.

An excused absence means that you will receive points for attendance but not for participation.

Assignments: More information will be provided for each assignment well before it is due.

Paper 1 will be a 2–3 page paper based on Davis.

Paper 2 will be a 4–5 page paper based on Davis and the other readings about Martin Guerre.

Exam 1 will be over the first eight weeks of the course on rural communities in Europe and our discussion of history and community. It will also have questions about Hoch. There will be short answer and essay questions.

Exam 2 will be over the second six weeks of the course on rural communities in the United States. It will also have questions about Faragher. There will be short answer and essay questions.

In-Class Presentation will be a brief (no more than 10 minutes) talk to the class about the communities in which you grew up. You will use the knowledge gained from class to evaluate the nature and characteristics of those communities.

Presentation Preview will be a 1–2 page paper about what you expect to talk about in your in-class presentation.

Late assignments will be penalized one letter grade for each day they are late.

History Writing Center: The History Department has a writing center to assist you in writing papers for History courses. It is staffed with History graduate students who will help you think about writing or critique a draft of a paper. It is located in _____ Hall. Hours of service will be posted on the office door, or you may call to make an appointment at _____.

Plagiarism/Cheating: Any student who plagiarizes or cheats on any assignment faces penalties that may include an F on the assignment or an F in the course. If I suspect plagiarism or cheating, I am required to inform you in writing and to give you a copy of the report on the incident that I submit to the History Department and to the College of Liberal Arts.

Students with Disabilities: I would like to hear from anyone who has a disability that may require some modification of seating, testing, or other class requirements so that appropriate arrangements may be made. Please talk with me after class or during my office hours.

Questions/Problems: Please visit me during my office hours (or other times by appointment) to discuss your work or anything concerning the course. If you feel that we have not resolved the issue, you should talk to Professor _____, the Issues Coordinator. His office is _____ Hall and his telephone number is _____. You may also contact the Chair of the History Department, Professor _____. His office is _____ Hall, and his telephone number is _____.

Schedule: Each assignment should be read before the date listed. You should bring the discussion questions for the day with you to class and come prepared to discuss.

PART I—RURAL COMMUNITIES IN EUROPE

Week 1   **Introduction to the History of Rural Communities**

T, Aug 28	Class Topics:	Introduction to Course, Pass Out Syllabus, Introductions
		History and Sources
		Timeline of World History, Western Civilization
Th, Aug 30	Reading Assignment:	Coras, "A Memorable Decision . . . ," *Triquarterly* 55(1982): 86–103 (Handout, Web)
	Class Topics:	Preliminary Discussion of Coras
		Why Should Anyone Believe Anything at All?

Week 2   **Medieval Rural Communities in France**

T, Sep 4	Reading Assignment:	Davis, 1–61; Strunk and White, 1–14
	Class Topics:	Medieval European Agriculture
		Martin Guerre's France
		Martin and Bertrande
		Strunk and White on Usage
Th, Sep 6	Reading Assignment:	Davis, 62–125; Strunk and White, 15–33
	Class Topics:	Medieval Peasant Communities
		Law and Community
		Strunk and White on Composition

Week 3   **Writing History**

T, Sep 11	Reading Assignment:	Strunk and White, 66–85
	Class Topics:	Davis and Coras
		Communities in Davis—Family, Church, Village, Others?
		Strunk and White on Style
		Writing a history paper
Th, Sep 13	**PAPER 1 DUE**	2–3 page paper about Davis
	Reading Assignment:	None
	Class Topics:	The practice of history
		Thinking historically
		Asking questions
		Electronic sources for history

Week 4   **Disagreements Among Historians**

T, Sep 18	Reading Assignment:	Robert Finlay, "The Refashioning of Martin Guerre," *American Historical Review* 93(3)(1988): 553–571 (Web)

	Class Topics:	Disagreements among historians Constructing an argument Finlay vs. Davis
Th, Sep 20	Reading Assignment:	Natalie Zemon Davis, "On the Lame," *American Historical Review* 93(3)(1988): 572–603 (Web)
	Class Topics:	Davis vs. Finlay Critiquing an argument Writing an argumentative paper

Week 5   **Types of History**

T, Sep 25	Reading Assignment:	Hoch, 1–14
	Class Topics:	Intro to Hoch Questions about Paper 2 Reading academic books
Th, Sep 27	**PAPER 2 DUE**	5–6 page paper about Martin Guerre
	Reading Assignment:	None
	Class Topics:	Types of history: cultural, demographic, social, political . . . Asking questions

Week 6   **Rural Communities in Russia**

T, Oct 2	Reading Assignment:	Hoch, 15–64
	Class Topics:	Demographic History Nineteenth-Century Russian Peasant Agriculture
Th, Oct 4	Reading Assignment:	Hoch, 65–90
	Class Topics:	Serfdom and slavery Peasant families

Week 7   **Serfdom and Social Control in Russia**

T, Oct 9	Reading Assignment:	Hoch, 90–132
	Class Topics:	Peasant Communities—Family, Others?
Th, Oct 11	Reading Assignment:	Hoch, 133–159
	Class Topics:	Peasant Communities—Village, Others? Wrap-up on Hoch

Week 8   **Midterm Exam**

T, Oct 16	Reading Assignment:	None
	Class Topics:	Choose dates for in-class presentations Review for exam
Th, Oct 18	**EXAM 1**	Material covered to this point, one section on Hoch

PART II—RURAL COMMUNITIES IN THE UNITED STATES

Week 9   **Rural Communities in the U.S. North and South**

T, Oct 23   Reading Assignment: David Danborn, *Born in the Country,* pages
                                      1–38 (Reader)
              Class Topics: Early American Rural Communities
                                      U.S. Rural History
                                      U.S. Regions

Th, Oct 25   Reading Assignment: Peter Kolchin, "Reevaluating the Antebellum
                                      Slave Community," *Journal of American History*
                                      70(3)(1983): 579–601 (Web)
              Class Topics: Rural Communities in the South

Week 10   **The U.S. Midwest**

T, Oct. 30   Reading Assignment: Faragher, xiii–36
              Class Topics: Westward expansion
                                      Indians in the Midwest

Th, Nov 1   Reading Assignment: Faragher, 37–75
              Class Topics: Westward expansion
                                      Rural settlement

Week 11   **Rural Communities in the U.S. Midwest**

T, Nov 6   Reading Assignment: Faragher, 76–118
              Class Topics: The Midwestern Rural Family
Th, Nov 8   Reading Assignment: Faragher, 119–170
              Class Topics: Rural Communities in the Midwest:
                                      School Neighborhood, Church

Week 12   **Rural Communities in the Midwest/Far West**

T, Nov 13   Reading Assignment: Faragher, 171–237
              Class Topics: Continuity and Change
                                      Historical Memory

Th, Nov 15   **PRESENTATION PREVIEW DUE**
              Reading Assignment: David Vaught, "Factories in the Field Revisited,"
                                      Pacific Historical Review 66(2)(May 1997):
                                      149–184 (Reader)
              Class Topics: Rural Communities in California

Week 13   **Rural Communities in Twentieth Century**

T, Nov 20   Reading Assignment: Valerie Grim, "From Plantation to Society,"
                                      Locus 7(1)(1994): 1–30 (Web)
              Class Topics: The South after the Civil War

Th, Nov 22   NO CLASS—HAPPY THANKSGIVING

Week 14   **Rural Communities in the Twentieth Century**

T, Nov 27   Reading Assignment: Paula Nelson, "Rural Life and Social Change in
                                    the Modern West," in *The Rural West Since
                                    World War II*, 38–57 (Reader)

             Class Topics: The Twentieth-Century Midwest and West
Th, Nov 29   **EXAM 2**   Material in Second Half of Class, Section on
                                    Faragher

             (The final exam was originally scheduled for Friday, December 21,
             at 7:00 PM.)

Week 15   **In-class presentations**

T, Dec 4   In-class presentations

Th, Dec 6   In-class presentations

Week 16   **In-class presentations**

T, Dec 11   In-class presentations

Th, Dec 13   In-class presentations

Paper 2 Assignment: Martin Guerre

Due: At the beginning of class, Tuesday, September 27 (Different from Syllabus)

Assignment: This paper is to be based on Jean de Coras's "A Memorable Decision," Natalie Zemon Davis's *The Return of Martin Guerre,* Robert Finlay's "The Refashioning of Martin Guerre," and Natalie Zemon Davis's "On the Lame."

Your assignment is to assess Davis's and Finlay's arguments about what happened in the case of Martin Guerre. Answer one or more of the following questions: What do you think actually happened in this case? Do you believe Davis's narrative or Finlay's? Do you find some parts of both of their arguments believable? What do you find convincing in their accounts? How do they use Coras's narrative differently?

Be sure to support your argument with evidence from the sources. Please feel free to talk to me or visit the History Writing Center at any stage of your writing.

Length: 5–6 pages, typed, double-spaced

Writing: Your paper should have the following:
1. An introduction that presents your thesis—the argument that you are going to make—and previews your main points.
2. A body that gives evidence from the readings and explains how it supports your thesis.
3. A conclusion that restates your thesis and briefly reviews how you supported it.

Follow the rules for usage and composition in Strunk and White's *The Elements of Style.* Edit your own work.

Grading: I am looking for:
1. A strong, solid argument, supported by evidence.
2. Good organization: your thesis is presented in an introduction, is developed and supported throughout the paper, and leads to a solid conclusion.
3. A satisfactory understanding of the source's content.
4. Correct spelling, punctuation, and grammar.

– OVER –

Please note that according to the College of Liberal Arts:

A – Superior work   D – Below average work

B – Above average work   F – Failing work

C – Average work

Quotations: Include quotes from the sources that support the point you are trying to make, but don't just use quotes to pad your paper. Make sure that you explain why you used each quote.

Citation: To cite a quote or an idea, put the author's last name and page numbers in parentheses.

Examples: Coras – (Coras, 88)

Davis, *The Return of Martin Guerre* – (Davis, *Return*, 50)

Davis, "On the Lame" – (Davis, "Lame," 574)

Finlay – (Finlay, 556)

If you use a source outside those assigned, provide a bibliography. Please see me or consult *A Manual for Writers of Term Papers, Theses, and Dissertations* by Kate Turabian (6th ed., Chicago, 1996), pp. 185–213 for more information.

Plagiarism: Any student who plagiarizes faces penalties that may include an F on the assignment or an F in the course. Plagiarism is using the words or ideas of someone else without giving them credit.

Format: In preparing the paper, please do the following:

1. Have a cover sheet with the following information:
   a. Your name
   b. The title of the paper
      (You may include the date, course title, etc., if you like.)
2. At the top of the first page of text, put the title of the paper **but not your name.**
3. **Do not put your name on any pages of the paper.** (Except the cover sheet.)
4. Number your pages.
5. Use a 12 point Times or Times New Roman font and 1-inch margins.
6. Staple the pages together in the upper-left-hand corner.
7. **Staple this paper on top of Paper 1.**

A Silent Partner

It is hard to extract the truth from a story like Martin Guerre. It seems as though much is left to the imagination. Reading three different perspectives of the story just made me even more cautious and confused as to what is the real truth. After studying all the authors I have to come to the conclusion that Bertrande was not as innocent as she seemed but rather a key participant in Arnaud du Tilh's scheme. Although others may disagree, I believe there is more to the story than just the account given by Coras. It is not as black and white as Finlay interprets it. There are four key points to look at when looking at Bertrande's role in Arnaud's plot: the "touch of a man" on a woman, the characteristics of Bertrande's personality, her actions during the trial, and her independence as a woman. I believe that Bertrande participated in Arnaud's plot in ways that would only benefit herself and that may be the reason that she is looked at as dupe. She finally decided to go along with the accusations that Arnaud was not her real husband but in fact she was just covering for herself. Therefore, I believe Bertrande was an accomplice in Arnaud's scheme to impersonate Martin Guerre.

When Arnaud and Bertrande began to have a sexual relationship it is hard to believe that she took Arnaud to be the real Martin without question. How could a spouse not remember the ways of her man? The "touch of a man theory" created by Davis, however, does not just apply to actually having intercourse but it also relates to the ways that Martin might have held her prior to his departure. (Davis, "Lame," 578) "Thus when Bertrande finally found herself in the embrace of Arnaud du Tilh, she was feeling a body unlike the one she had lain next to and held for nine or ten years, unclothed as well as clothed." (Davis, "Lame," 578) Even a more obvious difference between Arnaud and Martin were the different physical characteristics Arnaud displayed. "The village shoemaker also testified that Martin Guerre's shoe size was larger than that of the man claiming to be the husband of Bertrande do Rols." (Davis, "Lame," 578) There was also evidence that permanent marks, such as scars and warts also differed between Martin and Arnaud. Arnaud also lacked the ability to fence and perform acrobatics. He had two real legs as opposed to the wooden one that a soldier claimed Martin Guerre had received from a battle he fought in. (Davis, "Lame," 580) With these different physical characteristics in mind Bertrande must have realized that Arnaud was truly an imposter, however, she went along with his plans. "I think more plausible for a wife, since Arnaud was not just stockier but shorter and squatter than her husband and she washed those smaller feet—is that Bertrande 'knew,' despite the passage of years, that she was not being held by the real Martin Guerre." (Davis, "Lame," 578)

Bertrande continued to support Arnaud through all the allegations that arose after Pierre Guerre accused Arnaud of being an imposter. She was determined to keep him as her husband, and I believe it is because she was an accomplice, not a dupe. Bertrande finally gave in the morning Arnaud was arrested. (Davis, "Lame," 580) "The stubborn woman calculated and made her plans. She would go along with the court case against the imposter and hope to lose it. She would follow the strategy she had worked out with the new Martin about testimony and hope that the judge would declare him her husband." (Davis, *Return*, 60) There wasn't any new evidence that had surfaced that would give reason for Bertrande to think any differently of Arnaud when her decision was made. (Davis, *Return*, 61) Actually, according to Coras: Pierre Guerre and his wife (Bertrande's mother) were "even threatening her with dragging her out of the house if she did not say it." (Coras, 95) Bertrande was left with no choice but to testify. "Beyond this threat to her access to her children, to her relatives, and to family property was the threat to her reputation and even to her life if Pierre and her mother went so far as to accuse her of complicity in a serious case of adultery and fraud." (Davis, "Lame," 581) Although Bertrande eventually went along with the accusations that Arnaud was an imposter, her support in other ways failed to stop. The day of Arnaud's incarceration she sent money and clothing to his jail cell. (Davis, 61) This is a strong signal of her support for the imposter. I believe this was the only thing Bertrande could still do to support Arnaud. I argue that Bertrande may have feared she would be questioned as an accomplice if she did not go along with her family. Bertrande was looking out for herself and she could not risk her reputation in the village, or take the risk of being jailed herself if she was questioned or found guilty as a co-conspirator.

Another convincing piece of evidence that supports my argument is the way Bertrande acted in court. When she testified she refused to take an oath that said Arnaud was not her husband. While being questioned Bertrande spoke of private relationships she had with the real Martin Guerre. (Davis, "Lame," 581) After the real

Martin Guerre testified, "the justices had the prisoner brought, to whom they put the same questions, as many as ten or twelve, to which he replied completely like the other." (Coras, 98) I do not think it was a coincidence that Arnaud could also relay the same information. Bertrande and Arnaud must have conspired before the trials. Surely Bertrande could have told of some instances that Arnaud couldn't have known about from his own studies of Martin Guerre. Davis provides another possible theory of why Arnaud could have given such compelling testimony "Are we to imagine one of the judges or a scribe feeding plaintiff and defendant each other's words?" (Davis, "Lame," 582) I think this is a very unrealistic theory. Bertrande must have discussed her testimony with Arnaud prior to the trial. Bertrande was also covering herself by not taking the oath. If she was later found to be an accomplice, they could not hold perjury against her. "She did her best to help Arnaud be declared her husband by the court, while protecting her own life and reputation whatever the outcome." (Davis, "Lame," 583)

According to Davis, Bertrande was a woman of independence. (Davis, "Lame," 584) While Martin Guerre was away she remained faithful. Bertrande wanted to keep her status as a married woman, for her large inheritance would be lost if she became a single woman or an adulteress. When Arnaud appeared claiming to be Martin Guerre, this was the perfect opportunity for her to reclaim her social status. "On occasion a distinctive independence and willingness to take some risks to escape from her predicament." (Davis, "Lame," 584) I believe the "willingness to take some risks to escape from her predicament" is best shown in the way Bertrande took Arnaud in as her husband. Bertrande was taking a chance that Arnaud's true identity would never be questioned and that she could go back to a normal life. She also took chances by giving Arnaud information that she thought might be helpful in his testimony. However, she was smart enough and independent enough to go along with her family's accusations that Arnaud was an imposter, for fear that she may lose her freedom if she was found to be an accomplice. To help justify her actions of deceit, Natalie Zemon Davis speculates that Bertrande may have changed her religious views to those of Protestantism. (Davis, *Return*, 48) Because Bertrande wouldn't have to speak directly to God, she would never have to reveal the real truth to a priest. "It is probable even possible that the new Martin and Bertrande de Rols were becoming interested in the new religion, in part because they could draw from it another justification for their lives." (Davis, *Return*, 48)

Robert Finlay may disagree on some of these arguments but I believe that is because he only looks at Coras's account and his interpretation is based on moral values. One of Finlay's arguments is that because Martin and Bertrande were married at such a young age and did not have sexual intercourse for the majority of the time, that Bertrande would not recognize Arnaud as the imposter by the way he touched her. Like I have stated earlier, the "touch of a man" does not only deal with sexual intercourse but also the way a husband might hold his wife or touch her in any nonsexual manner. (Davis, "Lame," 578) It is absurd to think that Bertrande would not have recognized her own husband even after a few years. She spent adequate time with Martin before his departure, she surely would have recognized Arnaud's touch as that of a stranger.

Another of Finlay's arguments pertains to the way Davis portrays Bertrande. Finlay believes Davis depicts Bertrande's character "as an instance of the ingenuity and calculation commonly shown by peasant women who must maneuver within a patriarchal system."(Finlay, 556) It is true that Davis depicts Bertrande as calculating, however, she does it with good reason. Bertrande has shown her personality to be very deceitful and crafty. She helped Arnaud with his testimony, but in a subtle way that she would not be questioned for adultery. It is also evident that she must have known within a few days that Arnaud was truly an imposter by his physical characteristics, but rather than accuse him of being an imposter she went along with his scheme. Finlay also believes that because Davis is the first woman to comment on the story of Martin Guerre until the twentieth century, it may have impaired her judgment of Bertrande. (Finlay, 557) I, on the other hand disagree. Although Davis' gender might have played a small role in her perception of Bertrande, it does not mean that her interpretation of the story is incorrect. It is unfortunate that Davis may be the first person to give Bertrande enough credit to think she could pull off such a scheme like I believe she did, however, this does not mean it is not possible. I believe that it is very possible, and most likely what happened because of the evidence I have stated.

As a result of analyzing all the interpretations of Martin Guerre I have come to the conclusion that Bertrande was in fact the accomplice of Arnaud. There is substantial evidence to support my theory such as Bertrande's personality, her actions in and out of the courtroom, her independence and the fact that she would have recognized the real Martin by his touch. The story of Martin Guerre is not as black and white as it seems. Looking at the story with an open mind is all that is needed to understand my argument. Coras' account is not the truth, but rather the evidence he had and how he interpreted it. Bertrande was a calculating, intelligent, woman who succeeded in her plot to have Arnaud become her new husband.

Social Sciences Work Sample: History

This work sample was for a course surveying rural communities in history. We studied the history of five hundred years of rural communities and applied knowledge about those communities (family, locality, church, school) to the communities we live in today. The syllabus laid out the expectations for the course: in general, students had to read texts carefully, think about them critically, talk about them in class intelligently, and write about them persuasively.

This paper gives a very good idea of how a college student should be able to think about a difficult issue, formulate an answer to a question, and support an argument with evidence from the past. The assignment was not an easy one; we had read three different accounts of a very confusing historical event: a man in late medieval France was accused of impersonating another woman's husband. One of the accounts was written shortly after the event; the other two were written by historians in the last twenty years. Students had to weigh the evidence and the interpretations and make an argument about what they believed actually happened.

The paper shows that the student was able to perceive events and circumstances from the vantage point of people who lived five hundred years ago with historical empathy. (Standards I. A. 5 and I. C. 4) The student evaluated different historical interpretations and chose the one she thought was most reliable. (Standards I. C. 7 and VII. C. 3.) She then constructed an argument that supported the thesis she had chosen.

Organizationally, the student laid out the paper's thesis and previewed the main points of the argument in the first paragraph. The paper then addressed each point, providing evidence from the sources. Quotations and other important pieces of information are cited in parentheses. This student even provided some possible counterarguments and responded to them. She then brought all of the arguments together again in the final paragraph. (Standards VIII)

Samples: Elementary Spanish Review

Background information about the course and the student population

The General Education requirement in foreign language is fulfilled when a student passes the fourth-semester course. It is possible to fulfill the requirement by studying four years of a language in high school, or by getting a qualifying score on a locally developed placement test. Students who do not fulfill the requirement before entering the university may continue with the language they studied in high school or may start a new language here. Most entering students who choose to continue their study of high school Spanish place into one of two courses: Elementary Spanish Review or Intermediate Spanish I.

Elementary Spanish Review is composed entirely of students who have studied Spanish in high school for two years or longer but who are not yet ready for Intermediate Spanish. Elementary Spanish Review is characterized by a wide range of student profiles. In a section of 20 students, some may have allowed several years to pass since their last Spanish class in high school; others may not have taken their high school Spanish study seriously; still others could have started with Intermediate Spanish I, but prefer to start with a course at the elementary level to consolidate their skills and knowledge.

Elementary Spanish Review classes, which meet daily for 50 minutes, are conducted entirely in Spanish. The course carries 5 semester hours of credit. Course materials include a textbook, workbook, lab manual with audio tapes, web site, and video. Students are expected to spend at least 2 hours per day outside of class studying on their own and completing homework assignments. The following is a summary of the goals of Elementary Spanish that is included in the course overview:

> The primary goal of the first-year Spanish program is to enable students to achieve basic communicative skill in Spanish. The various activities in the program are designed to provide you with many models of written and spoken Spanish and to give you many opportunities to interact with both your instructor and your fellow students.

> By the end of first-year Spanish, you should be able to do the following:
> (a) understand spoken Spanish in simple conversations directed to you, and understand the main ideas of videos about Hispanic cultures;
> (b) speak Spanish well enough to communicate simply and survive in a Spanish-speaking country;
> (c) handle the basic tenses and other grammatical forms in simple sentences in speaking and writing;
> (d) understand the main ideas and some details of short printed texts such as announcements, newspaper articles, advertisements, brochures, etc.

(e)   write short compositions;

(f)   understand some of the cultural values and practices of the Hispanic world.

Writing in Elementary Spanish Review

The formal writing component of the course consists of four essays, all of which are written during one class period. Each writing activity is linked to a course theme and (tangentially) to structures that are taught in that segment of the course. Some writing activities, like the one from which the work samples below are drawn, involve interviewing a classmate and then incorporating the information obtained through the interview into the essay.

Explanation of the writing activity from which the samples of student work come:

This writing activity takes place shortly before the midpoint of the semester (week 6). First, students read and discuss in class an article on healthful eating. Then they interview a partner about his or her eating habits. Following guidelines suggested by the article, students find out as much as they can about what their partner eats on a regular basis for meals and snacks. Then, the following day, they write in class an essay in which they describe their partner's diet and analyze it for healthfulness (or lack thereof) according to the information in the article. [**Note:** If a student missed the previous day's class (and therefore has no partner), that student should write about his/her own diet and otherwise follow the guidelines below.]

The guidelines for writing are as follows:

Writing Activity #2: ¿Come inteligentemente mi compañero/-a de clase?

Your composition will have four parts:

- An opening paragraph, in which you briefly explain the importance of a having a good diet, and make a transition to the second paragraph

- A detailed description of your partner's eating habits

- An analysis of your partner's diet in terms of the criteria in "Coma inteligente ¡y viva más!."

- A brief conclusion

Elementary Spanish Work Sample

This is a strong introduction that [pre]sents the topic of the essay and [ma]kes a transition to the example; [tha]t is, the diet of the writer's friend [Kar]i. The introductory paragraph [cou]ld be further strengthened by a [lin]e that put the reader in an appro-[pria]te frame of mind.

(1) Es muy importante que las personas tienen una dieta muy buena. Necesi-tan muchos nutrientes y poco grasa, sal, y colesterol para una vida buena y larga. Muchas personas la conocen pero no tienen una dieta buena. Aquí está la dieta de mi amiga, Kari.

[The] high level of [ling]uistic accuracy [and] skill in discourse [can] be seen here in [the] appropriate use [of c]onnectors (tam-[bié]n), the accurate [use] of compound [ver]bs (debe comer), [and] ability to use di-[rec]t object pronouns [(no] lo come) to create [com]plex sentences. [Som]e errors do re-[ma]in, however, con-[trol] of the gustar [con]struction takes a [lon]g time to acquire.

Kari tiene una dieta regular. Es más buena que mala, pero ella necesita más nutrientes. Kari debe eliminar nada de su dieta. Todo la comida que Kari come es buena y conjunto de nutrientes. Kari necesita comer mucho carne más porque ella no lo come. También, ella debe comer más pescado porque no lo come (1a). Pero, Kari no le gusta pescado. Kari le gusta pan mucho. Ella come mucho. Pero, necesita comer un poco más para una buena dieta. Kari debe comer más arroz y más verduras también. (2)

(2) The writer in-cludes what the part-ner eats regularly and also what she does not eat. The writer both describes and evaluates his/her partner's diet. The evaluation consists of unsupported state-ments. To be convinc-ing, the evaluations should be justified, ideally by references to the article.

"Coma inteligente ¡y vida más!" dice que es importante que las personas tienen una dieta buena. Dice que las _____ (3) no deben comer grasa, sal, y colesterol. Kari no come comida mala. No come mucho grasa, sal, o colesterol. Ella come cinco raciones de frutas todos los días, pero ella necesita comer dos más raciones de verduras todos los días porque necesita seís raciones. También, Kari bebe la leche descremada y el artículo nos dice que la es buena y no tiene mucha grasa. Kari no come las yemas de nuevos porque tienen mucho colesterol. Pero, ella come las claras con mucha proteína. (3a) Kari debe comer más carne con color de mármol porque es muy importante y ella no lo come. Tambien, ella debe comer pescado. (4)

[This] is a simple [dra]ft writing activity [tha]t students produce [in c]lass. If there had [bee]n an opportunity [to r]evise, the student [cou]ld have been [ask]ed to tighten up [the] organization by [elim]inating repetition [suc]h as this.

(3) Something went wrong here. It looks like the writer needed a word and did not use the dic-tionary or the in-structor (who serves as a resource during writing activities).

En conclusión, Kari tiene una dieta regular pero necesita más de las comidas importantes con nutrientes. Ella tiene una dieta más buena que yo. No tenho una dieta buena. Me gusta más las comidas con grasa y sal. También, hay mala comida en mi resedencía y no la como. (5) (6)

[The] references to [the] article are clear [and], for the most [par]t, persuasive. [The]re is still no [exp]lanation of why [ma]rbled meat and [fish] are important [in a] sound diet.

(5) The conclusion summarizes the foregoing discus-sion, and briefly draws a comparison between the part-ner's diet and the writer's diet. The last sentence leaves us hanging; it does not sum up the con-tent of the essay.

(6) This is an excellent sample of writing for a student at this level. The writer has presented a good level of information from the article, has described and evaluated the information, and has few linguistic errors.

Second Language Work Sample Comments: Elementary Spanish

This assignment required students to use their listening, speaking and writing skills. They were asked to conduct interviews in Spanish with their classmates, asking about their eating habits as a basis for the writing activity.

The sample shows that, despite some grammatical errors, the student can write simple sentences, using basic tenses and other grammatical forms well enough to convey meaning to the reader. Further, the student shows writing skills in organizing the composition with an introductory paragraph, followed by a description and analysis of the partner's eating habits and then a short conclusion. As students develop proficiency in a second language, they should be able to analyze information, express ideas, and defend personal opinions, as the student does in this work sample.

APPENDIX A: CHECKLIST FOR COLLEGE READINESS

The Checklist for College Readiness is composed of specific examples of college readiness indicators that correspond to one or more of the KSUS foundational skills and content standards. All were written by university faculty who teach courses to first-year students. They describe the knowledge and skill levels and assignments expected from students in entry-level university courses. As a result, many are at a level that students are unlikely to reach by the time they graduate from high school. Nevertheless, these examples are illustrative of the expectations students face when they arrive at college. Students should be striving to gain competence in or at least familiarity with as many as possible. The senior year is a particularly good time to expand and consolidate knowledge in these areas and strive toward these expectations.

The statements in the checklist are written from a student's perspective. High school students can read each statement, then determine which of four performance levels best describes their knowledge and skill level relative to the statement. Teachers can share the statements with students in their classes as a way to illustrate what will be expected of them in college and why they should work hard in high school to develop the necessary knowledge and skill. Alternatively, teachers or members of a task force charged with assessing the school's college prep program can score each statement based on their judgment of which performance level best describes the school's students collectively. The individual scores can be summed to a total that can be averaged by discipline or across all disciplines. The average score helps suggest how close a typical graduate of the high school is to college readiness.

- 3. Mastery: *I do this well or I understand this well. I can apply this knowledge/skill appropriately with deep conceptual and procedural understanding.*

- 2. Competence: *I do this pretty well or I understand this pretty well. When I apply this knowledge/skill, I have to think about it carefully. I do not necessarily have a deep understanding of the conceptual basis underlying the knowledge/skill.*

- 1. Developing: *I cannot apply this knowledge/skill yet with consistency. I do not do this well or understand this well, but I understand what is required to do this well, and I am working to develop competence and eventual mastery of this knowledge/skill.*

- 0. New knowledge: *I do not have this knowledge/skill. I have not yet encountered this knowledge/skill in my high school education, or if I have, I do not recall it well enough to use it.*

An average score of 2.0 overall would indicate to teachers or the members of a task force that their school's college preparatory curriculum is strong, although this still suggests much room for improvement because half the graduates are below this point. A score much below 2.0 would point to the need to make substantive changes in the curriculum. A score above 2.5 would indicate the school is doing a good job overall covering content and may want to focus on deepening student understanding.

The checklist included here is designed to be illustrative and not comprehensive in nature. It contains many good examples of what students are expected to know and do to succeed in entry-level college courses. Its content is limited to standards for which reasonably clear examples could be generated. Some of the KSUS standards are more integrative in nature and do not lend themselves to specific examples, such as many of those in the mathematical reasoning section. Some of the statements encompass more than one KSUS standard. Work samples provide additional insight into what is expected in entry-level courses (see Chapter Seventeen). More statements can be reviewed on the Standards for Success Web site at http://ww.s4s.org.

English

Reading and Comprehension

When I read a difficult passage, I take the time to make sure I understand it before moving on. I attempt to relate it to prior learnings and personal experience, when possible.

I make notes on the page of the book I am reading (if I own it) or on a separate sheet of paper as I read, identifying key points as well as questions I have about what is written and observations about main points.

When I read something, I think about whether I agree with the point the author is making. I think critically about what is written and how it is presented, including the quality of the logic, the writing style employed, and the manner in which the author attempts to engage the reader.

As I read, I am able to figure out the point the author is trying to make, and I can also see the implications the author's point has for other similar situations.

To do this, I observe what proof or evidence the author includes, the kind of language used to influence my thinking, and whether the author's point of view or argument has a logical structure to it and is convincing.

When I read a poem or story, I think about how the plot and style resemble other works I've read. I look at conventions like the structure of the plot, the types of characters, and lengths and numbers of lines in poetry. I use these observations to decide if the author is writing in a specific literary form.

When I read a poem or story, I ask myself what ideas the author is trying to express through her language, style, and characters. When I think about qualities of a text such as character development or tone, I ask myself how these qualities allow the author to express or emphasize particular ideas.

I look for clues in the plot, language, and style of the texts I read that might give me insight into the moral, religious, or philosophical views of the author. I try to keep in mind that texts from different cultures and time periods might be influenced by religious or social conventions that are different from my own.

When I encounter a word I don't know, I try to figure out what it means by looking at the context of the line or sentence in which it appears and by associating the word with similar words I do know. If that doesn't work, I circle the word. After I've read the whole text through once, I go back and look up all the words I didn't know in the dictionary.

When I read narrative, I think about how the imagery, the tone, and the details of the story affect the way I react to it. I don't assume that the author and the narrator are the same person. Instead, I think about how the author might be using the narrator along with the other aspects of the narrative to add particular spins or shades of meaning to the story.

When I read a text, I think about how the author's culture and historical period might have influenced the ideas she expresses through her writing. I particularly look for places where the author's attitudes, morals, or political beliefs are different from mine, and I take these differences into account when I analyze the text.

I feel comfortable with my ability to interpret graphs, charts, and illustrations. When I encounter these things in a text, I examine them carefully and ask myself what they add to my understanding of the author's points.

Writing

I know the definition and function of each part of speech—noun, verb, adverb, adjective, pronoun, preposition, and interjection. I know how to change a word from one part of speech into another (for example, an adjective into an adverb or a noun into an adjective) by adding, changing, or removing suffixes.

I understand what subject/verb agreement and pronoun/antecedent agreement are. I am confident in my ability to maintain agreement in my writing.

I know what prewriting strategies work best for me. I know when and how to brainstorm for ideas, and I know how to develop an outline to focus and structure my ideas.

I am confident in my ability to construct paragraphs. I know how to write effective topic sentences that introduce my ideas and concluding sentences that create logical connections between my paragraphs. When I revise, I know how to look for paragraphs that are too long, too short, or awkwardly constructed.

I am confident in my ability to construct sentences without grammatical errors. I can avoid sentence fragments and run-on sentences. I understand the different types of sentences (simple, compound, etc.), and I can use all of these types.

I know how to develop my ideas effectively throughout an essay or a single piece of writing. I know how to break down my ideas into clear individual points. I know how to put these individual points into the order that will be most effective for the piece as a whole.

I am able to find the right words to express my ideas. I understand how and when to adjust my choice of words for different audiences and different types of writing. When necessary, I can use a dictionary or a thesaurus to help me choose the most appropriate word for a given situation.

I am comfortable with the style I am developing in my writing. I am able to write essays that meet the requirements of a given assignment but still express my own ideas and personality. When I read my writing, I feel that it reflects me.

I can use a formal documentation style (i.e., MLA or APA) to format my essay, document my use of outside sources, and construct a bibliography.

I know how to focus all of my ideas for a particular essay into a single clear thesis statement.

I can use a thesis to add structure to an essay. I understand how to go from having a thesis to developing individual points that support the thesis. I know how to make connections throughout my essay between my evidence, my individual points, and my thesis.

When I write, I give at least some thought to how my audience will react to my writing. When I revise, I make it a point to look for places where awkward grammar, sentence construction, or paragraph construction might make it difficult for readers to comprehend my ideas.

When I write, I think about the type of audience who will be reading my work, and I adjust my writing style to best fit that audience's expectations while still expressing my ideas.

I understand what elements make a piece of writing more or less formal, and I am able to adjust the formality of my writing as the occasion demands.

When I proofread my writing, I am able to catch and correct all spelling, punctuation, and grammar errors.

When I revise, I am able to make substantial changes that improve the overall structure or content of my writing.

As I revise, I can identify places where my ideas need to be expressed more clearly, developed more fully, or integrated more effectively into the essay as a whole.

When I receive comments on a draft from my instructor or my peers, I can use these comments to help direct my revisions.

Research Skills

When I am presented with a research assignment, I can quickly decide what research tools will be most useful for completing that assignment, and I can formulate a plan that will allow me to find the information and sources I need quickly.	
I can use the library and the Internet to find both print and electronic sources. I understand the strengths and weaknesses of books, periodicals, electronic databases, and Web sites as sources of information.	
I understand what plagiarism is. I know how to use outside sources to support my ideas without stealing or misusing other people's work. I understand how and why to document all the sources I use in my writing.	
When I find sources on the Internet, I know how to evaluate the currency and credibility of those sources. I have a solid understanding of when to trust and when not to trust information from the Internet.	

Critical Thinking

When I read new texts or encounter new ideas, I consciously compare them to my own ideas and experiences rather than passively absorbing the information.	
When I read texts, I can identify whether a theory is used to frame the ideas and information presented, and I can understand how the author has used various elements including evidence to support the theory. In the process, I can judge if the author is credible and the theory reasonable.	
I am comfortable expressing my ideas and opinions to others, even when I am just forming them.	
I can put forth an argument that is supported by evidence and a logic framework that makes the argument reasonable and compelling. When I present my argument, I do so in a way that anticipates the major criticisms the argument will encounter, and I have some awareness of any weaknesses in my argument.	
I am able to think about the assumptions underlying my own beliefs. I am willing to consider how my opinions are viewed from the perspectives of those who may not agree with me, no matter how strongly I believe them.	

Mathematics

Computation

Compute and simplify: $\dfrac{5}{12} - \dfrac{3}{8}$

Simplify: $\dfrac{75,600}{15,876}$

Simplify: $\dfrac{2^4}{6^3}, \left(\dfrac{2^3 \times 3^2}{3^3 \times 2^2}\right)^{-1}$.

Simplify: $2\sqrt{8} - \sqrt{18}$

Write the following in decreasing order:

$-1, 10^{-2}, 0.01, \pi, -\dfrac{1}{10}, 10^{-3}, \dfrac{1}{\pi}, \dfrac{1}{10}, \pi^2$.

Compute: $2 - |1-4| - |5-1|$

Compute: $2\left(3 - 4(1-2) + 3(1-2)\right)$

Which of the following numbers are rational numbers?

$0, -\dfrac{1}{2}, \sqrt{2}, \dfrac{\sqrt{9}}{2}, -\dfrac{7}{3}, \dfrac{3}{\sqrt{8}}, \sqrt[3]{8}, 2.\overline{66}$.

Compute and simplify the following expression for the given values of a, b, and c.

$\dfrac{-b \pm \sqrt{b^2 - 4ac}}{2a}$ when $a = 1$, $b = -1$, and $c = -1$.

Find the remainder when $(x^3 + 1)$ is divided by $(x - 1)$.

If $A = \{0, 3, 6, 9, 12, 15\}$ and $B = \{0, 2, 4, 6, 8, 10, 12\}$ find $A \cup B$ and $A \cap B$.

If $h = (m + n)$ and $k = (m - n)$, find and simplify: $hk + \left(\dfrac{h - k}{2}\right)^2$ in terms of m and n

Algebra

Distribute: $-2(2x-1)(x^3-x-2)$

Compute and simplify the following expression: $\left(\dfrac{x}{x-2}-\dfrac{x-2}{x}\right)\div\dfrac{2-x}{x}$

Simplify whenever possible. Do not factor out.

a) x^3-x^2 b) $\dfrac{x^{-2}}{x^{-3}}$ c) $\sqrt{\left(x^{-1}\right)^{-2}}$

Prove the following statement: $\left(\dfrac{1}{25}\right)^m=\dfrac{5^{n-m}}{5^{n+m}}$

Factor out completely. $P(x)=x^4-1$ $Q(x)=x^6-1$

Solve for x. $3(x-2)-2x=5-2(x-3)$

Solve for x. $20-|3-2x|\le 10$

Solve the following system of equations.
$\begin{cases}2x-3=15\\3x+5y=32\end{cases}$

Solve the following equation. Exact answers only (no decimals).
$2u^2-7u=5$

Solve the following equation: $(2x-3)^2(x^2+1)(x+2)=0$

Graph $y=x^2-3x-1$

Find the range of the function defined by $f(x)=2x^2+3x-3$

Find the domain of the function defined by $f(x)=\dfrac{\sqrt{x-1}}{x+2}$

Find both intercepts of the line with equation $2x-3y+5=0$

Find all the intercepts of the parabola with equation $y=2x^2-5x-3$

Find the speed of the current in a river if it takes twice as long for a boat to cover a distance upstream than it takes to cover the same distance downstream, if the speed of the boat in still water is 5 mph.

Geometry

In the figure below, find the length of segment DE with the given hypotheses.

ABE is a right triangle. CD is parallel to AB. $\overline{AE} = 10$. $\overline{AB} = 3$. $\overline{CD} = 2$.

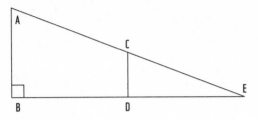

The square below is inscribed in a circle of radius of length 3. Find the area of the shaded region.

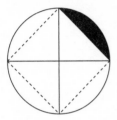

If the measure of angle D is five times the measure of angle C, what is the measure of angle A?

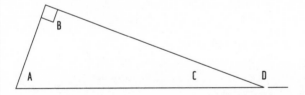

The volume of a cylinder is 16π cubic inches. If the height and the diameter of the cylinder are equal, what is the radius?

Find the slope of the line that is perpendicular to the line with equation $2x + 3y = 6$ and goes through the point $(1, -2)$.

Find the perimeter of the triangle whose vertices are: A $(1, 2)$ B $(4, 1)$ C $(0, 1)$

How long is the shadow of a 6-foot-tall person who stands 3 feet away from a 10-foot-high street light?

Mathematical Reasoning

A, B, C, D are points on the circle with center O. Prove that measure of angle CAD plus measure of angle CBD is equal to 180°.

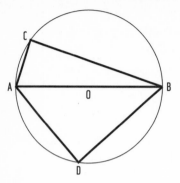

Prove or disprove the following statement: $|a+b|=|a|+|b|$ for all real numbers a and b.

Natural Sciences

General Foundation Skills

I understand what is meant by the scientific method, the general steps to utilize (the steps are _____, _____, _____, _____, _____), and the kinds of questions that can (and cannot) be addressed by using the scientific method. For example, given the observation that tree leaves turn color in autumn, I can formulate a question and hypothesis(es) to address the natural cause(s) of this phenomenon.

I am capable of carrying out deductive reasoning ("if . . . , then . . . " logic) and know how this differs from inductive reasoning. Specifically, I can make predictions based on existing knowledge. For example, if all known life forms on earth are made of cells, then I can predict that. . . .

I know that all hypotheses must be testable and am capable of using my existing knowledge to formulate hypotheses about natural phenomenon. For example, for the observation that my computer did not start up when I pressed the power button, I could formulate at least one testable hypothesis to explain why it did not.

I recognize that there are different procedures, devices/instruments, and means of data collection for answering different kinds of questions and that the appropriate procedures and devices/instruments must be chosen for an experiment to provide meaningful, reproducible results. I am able, with the guidance of instructors, to design an experiment. I always thoroughly familiarize myself with the devices/instruments before beginning so that I use them correctly and understand the kind of data that I will be collecting.

I understand the difference between dependent and independent variables in an experiment and could explain those differences to someone else. I also understand what a "control" is and can explain its purpose. For example, in an experiment to investigate the effect of temperature on the rate of germination of pea seeds, the independent variable is _____ and the dependent variable is _____. A good control for this experiment would be

_____.

I am able to organize and present experimental data in a variety of ways, including in tables, graphs, and figures. I have a good sense of how different forms of data and information are best presented so that other people can understand what I have done.

I can critically examine data that I, or others, have collected, and draw conclusions from that data. For example, I can look at illustrations, graphs, or charts, and interpret them. With the guidance of an instructor, I am able to choose the appropriate methods of additional analysis (such as statistical tests) to test the significance of test results.

I understand that hypotheses cannot be "proven," but rather only falsified. I understand that hypotheses are revised, refined, or even discarded as data is collected, and that results of an experiment generally lead to more questions, new hypotheses, and more experiments.

I can communicate, both orally and in writing, about scientific investigations I have conducted, and I seek critiques of my investigations from my peers and superiors as a way of deepening my understanding of the concept or question that I have investigated. For example, if I have to develop a science project or experiment, I discuss my ideas with others, ask for feedback, and accept recommendations for improvement when they are given. When my project or experiment is complete, I can readily explain what I did, the specific question(s) I addressed, the results I obtained, and if those results supported my hypothesis(es).

I know that for the findings of a scientific investigation to be accepted as "fact" that the results must be reproducible by others and also be verifiable by other methods.

I can explain the difference between hypothesis and theory. I also know and can explain how "scientific theory" differs from the everyday usage of the term theory (for example, speculation or a hunch).

Science and Society

I know the difference between science and other ways that people describe and make sense of nature (e.g., religious or philosophical explanations).

I understand that science and theories of science are not absolute, but should be questioned and challenged. For example, I am able to evaluate new information objectively, relate it to what I already know, and ask questions about it. I am willing to change my mind and challenge what I had previously thought about something when given new information or evidence.

I know that for a scientific theory to be widely accepted it must meet certain criteria including: _____.

I know that science and society influence each other in a variety of ways, and for *each of the following statements* I can describe an example in my own life or community that illustrates this:

- Scientific methods and the knowledge they produce influence how people think about themselves and their world.

- Technology can contribute to the solution of an individual or community problem.

- Social and economic forces strongly influence which science and technology programs are pursued, invested in, and used.

I understand that science involves different types of work in many different disciplines (for example, biology, chemistry, environmental science, and physics).

I understand how these different disciplines of science approach investigations (for example, how in general the methods, questions, and evidence differ in each discipline).

I understand how contributions from different disciplines complement each other and often are required to complete an investigation (for example, how the work of different disciplines can produce a full understanding of the impact of an oil spill on the health of an ecosystem).

I understand that when traditional disciplines meet, new branches of science are often formed (such as geophysics), and I can think of at least one other example: _____.

I know that scientists throughout history have had many difficulties convincing their contemporaries to acknowledge what are now generally accepted scientific ideas. Two examples that I am aware of are: _____ and _____.

I understand that a host of complex new problems are generated by our society's capabilities (for example, the ability of modern medicine to fight many diseases and efficient food production by modern agricultural techniques have both contributed to increasing population growth). I can think of at least two other examples of this.

If asked, I could define the term "technology" and give several examples of technologies that have been developed in the past several decades.

I understand that interactions between science and technology have led to refined tools (e.g., precision instruments, measuring techniques, data processors, etc.) that benefit society. I can describe some examples of such interactions and discuss the developments that have led to a safer, more comfortable life for more people.

I know that investigations and public communication among scientists must meet certain criteria in order to result in new understanding and methods. These criteria generally are:_____.

Environmental Science

I can describe the earth as a body in space (e.g., how it is part of the larger solar system and the importance of its position in the solar system).

I can define and describe the different parts of the earth's environmental system—atmosphere, lithosphere, cryosphere, hydrosphere, and biosphere.

I can describe the earth's current environment (e.g., geography and climate) and ways that it has changed over time or might change in the future (e.g., global warming, continental drift).

I am familiar with the biological and geological processes of nutrient cycling (for example, the carbon and nitrogen cycles) and their role in processing matter crucial for sustaining life. For example, I could describe where I fit into the cycling of carbon atoms.

I know that specific relationships exist among the earth (geology and soil science), the water (hydrology and oceanography), and the atmosphere (meteorology and atmospherics), and can describe these relationships using the water cycle as an example.

I understand basic concepts related to geology.

I have a general understanding of the history of the earth (age, major geological periods, and major episodes in the history of life on earth).

I have a general understanding of the history (age and formation) of our solar system.

I can define the process of erosion (both wind and water erosion) and describe how this process affects the local and global environment.

I can define the process of volcanism and describe how it has contributed to the earth's climate and geography over time.

I understand the interaction of the environment and biota (living organisms).

I understand the notion of habitats and can describe several specific examples of habitats and some of the organisms found there (for example, the difference between a desert and a wetland habitat).

I am familiar with the impact of humans and other environmental changes on some of the earth's habitats. I could describe at least two specific examples of habitat loss.

I understand the role of changing habitats in evolution (for example, how change in habitat makeup or size can change the distribution of species that live there). I also understand the causes of extinction and how human activities can lead to extinction of species.

Biology

I can explain why the cell is described as the fundamental unit of life. (Hint: Most biology teachers would give at least two reasons.)

I can give examples of unicellular organisms and of some of the cell types found in multicellular organisms such as myself.

I can draw or describe the chemical structure of water, and describe the properties that arise from that chemical structure. I can relate these same chemical properties of water to several important roles it plays in living things (as a solvent, in evaporative cooling, in water transport in plants).

I can draw or describe the carbon atom and explain how it can form chemical bonds with a variety of other atoms to make organic molecules (for example, a molecule of methane).

I know the four different carbon-based macromolecules (carbohydrates, lipids, proteins, and nucleic acids) that are found in cells and have a general understanding of the properties and functions of those macromolecules in cells. For example, lipids as a group have the common property of _____ and are important in the construction of _____ of cells.

I understand that both unity and diversity exist among cells, and can describe the common features of all cells.

I can describe the major differences between prokaryotic and eukaryotic cells and give examples of organisms that are prokaryotes or eukaryotes.

I can name and describe specializations that are: (a) unique to eukaryotic cells, (b) unique to plant cells, (c) unique to animal cells.

I know that within a multicellular organism such as myself there are many different types of cells that perform different functions. I can name several different types of cells in my own body and the specialized function that they perform.

I know that mitosis and meiosis are two different cellular division processes. I can describe and/or draw each of these processes (including what is happening to the DNA and chromosomes), distinguish between what is the same and different for each process, and discuss the purpose of each process for an organism. For example, I could describe to someone which cells of my own body are made by mitosis, which are made by the process of meiosis, and how the cells made by these two processes differ from each other.

I know and can describe how DNA is organized into chromosomes and why this organization is important for distribution of the DNA to new cells.

I know that cells must exchange materials with their environment or with other cells. I know of and can give a simple description of the following mechanisms of exchange: diffusion, osmosis, facilitated diffusion, active transport, endocytosis, and exocytosis.

I understand the ways that cells capture and transform energy (ultimately obtained from the sun) for their use. For example, I understand the big picture of photosynthesis (i.e., how plants capture the energy of sunlight and use that energy to make sugar from carbon dioxide and water). I understand the big picture of cellular respiration (i.e., how organisms use this process to transform the energy of food to a form that cells use [ATP]).

I understand that ATP is needed by all cells to power a variety of cell processes (cell work). I can explain how energy is stored and released in the ATP molecule (i.e., through making and breaking of the phosphate bond.)

I know the general kinds of chemical reactions involved in cellular metabolism and functions (for example, condensation and hydrolysis reactions, oxidation and reduction reactions) and how these different reactions are used to (a) break down food to obtain energy and building blocks or (b) manufacture new cell structures or molecules.

I understand the role of enzymes in the metabolic reactions of cells and can give a concise definition of an enzyme.

I have a solid understanding of Mendel's laws of heredity: *law of segregation and law of independent assortment.* I could explain these laws to someone else using a specific example or a diagram. For example, I can explain why when Mendel crossed garden peas that differed for two characteristics (e.g., tall with purple flowers to short with white flowers), the hybrid offspring were all the same (tall with purple flowers), but when these hybrid offspring were crossed to each other or self-pollinated, the next generation had four offspring types (tall/purple; tall/white; short/purple; short/white).

I can define and distinguish between the terms *gene, allele,* and *chromosome.* For example, I can fill in the blanks correctly in the following sentences using these terms: In referring to genetics of blood type, a person with type AB blood possesses two different _____ of the blood type _____. Each of the 46 _____ in my body cells is composed of a long molecule of DNA and contains many _____.

I can define the terms *genotype, phenotype, dominant trait, recessive trait, homozygous,* and *heterozygous.* For example, I can interpret the following passage: Mary has the AB blood type. Is her blood type an example of a genotype or phenotype? Is she homozygous or heterozygous for blood type?

I understand how Mendel's laws relate to the movement of chromosomes into separate gametes during meiosis. For example, the woman with type AB blood will produce eggs of the types: _____. This can be explained because the A and B forms are on different _____ and segregate into different _____ during meiosis.

I understand the chromosomal basis of sex determination. For example, I can describe how my sex (male = XY, female = XX) was determined through the union of my parents gametes. My mother's egg that formed me contained ___ sex chromosome(s) and my father's sperm that formed me contained ____ sex chromosome(s). A person who is XO (a female with the rare condition known as Turner's syndrome) would have failed to get a sex chromosome from the mother? the father? either parent?

I know the chemical and structural properties of DNA and how these properties relate to the function of DNA in heredity and protein synthesis. For example, I can describe the aspects of DNA structure that allow it (a) to be faithfully copied and transmitted to new cells/generations and (b) to provide the information for making proteins.

I can give a general description of each of the following processes, including where they occur and how they are similar and different from each other: *DNA replication, transcription, translation.*

I have a general understanding of the genetic code (e.g., it is triplet, redundant, universal) and how the information in DNA is transferred from the cell's nucleus to the cytoplasm through mRNA, and how the codons in mRNA are translated into a sequence of amino acids in proteins. I also understand how mutations (changes in the DNA sequence) can alter the sequence of amino acids in proteins.

I understand how DNA technologies, such as recombinant DNA and cloning, allow scientists to analyze the structure and function of genes as well as to mass-produce drugs and other useful products for society. For example, I have sufficient understanding of recombinant DNA technology to read a newspaper or magazine article on the topic and understand it.

I know the different levels of the organizational hierarchy of life (beginning with atoms and ending with the biosphere) and how at each level there is interaction and integration of the parts to create new properties. For example, the level below the cell is the _____, while the level above the cell is the _____.

I know that in multicellular organisms there are a variety of specialized cells and that these are organized into tissues, organs, and organ systems, which each perform specialized functions. For example, I can name and describe at least one example of a specialized cell or tissue found in each of the systems of my body: digestive system, circulatory system, immune system, nervous system, reproductive system, etc.

I know ways in which living things can be classified (e.g., internal and external structure, pattern of development, relatedness of DNA sequence) and how this can be used to infer relationships among organisms, both living and extinct.

I am able to describe how DNA and protein sequences are used to infer evolutionary relationships among organisms. For example, if I was asked to examine the amino acid sequence of the same protein (such as hemoglobin) from three different mammals, I could tell which two, if any, were more closely related.

I understand and can discuss at least two examples of natural selection. I can describe how natural selection can lead to origin of new species over time.

I can explain the Darwinian theory of evolution (for example, how the earth's present-day life forms evolved from earlier, distinctly different species). I can explain the role of each of the following factors/forces in evolution of new forms: *mutation, natural selection, genetic drift, nonrandom mating.*

Chemistry

I know that all matter is composed of tiny particles. The characteristics of these particles govern how they interact with one another and these interactions control how a material looks and behaves at the macroscopic level. For example, because oppositely charged ions attract one another very strongly, ionic substances tend to be hard crystals under room conditions.

I know that the particles that make up matter may be separate atoms, molecules, or combinations of ions, and that these particles have characteristic sizes, shapes, and polarities that determine how they will interact with one another. For example, helium atoms hardly interact at all, but water molecules attract one another quite strongly.

I know that the states of matter, solid, liquid, and gas are related to the freedom of motion of the particles that make up a material:

- If the submicroscopic particles attract one another so strongly that they cannot move relative to one another, then the material will be a solid. Strong attraction between oppositely charged ions leads to solid ionic compounds. For example, table salt (sodium chloride) is an ionic compound and it remains solid over a wide range of temperatures.

- If the submicroscopic particles attract one another strongly enough to stay together, but they are able to slide past one another, the material is a liquid. For example, water molecules attract one another strongly enough to stay close together but have enough freedom of motion for water to flow.

- If the submicroscopic particles exert forces too weak to keep them together, the material will expand freely and will behave as a gas. For example, helium atoms exert almost no forces on one another and move independently.

I understand the structure of the periodic table:

- I know that the elements are listed in order by atomic number, which is the number of protons in each atom.

- I know that when the elements are listed in order of increasing atomic number, a recurring pattern of chemical properties appears. When each sequence of properties is laid one above the other, elements with similar chemical properties lie in the same column.

- I am familiar with the properties represented by each column, so that by knowing which column an element falls within, I can predict many of the properties of that element. For example, I know that any element in the leftmost column of the periodic table is a very reactive metal (except hydrogen), and I know that any element in the rightmost column of the periodic table is an unreactive gas.

I know that acids are substances that produce hydrogen ions and I know that bases are substances that produce hydroxide ions. I know that hydrogen ions and hydroxide ions combine to form water. I understand the pH scale, and given a pH value, I can identify the solution as acidic, neutral, or basic. For example, any solution with a pH below 7.0 is acidic.

I understand the behavior of ideal gases, and I can use the ideal gas law and the gas laws derived from it. For example, I know that Boyle's law says that the pressure and volume of an ideal gas are inversely proportional.

I know and understand the relationship between atomic structure and the bonding of atoms:

I know that atoms are composed of three types of particles: positively charged protons, negatively charged electrons, and chargeless neutrons. I am aware that:

- The electrons of an atom are in constant motion about the nucleus, and the region of space in which they move is much larger than the nucleus.

- The neutrons and protons exist together in the very small, central region of the atom known as the nucleus.

- Neutrons and protons are each about 2000 times heavier than an electron, so that the great majority of the mass of the atom is concentrated in the nucleus.

- The attractive force between the positively charged nucleus and the negatively charged electrons keeps the atom together.

I know that atoms are able to form chemical bonds with one another by either transferring or by sharing electrons. When electrons are transferred, the ions that form attract one another and remain together. Atoms that share electrons form small clusters known as molecules. When molecules are attracted to other molecules, they tend to stay together. A large collection of ions or a large collection of molecules will often form a crystalline structure. For example, sugar crystals are huge, ordered collections of molecules, each one of which is a set of carbon, hydrogen, and oxygen atoms that are sharing electrons with one another.

I know that chemistry is concerned with the behavior of electrons. I understand that:

- Different types of atoms that have similar arrangements of electrons will lie in the same column in the periodic table, and they will behave similarly in chemical reactions. For example, all elements in the first column of the periodic table have one electron outside of a closed shell of electrons. Each of these elements will react with chlorine in a one-to-one combination.

- When atoms form bonds they may do so by transferring electrons—forming ions and ionic bonds—or by sharing electrons and forming covalent bonds. In either case, it is only the outermost, or valence, electrons that interact.

I know that when two or more substances react chemically, the products of the reaction will be unlike any of the reactants. For example, when oxygen and hydrogen gases, both of which are highly reactive, form water, the result is a moderately reactive liquid.

I know that chemical reactions can be represented by chemical equations; reactants are shown on the left and products are shown on the right. With a chemical equation I can show that:

- Mass is conserved in any chemical reaction. The sum of the masses of the reactants must equal the sum of the masses of the products. For example, 4 g of hydrogen gas and 32 g of oxygen gas will produce 36 g of water.

- Chemical equations may be interpreted in two ways:

  1. A description of how atoms, molecules, and ions combine at the submicroscopic level

  2. A description of how moles of substances will combine at the macroscopic level

- I must always balance a chemical equation because atoms are neither created nor destroyed during a chemical reaction. For example, if my equation shows a particular number of hydrogen atoms among the reactants, that same number of hydrogen atoms must appear among the products.

I understand that a mole is a collection of objects, in much the same way that a dozen is a collection of objects. I understand that the mole concept allows me to relate the large collections of atoms with which we work at the macroscopic level to the interactions between individual atoms, molecules, and ions that take place at the submicroscopic level. Using the mole concept, I know:

- The coefficients in a balanced chemical equation show the relative numbers of moles of the substances that react and of those produced. I understand that the subscripts in chemical formulas indicate how many moles of atoms of a particular element are present within a mole of a compound. For example, if I find the term "$3H_2O$" in a chemical equation, I know that three moles of water are reacting, and that each mole of water contains two moles of hydrogen and one mole of oxygen.

- A mole of a substance is a collection of 6.022×10^{23} (or Avogadro's number of) particles. The molar mass is the mass, in grams, of that collection of particles. The molar volume is the volume occupied by that collection of particles.

Physics

I know that energy is the capacity to perform work and that it has many forms. I understand that:

- Temperature is a measure of the amount of heat, or thermal energy.

- Heat is a type of kinetic energy. It is the kinetic energy due to the random motion of the atoms, molecules, or ions that make up a sample of matter. For a solid, where the particles are held in fixed, relative positions, this motion is merely vibrational. For liquids and gases, where relative motion is possible, it will be translational and/or rotational.

- Temperature is proportional to the amount of heat. Since heat is kinetic energy, that means that the higher the temperature, the faster will be the motion of the particles.

I know that the first law of thermodynamics is the same as the law of conservation of energy: energy cannot be created nor can it be destroyed. The total amount of energy in the universe is constant. It can be moved from place to place through the flow of heat and it can be changed in form through the performance of work.

I understand that the second law of thermodynamics says that energy and matter are dispersed in any process, and that our measure of this dispersal is entropy. In any process, some energy will become so dispersed that it is no longer useful to us, and this means we can never attain 100% efficiency.

I know that kinetic energy is related to the motion of an object. I know that potential energy is related to the position of an object, generally in a force field, such as the gravitational field of the earth.

I know that energy can be converted from one form to another. For example, an object on a hill has potential energy, but as it rolls downward and loses potential energy, it gains kinetic energy by rolling faster and faster. The potential energy has been converted into kinetic energy.

I understand the principles of optics, and I can draw a ray diagram that will predict the location and orientation of an image produced by a lens or mirror. For example, a convex lens will both invert and enlarge the image of an object placed further away than the focal length of the lens.

I understand the basic principles of electricity and magnetism. For example, I know that opposite electrical charges attract, while like charges repel, and that the opposite poles of two magnets will attract, while like poles will repel.

I know that in a series circuit, the electric current flows along a single path through all of the resistances, such as lightbulbs, motors, etc. I know that in a parallel circuit several pathways are available and that the current is distributed among those pathways so that a particular moving charge will not pass through all of the resistances. For either type of circuit, I am able to calculate the relationships between current, voltage, and resistance.

I understand the laws that govern moving objects. I am familiar with:

Newton's laws of motion, which say that:

- The motion of an object will be changed, or undergo an acceleration, only if the object is acted upon by an external force ($F = ma$).

- Objects have inertia and will remain at rest or move with constant velocity unless acted upon by an external force.

- Forces have both magnitude and direction (they are vectors), and the effect of several forces acting upon a single object is the same as that of a single force equal to the sum of those forces.

I know that a wave, such as sound, is a disturbance that travels from place to place without any net displacement of the medium. Matter that is struck by the wave is put into motion, so that energy has been moved from place to place. I know that electromagnetic radiation does not require a medium (it can travel through a vacuum).

I understand the properties shared by all waves (wavelength, frequency, amplitude, and speed of travel), and I know that when waves interact with matter they can undergo reflection and refraction.

I know that electromagnetic radiation is a traveling oscillation of an electric field and a magnetic field and that:

- We categorize electromagnetic radiation in terms of its wavelength. For example, in order of decreasing wavelength, the electromagnetic spectrum is broken into the categories of radio waves, microwaves, infrared radiation, visible light, ultraviolet radiation, X rays, and gamma rays.

I know that electromagnetic radiation can be produced when an object with an electrical charge is accelerated. For example, when electrons are accelerated back and forth along an antenna, electromagnetic radiation, such as a radio signal, is emitted.

I understand the various types of forces that can act upon objects.

I understand that gravitational attraction exists between every pair of objects and that the magnitude of the force is proportional to the mass of each of the objects, and is inversely proportional to the distance between the objects.

I understand that electrostatic forces exist between electrically charged particles, that particles having the same charge, such as two positively charged particles, repel one another, and that particles having opposite charges, a positively charged particle and a negatively charged particle, attract one another.

I understand that the behavior of both magnets and electric charges are governed by the electromagnetic force. I know that an electric charge in motion produces a magnetic field, and that a magnet in motion produces an electric field. For example, when an electric current, which is a stream of electrons in motion, is passed through a coil of wire, a magnetic field is created and we call this an electromagnet.

I understand that the laws of classical physics, such as Newton's laws of motion, do not apply to objects that are extraordinarily small or that are moving at very high speed (close to the speed of light). For very small particles, I understand that quantum mechanics apply, and that for very fast moving objects, the theory of relativity applies.

I know that special relativity is based on two postulates:

- Physical laws are the same in all frames of reference.

- The speed of light is constant and has the same value for all observers, regardless of how they are moving.

I know that atoms are composed of three types of particles: positively charged protons, negatively charged electrons, and chargeless neutrons. The electrons of an atom are in constant motion about the nucleus, and the region of space in which they move is much larger than the nucleus. The neutrons and protons exist together in the very small, central region of the atom known as the nucleus.

I know that whenever I observe the characteristics of matter or perform measurements, I am noting the properties of that sample. Examples of properties are color, texture, mass, volume, temperature, etc.

I know that mass is a measure of the amount of matter present in an object and is independent of the location of the object. I realize that weight is the force of gravity acting on an object, and that while it is proportional to the mass, it also depends on the strength of the gravitational field. For example, I know that I would weigh less on the moon, but weigh more on Jupiter, than I do on earth, though my mass would be the same in all locations.

I know that density is the ratio of the mass and volume of an object and that its value does not depend on sample size. For example, the density of a liter of water is the same as the density of 1000 liters of water.

I understand that the properties of matter and waves are either scalar (with magnitude, but independent of direction) or vector (having both magnitude and direction). For example, the mass, volume, and temperature of an airplane in flight are scalar, but its velocity and acceleration are vectors.

I understand that different materials respond differently to the absorption of heat. The amount of heat required to raise the temperature of 1 g of a material by 1°C is the specific heat capacity of that material. For example, metals have low specific heats and undergo large temperature changes, while insulating materials undergo small temperature changes, for the same amount of heat absorbed.

I know the basic laws of physics.

I understand that certain quantities do not change, or are conserved, during any process. For example, the law of conservation of mass states that in a chemical reaction the mass of the products must equal the mass of the reactants. Energy and momentum are also conserved in any process.

I understand the laws that govern electricity and magnetism, such as Gauss's laws, Faraday's law of induction, and Ampere's law. For example, I understand that Gauss's law of magnetism says that isolated magnetic poles do not exist.

I understand the relationship between electrical currents and the magnetic fields that they produce. For example, I can apply the "right hand" rule, which relates the direction of motion of the current to the direction of the magnetic force.

Social Sciences

I am able to start with a vital current issue such as terrorism, then select a major scholar from each of three social science disciplines. After describing the basic concepts and hypotheses of each scholar, I can apply each "theory" to the issue in question in an attempt to explain the issue. Finally, I can evaluate the three theories based on empirical evidence.	
I can read Albert Hastorf and Hadley Cantril's case study "They Saw a Game," which illustrates the phenomenon of multiple realities. With the teacher providing me background on Plato's cave image and current social construction of reality theorists like Berger and Luckman, I can examine the 1915 Turkish/Armenian conflict and read the *New York Times* article on Atom Egoyan's movie *Ararat* (Jan. 2002, which implies that it was a matter of perspective whether one viewed the deaths of a million Armenians as genocide or as war casualties). I am able to try to see the conflict through both Turkish and Armenian eyes. Finally, I can review the historical evidence and decide which perspective, if any, is correct. Throughout this process, I am able to cite scientific principles of evidence (objectivity, valid measurement, etc.) to back up any choices or assertions.	

History

I am able to review United States history, then define general criteria or principles for choosing the top 20 historical events/people that shaped the society and the world. I can then show the connections between the early historical events and the modern society.	
I could participate in an activity such as a scavenger hunt at an archeology or ancient history museum. Armed with particular people and events, I could find appropriate artifacts related to specified persons/events. I could then write a description of the artifacts and describe the role the artifacts played in the events of the lives of the historical figures.	
I can critique a major world history text's portrayal of a social movement by reading a primary historical document. For example, I can read a description of the Atlantic slave trade in the textbook, and then read Olaudah Equiano, *Memoirs of a Former Slave*. Or I can compare the text's treatment of the rise of factories and capitalism and that of Marx and Engels in *The Communist Manifesto*.	

Economics

In economics, I can conduct a needs assessment of my hometown preparatory to designing an intergenerational day care program. In the process, I can document from data sources the demand for child care, adult day care, and transportation. I can then write a business plan for the intergenerational day care program.

I can research and describe empirically the U.S. health care industry, e.g., how a dollar spent on health care is broken down, inflation, insurance coverage, Medicare and Medicaid budgets, drug company revenue streams and expenditures, etc. I can then apply the principles and concepts of the market economy to the health care system and critique the explanatory power of those concepts.

I can study U.S. farm policies with price supports and tariffs, etc., then link those policies to the global farm economy with particular attention paid to the European Union farm market and the developing world farm markets.

Geography

I can design and model a European Union–like organization that would establish international immigration policy and govern immigration disputes. I can create a multimedia "tool chest" for member nations, including interactive maps like GeoQuest, GPS mappers, and demographic profiles and trends for major "exporters" and "importers" of immigrants.

Political Science

I can identify oligarchic societies, e.g., Arab emirates, and then describe the strengths and weaknesses of the political and economic institutions of that kind of society in comparison to the U.S. I can develop a hypothetical plan to import and export various aspects of the two societies' political and economic institutions in ways that improve the political and economic stability of both societies.

Sociology

I can define a research problem around structured inequality (race, gender, age, ethnicity) in my community. I can create a literature review, develop and test data-gathering instruments, design the sample plan, implement the fieldwork, and then analyze the data using SPSS or Statview. I can create a final report with tables, charts, and other explanatory graphical material.

I can identify the similarities and differences between the peer mediation program at the local elementary school and the major league baseball salary mediation program in terms of the sociological principles behind the programs and how the programs function in practice.

I can query the Human Relations Area File database and analyze the different forms of family and kin networks along with the numbers of societies in each type or category. I am able to draw conclusions about the diversity of the forms observed.

Inquiry, Research, and Analysis

I can read Laud Humphreys's *Tearoom Trade* and critique its implications for ethical principles such as informed consent, confidentiality, full disclosure, and J. S. Mill's Least Harm Principle.

Using the General Social Survey example data set in SPSS, I can formulate a research question, state the major hypothesis, and then run a cross-tabulation or correlation analysis to test the hypothesis. I can draw conclusions about statistical significance and substantive significance.

I can conduct an observation at a public meeting of an organization of which I am not a member, participate and observe, recording physical properties and interactions. I can produce field notes immediately after the event. I can develop basic coding categories from the data and then code the observations. Using the coded data, I can write a paper using the codes as topic headings.

Communication

I can use PowerPoint to prepare a 10-minute class presentation with hand-outs on an empirical research project. The presentation would have an intro-duction, statement of the problem, methodology, findings, conclusions, and recommendations.

Second Languages

Communication Skills

I can actively interact in an interview in the target language. I can usually un-derstand another speaker, but if I can't, I know how to ask for a restatement or clarification.

In an interview in the target language, I am able to ask as well as answer questions about familiar topics, such as family, pastimes and other activities and interests in one's personal life. I can share information about most events in the present and about some in the past and future.

I am able to use the second language to participate and communicate in classroom activities with peers and teachers. I can respond to and ask ques-tions of my teachers or other students during learning activities. I contribute to class discussions by using the second language.

I can use the target language to carry out personal interactions in the classroom, such as agreeing or disagreeing, asking permission to do something, expressing confusion, seeking information, etc.

When preparing a writing assignment, I use prewriting strategies, such as brainstorming about and jotting down ideas and making an outline of the major points.

I write my ideas and all drafts in the target language, trying to avoid word-for-word translations from English.

Before handing in the assignment, I proofread it for possible errors in vocabulary choice, spelling, punctuation, and grammar, such as tense, usage, and agreement.

I use strategies to help a reader understand my writing, including an introductory sentence and a concluding one, a topic sentence in a paragraph followed by supporting points, sequencing words between paragraphs (e.g., *first, next, last*), and linking words between clauses and sentences (e.g., *therefore, but, nevertheless*).

When preparing a speech or composition, I choose a topic, vocabulary, and format that are appropriate to the assignment and to my audience. For example, I could write an informal letter to a friend but also write a more formal one such as a letter of introduction. I could give a prepared talk about one of my interests to my peers in a small group setting and also present an oral report on a research project (e.g., an important historical or cultural event) to the whole class.

I can write a prepared, carefully edited text to state and defend an opinion, argument, or point of view, for example, a discussion of a significant event in the target culture or my own, a reaction to a newspaper editorial from my own or another culture, an analysis of an important international issue, an evaluation of a literary work, or a discussion of an issue studied in another subject area.

I am able to recognize the genre of a variety of authentic materials in the target language and adapt my reading accordingly, skimming some for general meaning (e.g., advertisements or newspaper articles) and others for more in-depth comprehension (e.g., essays) and appreciation (e.g., poetry).

When approaching a written text, I use prereading strategies, including making word and memory associations with the title, using visual aids to get some ideas about the content of the text, and skimming and scanning to get the gist of the text.

When I come across unfamiliar words and phrases in the target language, I try to make an educated guess as to their meaning. With written texts, I use context clues (such as the topic, the sequencing of ideas, other words in the sentence or paragraph, root words, cognates, etc.) to help ascertain meaning. In oral interactions, I draw upon words I already understand, the context of the situation, the speaker's physical and facial gestures and intonation, etc.

I am able to distinguish main ideas from supporting details within a text written in the target language. I use the introductory paragraph to guide my reading as well as the concluding one, and I look for topic sentences in each paragraph followed by details.

I know how to identify literary devices in texts written in the second language, such as an author's point of view or narrative voice and an author's use of conventions typical of, and appropriate to, different genres.

I can analyze and appreciate an author's use of language (e.g., similes, metaphors, tone, informal versus formal use of language) and literary devices (e.g., foreshadowing, allegory, satire) in the text written in the target language.

Culture

Looking at a map, I can locate and identify in the target language the continents, various countries, and cities in which the target language is spoken, and geophysical landmarks in the primary target language country (e.g., rivers, mountains, provinces, etc.).

I know basic historical facts about the target language country, for example, the dates and events of its origin, the major figures in its history, and the dates and details of important events in its development.

I have knowledge about the target country's formal institutions (e.g., social, political, economic, educational). I also know about aspects of daily life (e.g., housing options, modes of transportation, work alternatives) and daily patterns of behavior (e.g., what people do when they go shopping, are socializing, are preparing and eating meals).

I know what dialects and other languages are spoken in the target language country or countries.

I feel confident about identifying and discussing major current events, issues, or problems (e.g., social, political, religious, ecological, etc.) in the second language's culture or cultures.

Using English, if necessary (or the target language, if possible), I can identify, talk, and/or write about *perspectives* (i.e., underlying beliefs and values) of the target culture. I can also discuss *practices* (behaviors) that reflect those perspectives. Some topics might include the values placed on family togetherness, the importance of religion in daily life, or attitudes about work and leisure time.

I am able to identify well-known physical artifacts of the target culture, including monuments and other famous buildings and architectural achievements as well as major artworks (in sculpture, painting, music, crafts).

I can identify cultural practices that influence daily life and that demonstrate how members of the target countries meet the needs of their body (e.g., food choices, health care, exercise), their minds (e.g., intellectual pursuits, typical topics of daily conversation, leisure time pursuits), and their souls (e.g., religious practices, hero worship).

Structure

I recognize most common parts of speech, including nouns, verbs, adjectives, articles, and adverbs, in English and in the target language. I can define each one and I understand the communicative functions that each one carries out (e.g., adjectives are used for description, adverbs for intensifying another word).

I am alert to the differences in morphology (forms of words) and syntax (word order) of the parts of speech between English and the target language, and I try to avoid carrying over points of interference from English usage to the target language.

I realize that knowing grammar rules is not an end in and of itself and that grammar exists to carry out communicative functions and interactions in English and in the target language, for example, using negatives to express disagreement, past tense to narrate events, or conditional forms of a verb to express politeness.

I know and can contrast the basic components of simple clauses in English and the target language, including syntax, morphology, and agreement. I avoid carrying over components of English usage to target language clauses.

I am able to identify and compare and contrast the coding of various tenses in English and the second language. I use the tenses in the target language that are appropriate to the linguistic context and communicative purpose, trying to avoid English interference.

I know that a second language cannot be thought of as a simple word-for-word translation of English or a replication of English grammar usage. I try to use basic sentences that I know in the target language and go on to construct other sentences from them.

Learning Behaviors

I understand the process of learning a second language, and I can identify a variety of successful strategies that help me in the learning process.	
I apply personal discipline to the language-learning enterprise, such as planning daily and regular study, breaking up longer assignments into short and focused work, completing assignments (oral and written) in detail and with care, reviewing often, reading a new word aloud while writing it down, and evaluating my progress.	
I work effectively in a group situation. I actively listen to others' ideas and I value and build on them. I contribute my own ideas in a positive manner. I encourage others' efforts and work toward cooperation with the group rather than competition.	
I am willing to speak in the target language in front of others (teachers, peers, and those fluent in the language). I encourage myself not to feel nervous about it and build my confidence by noting my success in communicating. When I can't think of a word, I use strategies like synonyms, circumlocution, paraphrase, or acting it out to get my point across.	
I am willing to take risks with the second language in practicing and using new grammatical structures and vocabulary. I recognize that making errors is part of the process in learning a second language, and I try to learn from my errors.	
I know how to use the dictionary effectively (e.g., looking at all the definitions and examples before deciding on the specific meaning of the word in question). I also know how to use resources in my textbook (e.g., the table of contents, charts, end vocabulary materials, verb tables) and those on the Internet.	
I am interested in and curious about other cultures and am willing to learn more about different cultures. I seek out opportunities to talk with people of other cultures, and if I know any words in their language, I try to use them to communicate with natives of the culture. I look for articles about other cultures in magazines or newspapers and find it interesting to discover how cultures are alike and different from my own.	
I use questions and other strategies to elicit responses from classmates and fluent speakers of the second language. I don't limit my communicative interactions only to answering questions but am ready and able to initiate interactions with others in the target language.	
I know and use mnemonic devices to enhance my learning, making active applications of them to form meaningful utterances in the target language. I employ memorization strategies of words and basic sentences, using that learning as a basis for creating new sentences to express myself.	

I use my knowledge of my first language to help form and test hypotheses about the second language. I compare and contrast the two language systems. I look for similarities, but I expect and note differences in vocabulary, pronunciation, and grammar.

I recognize and cope with ambiguity. I understand that more than one answer or option is possible, particularly when trying to understand the perspective of a different culture. I realize that each language has its own particular encoding system that I don't always understand but can make headway in learning. I do not expect that the values and attitudes of the second culture will always coincide with those of my culture, and I am open to trying to perceive and understand alternative ways of viewing reality.

I use metacognitive strategies to advance my language learning. That is, I think about and reflect on how best to learn a second language, and I apply those understandings and insights to my study of the language. For example, I review what I know before starting a new assignment, I identify the goal of the learning activity, I actively monitor my work to look for possible errors and I accept—and even ask for—corrections of my errors.

I also use metalinguistic strategies. That is, I engage in abstract thinking and generalizing about the workings of the target language, identifying and reminding myself of important linguistic features of the second language. I keep focused on those features that do not correspond with my first language (e.g., tense usage, formal/informal levels of verbs and pronouns) and consciously try to apply my knowledge about the second language to my use of it, in oral and written form.

I employ metacognitive and metalinguistic strategies to advance and enhance my cultural awareness. I look for similarities and differences in cultural practices, physical behavior, visual representation, and linguistic usage between the second culture and my own. I am able to discuss, in English and in the second language, similarities and differences that I note.

The Fine and Performing Arts

Art History

When I look at a work of art in a slide, book, or museum, I can identify the medium, e.g., painting, sculpture, print, or type of architecture.

I am confident in my ability to discuss the following qualities of the artwork in class and write about them in research papers. For example:

- I can describe when it was made, including the time period, such as late Renaissance, late 1600s.

- I can identify where it was made, including the country or region, such as in Florence, Italy.

I am familiar with the type of style, the particular details of the work of art, e.g., Greco Roman columns, and know the proper vocabulary, e.g., "sfumato."

I understand how the artwork was made, including the materials, e.g., clay, marble, fresco, and the tools or processes, e.g., "cire perdu," the lost wax style of casting bronze.

I can discuss how elements of design (e.g., scale, color, shape) are related to reasons for making the artwork, deciphering religious and cultural symbols (e.g., crosses, certain hand gestures).

I can also explain sociohistorical influences on art, such as wars, social movements, and scientific developments.

Dance

When I'm learning a new type of dance, I practice the routine in a slow tempo and then gradually speed it up to the original tempo.

I practice out of class so that I make improvements in my breathing techniques, flexibility, and certain choreographic movements.

I am comfortable performing most of the postures in the routine.

I can perform in both solo and group dance routines.

I can improvise new choreographic movements to communicate certain ideas that the audience can understand.

When I practice a dance that is new to me, I am able to accept constructive feedback from my peers and instructor.

I like learning about different types of dance forms performed in the community or viewing them on television or video.

When I go to dance performances, I can make an educated guess about the type of dance, its purpose, the history of the costume, and the cultural roots.

I can discern various elements of the dance: I can tell if the dancers are performing it in the traditional way, and when they incorporate their own personal style.

Music

I can read music notation. I can sing music written in four parts, with and without accompaniment.

When I sing in an ensemble, such as a choir, I know my part: I've memorized the words and can play in a variety of keys. I can accept constructive feedback from my peers and instructors.

I can vary my pitch, rhythm, timbre, texture, and form. I know the common Italian terms for music, including *tempo, piano, forte.*

I can experiment with various elements, compositions, and arrangements, comparing them to examples of well-known music.

I know how to develop my ideas effectively using music as my medium. I enjoy composing my own music.

I am cultivating a musical taste that is diverse and varied: I like to learn about local music concerts, as well as national and international music performances, by attending concerts or watching them on television and video, including more than what may be currently popular among others of my age group.

When I go to a music performance, I can identify the instruments and genre, or type of music being played.

I can describe the basic structure of the story, or narrative, of the music as well as the emotional ranges expressed in the music.

I can also explain the time period, the stylistic elements, and the evolution of the cultural traditions of that type of music.

I understand the relationship between classical genres and boundary-breaking genres: how popular musical forms such as hip-hop music utilize elements of certain traditions, such as African, jazz, and rock music as well as other creative forms of expression, such as poetry and the rhetoric of social movements.

I can describe the relationships between music and various other arts, such as the orchestra's role in operas or ballet theatre.

Theatre

When I read a play, I think about how the characters, the imagery, the tone, and the details of the story can be acted out or otherwise represented.

I examine the physical, emotional, and social dimensions of the characters.

I like to research aspects such as historical setting, location, cultural, and religious characteristics to better develop the character and bring him or her alive on stage.

I consider ways that the costumes, props, and stage lighting influence how the characters are represented.

When I am rehearsing a play, I can accept criticism from peers and instructors and incorporate it into my work. I don't let discouragement prevent me from improving my acting.

I know how to help create scenery, lighting, sound, costumes, and makeup to emphasize relevant symbols, colors, moods, and historical elements.

I can discuss and write about the ideas behind key aesthetic philosophies, such as Greek drama, Japanese kabuki, and Shakespearean forms.

I am interested in collaborating with actors and directors to create plays for different types of theatres and other media, such as film, television, or other electronic media productions.

I can recognize how drama is incorporated into other art forms such as rock concerts and other ceremonies.

Visual Arts

I know how to make a basic color wheel in acrylics or watercolor.

I know how to draw in two and three dimensions.

When I create a two-dimensional artwork, e.g., a painting, or three-dimensional artwork, e.g., a sculpture, I know how to use various elements, such as color, shape, line, pattern, movement, texture.

I can apply and distinguish between various principles, such as composition, rhythm, balance, and unity, to create a cohesive artwork.

I know how to focus my ideas and select media to create a single clear artwork.

I know how to use basic tools, such as brushes, paints, and charcoals.

I know to operate machinery safely, such as printing presses, kilns, and power tools, with the assistance of the instructor.

Once I've experimented in basic media, I can begin to experiment with combining them to make mixed-media artworks.

I can evaluate and discuss my artwork and those of my peers as a form of communication in informal and formal class critiques. This means I can describe the choices I made in selecting certain principles and elements of design, as well as the conceptual underpinnings.

As I work toward creating the final artwork, I am willing to take risks to make relevant or significant changes. To do this, I am willing to work out of class on my own schedule.

When I look at an artwork, I can make an educated guess about the artist's intentions, taking cultural and sociohistorical issues into account, and weigh it with my personal interpretation of the artwork.	
I understand the ways that art has been used as a form of social and political expression.	
I am familiar with the integral role of art in cultural festivals, ceremonies, and institutions.	
I like to go to gallery openings, local arts festivals, and new museum exhibitions.	

BIBLIOGRAPHY

Adelman, C. (1999). *Answers in the toolbox: Academic intensity, attendance patterns, and bachelor's degree attainment.* Jessup, MD: Education Publishing Center/U.S. Department of Education.

Adelman, C. (1999, November 5). Why can't we stop talking about the SAT? *Chronicle of Higher Education.*

American Council on the Teaching of Foreign Languages. (1995). *National standards for foreign language education.* Yonkers, NY: ACTFL.

Andrews, H. (2003). *Progress in Advanced Placement and International Baccalaureate in SREB states. College Readiness Series.* Atlanta: Southern Regional Education Board.

Andrews, H. A., & Davis, J. (2003). When high school is not enough. *American School Board Journal, 190*(8), 38–39.

Arenson, K. (2000, April 9). The learning gap. *New York Times,* 37–38.

Armstrong, W. B., & Carty, H. M. (2003, April 21–25). *Reconsidering the SAT-I for college admissions: Analysis of alternate predictors of college success.* Paper presented at the annual meeting of the American Educational Research Association, Chicago.

Association of American Colleges & Universities. (2002). *Greater expectations: A new vision for learning as a nation goes to college.* Washington, DC: Author.

Association of American Colleges & Universities. (2004). *Taking responsibility for the quality of the baccalaureate degree.* Washington, DC: Author.

Bailey, T., & Karp, M. M. (2003). *Promoting college access and success: A review of credit-based transition programs.* New York: Community College Research Center, Columbia University.

Bailey, T. R., Hughes, K. L., & Karp, M. M. (2002). What role can dual enrollment programs play in easing the transition between high school and postsecondary education? *Journal for Vocational Special Needs Education, 24*(2–3), 18–29.

Banta, T. W. (Ed.). (2002). *Building a scholarship of assessment* (1st ed.). San Francisco: Jossey-Bass.

Beecher, M., & Fischer, L. (1999, Spring-Summer). High school courses and scores as predictors of college success. *Journal of College Admission, 163,* 4–9.

Benjamin, R., & Chun, M. (2003, Summer). A new field of dreams: The collegiate learning assessment project. *Peer Review, 5*(4), 26–29.

Berkner, L., He, S., & Cataldi, E. F. (2002). *Descriptive summary of 1995–96 beginning postsecondary students: Six years later* (No. NCES 2003–151). Washington, DC: National Center for Education Statistics, U.S. Department of Education.

Boswell, K. (2001). State policy and postsecondary enrollment options: Creating seamless systems (pp. 7–14). *New Directions for Community Colleges,* no. 29. San Francisco: Jossey-Bass.

Bothun, G. (2004). Spotlight: Achieving an interdisciplinary general education. Retrieved September 1, 2004 from http://www.sunysb.edu/reinventioncenter/GE%20Spotlight.htm

Camara, W. J., & Millsap, R. (1998). *Using the PSAT/NMSQT and course grades in predicting success in the Advanced Placement program* (No. 98-4). New York: College Board.

Cavanagh, S. (2003). Oregon study outlines standards for college preparedness. *Education Week, 22*(25), 6.

Center for Community College Policy. (2001). *Postsecondary options: Concurrent/dual enrollment.* Denver: Education Commission of the States.

Conant, J. B. (1959). *The American high school today.* New York: McGraw-Hill.

Conley, D. T. (1996). Daddy, I'm scared: A prophetic parable. *Phi Delta Kappan, 78*(4), 290–297.

Conley, D. T. (1996). Where's Waldo? The conspicuous absence of higher education from school reform and one state's response. *Phi Delta Kappan, 78*(4), 309–314.

Conley, D. T. (1997, April). *Proficiency-based college admissions: Catalyst for reform in high schools and higher education.* Paper presented at the annual meeting of the American Educational Research Association, Chicago.

Conley, D. T. (1999). *Statewide strategies for implementing competency-based admissions standards. State strategies that support successful student transitions from secondary to postsecondary education.* Denver: State Higher Education Executive Officers Association, ACT Inc.

Conley, D. T. (2000, April 24–28). *Who is proficient: The relationship between proficiency scores and grades.* Paper presented at the annual meeting of the American Educational Research Association, New Orleans.

Conley, D. T. (2002, May 19). Equitable exams, not another test: There should be one set of measures of high school learning and college admission. *San Francisco Chronicle,* p. D4.

Conley, D. T. (2003). Connecting the dots: Linking high schools and postsecondary education to increase student success. *Peer Review, 5*(2), 9–12.

Conley, D. T. (2003). Improving signals and accountability across K–16 boundaries: PASS and Standards for Success. In R. Kazis (Ed.), *Double the numbers: Increasing postsecondary credential attainment for underserved youth.* Boston: Jobs For the Future.

Conley, D. T. (2003). *Mixed messages: What state high school tests communicate about student readiness for college.* Eugene: Center for Educational Policy Research, University of Oregon.

Conley, D. T. (2003). *Understanding university success.* Eugene: Center for Educational Policy Research, University of Oregon.

Conley, D. T. (2003). *Who governs our schools? Changing roles and responsibilities.* New York: Teachers College Press.

Conley, D. T. (2003, November). *When standards and assessments apply to all students.* Paper presented at the annual meeting of the University Council on Educational Administration, Portland, Oregon.

Conley, D. T. (2004). Proficiency-based admissions. In W. J. Camara & E. W. Kimmel (Eds.), *Choosing students: Higher education tools for the 21st century.* Hillsdale, NJ: Erlbaum.

Education Commission of the States. (2001). *Transfer and articulation policies.* Denver: Author.

Eves-Bowden, A. (2001). What basic writers think about writing. *Journal of Basic Writing, 20*(2), 71–87.

Feemster, R. (2003). Early colleges. *CrossTalk, 11*(1), 1, 8–10.

Ferren, A. S., & Kinch, A. (2003, Summer). The dollars and sense behind general education reform. *Peer Review, 5*(4), 8–11

Filkins, J. W., & Doyle, S. K. (2002). *First generation and low income students: Using the NSSE data to study effective educational practices and students' self-reported gains.* Paper presented at the annual forum for the Association for Institutional Research, Toronto, Ontario, Canada.

Gaff, J. G. (1991). *New life for the college curriculum: Assessing achievements and furthering progress in the reform of general education.* San Francisco: Jossey-Bass.

Gaff, J. G. (1999). *General education: The changing agenda.* Washington, DC: Association of American Colleges & Universities.

Gaff, J. G. (2003, Summer). Keeping general education vital: A struggle against original sin. *Peer Review, 5*(4), 31.

Gaff, J. G. (Ed.). (2004). Changing general education curriculum. *New Directions for Higher Education,* no. 125. San Francisco: Jossey-Bass.

Gaff, J. G., & Ratcliff, J. L. (Ed.). (1997). *Handbook of the undergraduate curriculum: A comprehensive guide to purposes, structures, practices, and change* (1st ed.). San Francisco: Jossey-Bass.

Gaff, J. G., & Wasescha, A. (2001). Assessing the reform of general education. *Journal of General Education, 50*(4), 236–252.

Gazda-Grace, P. (2002). Psst. . . . Have you heard about the International Baccalaureate program? *Clearing House, 76*(2), 84–87.

Gladieux, L. E., & Swail, W. S. (2000). Beyond access: Improving the odds of college success. *Phi Delta Kappan, 81*(9), 688–692.

Haycock, K. (2001). Closing the achievement gap. *Educational Leadership, 58*(6), 6–11.

Higginbottom, G., & Romano, R. (Ed.). (1995). *Curriculum models for general education.* San Francisco: Jossey-Bass.

Hoffman, N. (2003). College credit in high school: Increasing college attainment rates for underrepresented students. *Change, 35*(4), 42–48.

Horn, L., Kojaku, L. K., & Carroll, C. D. (2001). *High school academic curriculum and the persistence path through college: Persistence and transfer behavior of undergraduates 3 years after entering 4-year institutions* (No. NCES 2001–163). Washington, DC: U.S. Department of Education, Office of Educational Research and Improvement.

Hoyt, K. B. (2001). Helping high school students broaden their knowledge of postsecondary education options. *Professional School Counseling, 5*(1), 6–12.

Humes, E. (2003). *School of dreams: Making the grade at a top American high school.* New York: Harcourt/Harvest.

Huntley, H. J., & Schuh, J. H. (2003). Postsecondary enrollment: A new frontier in recruitment and retention. *Journal of College Student Retention, 4*(2), 83–94.

Hurwitz, N., & Hurwitz, S. (2003). Is the shine off the AP apple? *American School Board Journal, 190*(3), 14–18.

Johnson, J., Farkas, S., & Bers, A. (1997). *Getting by: What American teenagers really think about their schools.* New York: Public Agenda.

Kanter, S. L. (1997). *Revitalizing general education in a time of scarcity: A navigational chart for administrators and faculty.* Boston: Allyn & Bacon.

Kazis, R. (Ed.). (2003). *Double the numbers: Increasing postsecondary credential attainment for underserved youth.* Boston: Jobs For the Future.

Kazis, R., Conklin, K. D., & Pennington, H. (2004). Shoring up the academic pipeline. *Education Week, 23*(28), 56, 39.

Kendall, J. S., & Marzano, R. J. (2004). *Content knowledge: A compendium of standards and benchmarks for K–12 education.* Aurora, CO: Mid-continent Research for Education and Learning.

Keup, J. R., & Stolzenberg, E. B. (2004). *The 2004 Your First College Year (YFCY) survey: Exploring the academic and personal experiences of first-year students* (Monograph No. 40). Columbia: University of South Carolina, National Resource Center for the First-Year Experience and Students in Transition.

Kirst, M. (2000). *Overcoming the high school senior slump: New education policies.* Palo Alto: Stanford University.

Kirst, M. W., & Venezia, A. (2004). *From high school to college: Improving opportunities for success in postsecondary education.* San Francisco: Jossey-Bass.

Kuh, G. D. (2001). Assessing what really matters to student learning: Inside the National Survey of Student Engagement. *Change, 33*(3), 10–17, 66.

Kuh, G. D. (2003). What we're learning about student engagement from the National Survey of Student Engagement: Benchmarks for effective educational practices. *Change, 35*(2), 24–32.

Light, R. J. (2001). *Making the most of college: Students speak their minds.* Cambridge, MA: Harvard University Press.

Loveless, T. (2003). *Do students have too much homework?* Washington, DC: Brookings Institution.

Loza, P. P. (2003). A system at risk: College outreach programs and the educational neglect of underachieving Latino high school students. *Urban Review, 35*(1), 43–57.

Macy, B. (2000). *From rusty wire fences to wrought-iron gates: How the poor succeed in getting to—and through—college.* New York: College Board.

Manzo, K. K. (2004). Advanced Placement courses cast wider net. *Education Week, 24*(10), 1, 22.

Marinara, M., Duppalapalle, V., & Young, D. L. (2004). Making sense of the "loose baggy monster": Assessing learning in a general education program is a whale of a task. *Journal of General Education, 53*(1), 1–19.

Marshall, R. P., & Andrews, H. A. (2002). Dual-credit outcomes: A second visit. *Community College Journal of Research and Practice, 26*(3), 237–242.

Mathews, J. (2001, February 19). Schools trying new treatments for senioritis. *Washington Post,* p. B1.

Matthews, J. (2003, October 1). Not quite piling on the homework: Most students, studies find, should probably be hitting the books harder. *Washington Post,* p. A1.

McDonough, P. M. (1997). *Choosing colleges: How social class and schools structure opportunity.* Albany: SUNY Press.

McDonough, P. M., Korn, J., & Yamasaki, E. (1997). Access, equity, and the privatization of college counseling. *Review of Higher Education, 20*(3), 297–317.

McLeod, S. H., & Soven, M. (Eds.). (1992). *Writing across the curriculum: A guide to developing programs.* Thousand Oaks, CA: Sage.

McWhorter, K. T. (2000). *Successful college writing: Skills, strategies, learning styles.* Boston: Bedford/St. Martin's.

Meacham, J., & Ludwig, J. (2001). Faculty and students at the center: Faculty development for general education courses. *Journal of General Education, 50*(4), 254–269.

National Center for Education Statistics. (1999). *Students who took Advanced Placement (AP) examinations. Indicator of the month* (No. NCES-2000-001). Washington, DC: U.S. Department of Education.

National Center for Education Statistics. (2002). *Conditions of education 2002.* Washington, DC: U. S. Department of Education.

National Center for Education Statistics. (2003). *Conditions of education 2003.* Washington, DC: U. S. Department of Education.

National Center for Education Statistics. (2004). *Conditions of education 2004.* Washington, DC: U. S. Department of Education.

National Commission on Writing in America's Schools and Colleges. (2003). *The neglected "R": The need for a writing revolution.* New York: College Board.

National Committee on Science Education Standards and Assessment. (1995). *National science education standards.* Washington, DC: National Academy Press.

National Survey of Student Engagement. (2002). *From promise to progress: How colleges and universities are using student engagement results to improve collegiate quality. 2002 annual report.* Indianapolis: Author.

National Survey of Student Engagement. (2003). *Converting data into action: Expanding the boundaries of institutional improvement.* Bloomington: Author.

National Survey of Student Engagement. (2003). *2003 overview.* Bloomington: Author.

Naumann, W. C., Bandalos, D., & Gutkin, T. B. (2003, Fall). Identifying variables that predict college success for first-generation college students. *Journal of College Admission, 181*, 4–9.

Newell, W. H. (Ed.). (1998). *Interdisciplinarity: Essays from the literature.* New York: College Entrance Examination Board.

Nugent, S. A., & Karnes, F. A. (2002). The Advanced Placement program and the International Baccalaureate program: A history and update. *Gifted Child Today, 25*(1), 30–39.

Oesterreich, H. (2000). *Characteristics of effective urban college preparation programs. ERIC Digest Number 159* (No. EDO-UD-00-8). New York: ERIC Clearinghouse on Urban Education, Institute for Urban and Minority Education.

Olson, L. (2001). Universities seek "seamless" link with K–12. *Education Week, 20*(21), 5.

Oregon University System, Oregon Department of Education, & Oregon Department of Community Colleges and Workforce Development. (2003). *The first year: Student performance on 10th-grade benchmark standards and subsequent performance in the first year of college (2001–02).* Eugene: Oregon University System.

Osterlind, S. (1997). *A national review of scholastic achievement in general education: How are we doing and why should we care?* Washington, DC: Graduate School of Education and Human Development, George Washington University.

Palomba, C. A., & Banta, T. W. (1999). *Assessment essentials: Planning, implementing, and improving assessment in higher education* (1st ed.). San Francisco: Jossey-Bass.

Parke, B., Nichols, J., & Brown, A. S. (2002). Collegiate Connection: A program to encourage the success of student participation in high school/university dual enrollment. *Mid-Western Educational Researcher, 15*(2), 23–31.

Pedulla, J. J., Abrams, L. M., Madaus, G. F., Russell, M. K., Ramos, M. A., & Miao, J. (2003). *Perceived effects of state-mandated testing programs on teaching and learning: Findings from a national survey of teachers.* Chestnut Hill, MA: National Board on Educational Testing and Public Policy.

Quality in Undergraduate Education. (2004). *About QUE.* Retrieved December 1, 2004 from http://www.nc.gsu.edu/~wwwque/about/

Ratcliff, J., Johnson, D. K., & Richard, A. (2002). Florida breaking down walls between K–12, higher ed. *Education Week, 21*(22), 1, 26, 27.

Rothman, R. (2002). A test worth teaching to: The IB's course guides and exams make a good marriage. *American Educator, 26*(2), 28–36, 46.

Schneider, C. G., & Shoenberg, R. (1998). *Contemporary understandings of liberal educa-tion.* Washington, DC: Association of American Colleges & Universities.

School of Education, Indiana University. (2000). *NSSE 2000 report: National benchmarks of effective educational practice. National Survey of Student Engagement: The college stu-dent report.* Bloomington: Author.

Schroeder, C. C., Minor, F. D., & Tarkow, T. A. (1999). Freshman Interest Groups: Partner-ships for promoting student success (pp. 37–49). *New Directions for Student Services,* no. 87. San Francisco: Jossey-Bass.

Shapiro, N. S. (2003). Standards for a "C" paper: Standards and alignment in Maryland. *Peer Review, 6*(1).

Shapiro, N. S., & Haeger, J. (1999). The K–16 challenge: The Maryland case. *Metropolitan Universities: An International Forum, 10*(2), 25–32.

Siskin, L. S., & Little, J. W. (Eds.). (1995). *The subjects in question: Departmental organiza-tion and the high school.* New York: Teachers College Press.

Solomon, C. (2003, December 8). College-prep expectations don't mesh with realities. *Seat-tle Times,* p. A1.

Stevens, A. H. (2001). The phenomenon of general education and its contradictions: The influence of Hutchins. *Journal of General Education, 50*(3), 165–191.

Sutton, J. P., & Galloway, R. S. (2000). College success of students from three high school settings. *Journal of Research and Development in Education, 33*(3), 137–146.

Tafel, J., & Eberhart, N. (1999). *Statewide school-college (K–16) partnerships to improve stu-dent performance.* Denver: State Higher Education Executive Officers Association.

Tell, C. A., & McDonald, D. (2003, November 12–16). *The first year: Students' performance on 10th grade standards and subsequent performance in the first year of college (2001–02).* Paper presented at the annual meeting of the Association for the Study of Higher Ed-ucation, Portland, Oregon.

Tierney, W. G., Colyar, J. E., & Corwin, Z. B. (2003). *Preparing for college: Building expec-tations, changing realities.* California: Center for Higher Education Policy Analysis, Uni-versity of Southern California.

Tinto, V. (1996). Reconstructing the first year of college. *Planning for Higher Education, 25*(1), 1–6.

Tinto, V. (1999). Taking retention seriously: Rethinking the first year of college. *NACADA Journal, 19*(2), 5–9.

Tinto, V., & Goodsell, A. (1994). Freshman interest groups and the first-year experience: Constructing student communities in a large university. *Journal of the Freshman Year Experience, 6*(1), 7–28.

Tuma, J., & Geis, S. (1995). *High school and beyond: 1992 descriptive summary of 1980 high school sophomores 12 years later.* Washington, DC: U.S. Department of Educa-tion, National Center for Education Statistics, Office of Educational Research and Improvement.

U.S. Department of Education. (2000). *A forum to expand Advanced Placement opportunities: Increasing access and improving preparation in high schools. Transcript of proceedings.* Washington, DC: U.S. Department of Education/College Board.

Valverde, G. A., & Schmidt, W. H. (1997). Refocusing U.S. math and science education: International comparisons of schooling hold important lessons for improving student achievement. *Issues in Science and Technology, 14*(2), 60–66.

Valverde, G. A., & Schmidt, W. H. (2000). Greater expectations: Learning from other nations in the quest for "world-class standards" in U.S. school mathematics and science. *Journal of Curriculum Studies, 32*(5), 651–687.

Van de Water, G., & Rainwater, T. (2001). *What is P–16 education? A primer for legislators. A practical introduction to the concept, language, and policy issues of an integrated system of public education.* Denver: Education Commission of the States.

Venezia, A., Kirst, M., & Antonio, A. (2003). *Betraying the college dream: How disconnected K–12 and postsecondary systems undermine student aspirations.* Palo Alto: Stanford Institute on Higher Education Research.

Washington State Board for Community and Technical Colleges. (2002). *Running start: 2001–02 annual progress report.* Olympia: Author.

Williams, R. L., & Worth, S. L. (2001). The relationship of critical thinking to success in college. *Inquiry: Critical Thinking Across the Disciplines, 21*(1), 5–16.

Woodrow Wilson National Fellowship Foundation. (2001). *Raising our sights: No high school senior left behind.* Final report, National Commission on the High School Senior Year. Princeton, NJ: Woodrow Wilson National Fellowship Foundation.

Foundational skills: for arts, 235–237; for English, 175–180; for mathematics, 189–191; for natural sciences, 201–204; for second languages, 229–231; for social sciences, 217–221. *See also* Content standards

Freshman Inquiry (FRINQ) program, 144

Freshman schedules, 147–151

G

G.I. Bill, 35

Gaff, J. G., 135

General education requirements: changes in, 133–135; characteristics of effective, 135–138; examples of, 138–144

Government regulation, increasing, 154

Grade point averages (GPAs): and aspirations, 18; closer scrutiny of, 36, 37; of college freshmen, 109, 125; and placement tests, 146

Grading practices, 45–46

Grammar: for good writing, 80, 176–177, 183–184; and second languages, 94, 115

H

Habits of mind: critical thinking, 81, 187, 236, 306; description of, 6, 81, 165, 173; and intellectual maturity, 116–117; problem solving, 105, 173, 190–191, 203

High school counselors, 19, 25, 31

High school courses: academic challenge of, 36, 38; choosing, 40–41, 107–108; in rigorous curriculums, 115

High school educators: of arts programs, 98–99; as college advisors, 19, 32; English faculty, 82–84; feedback from,

39–40, 97, 104–105; math faculty, 86–87; recommendations for, 162–164; science faculty, 90–92; second languages faculty, 96; social sciences faculty, 94

High school graduates, increase in, 4

High school standards: exit standards, 76–78; expanding, 154–155. *See also* Content standards

High school students: aspirations of, 18; awareness of, 23–26; changes needed in, 165–166; intellectual maturity of, 116–117. *See also* Students' stories

High schools: Alignment and Challenge Audit for, 62–65, 72, 106–107; current strategies of, 6–9; early college, 61–62; intellectual coherence for, 101–110; purpose of, 9, 14

History and geography: checklist, 325, 326; content standards, 222–224, 225; general sense of, 218–219

I

Indexes, defined, 36

Information gathering, 177–178

Intellectual coherence: in art studies, 97–99; designing high schools for, 101–110; in English, 79–84; in entire curriculum, 78–79; exit standards for, 76–78; lack of, 73–76; in mathematics, 84–87; in science, 87–92; in second language programs, 94–96; in social sciences, 92–94

Intellectual maturity, lack of, 116–117

Intentionality and clear vision, 101–103

Interdisciplinary themes at universities, 140–144

International Baccalaureate (IB) program, 36, 37, 56–58, 71

K

K–16 educational system: desire to create, 158–160; policymakers' steps toward, 161–162

Kirst, M., 117

Knowledge and Skills for University Success (KSUS) standards: and Alignment audit, 62–65; and arts classes, 237–238; and Checklist for College Readiness, 174, 301; defined, 171–174; development of, 2, 5–6; and early college high schools, 61–62; and exit standards, 76–78; and hands-on learning, 108; and portfolios, 105; as reference point, 100. *See also* Content standards; Foundational skills

L

Lee Honors College (LHC) at Western Michigan University, 143–144

Light, R., 119

Loveless, T., 121

M

Majors, changing, 116

Math faculty, recommendations for, 86–87

Math phobia, 114

Mathematics: basic foundation for, 189–191; checklist, 307–310; and college success, 38; content standards, 192–199; feedback in, 105; intellectual coherence in, 74, 84–87; and problem solving, 105, 190–191; and science, 205–207

Mathematics placement tests, 146

Memorization of terms, 74, 123, 202

Mid-Continent Research for Education and Learning (McREL), 100

Middle college high schools, 61–62

Music: checklist, 333–334; content standards, 240–242

N

National Science Foundation (NSF), 91

National Survey of Student Engagement, 83, 119–120, 124

Natural sciences: checklist, 310–324; content standards for, 204–216; feedback in, 105; foundation for, 201–204; work sample, 274–280

No Child Left Behind Act, 154–155

O

Opportunities at colleges, 117–119

Oregon's Proficiency-Based Admission Standards System (PASS), xxi, 164

Orientation programs, 103–106

P

Parents: information for, 24–25; role of, 166–167

Physics: checklist, 321–324; content standards, 213–216; key concepts in, 88–89

Placement test policies, student knowledge of, 20–21, 109–110

Placement tests, description of, 144–147

Policymakers, 161–162

Portfolios, 105–106

Portland State's Freshman Inquiry (FRINQ) program, 144

Postsecondary faculty, interaction with, 164–165

Problem solving: as habit of mind, 173; in mathematics, 105, 190–191; scientific, 203

Proficiency-Based Admission Standards System (PASS), xxi, 164

Progress markers, 103–106

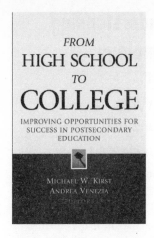

FROM
HIGH SCHOOL
TO
COLLEGE

IMPROVING OPPORTUNITIES FOR
SUCCESS IN POSTSECONDARY
EDUCATION

MICHAEL W. KIRST
ANDREA VENEZIA

From High School to College: Improving Opportunities for Success in Postsecondary Education

Michael W. Kirst, Andrea Venezia

Cloth   ISBN: 0-7879-7062-X
www.josseybass.com

"*From High School to College* reports on research findings that are changing the national policy conversation about higher education accessibility and quality. Michael Kirst, Andrea Venezia, and their colleagues examine the disjunctures between schools and colleges and the corrosive consequences for student learning and educational attainment. This study offers a critical examination of current policies and practices and a challenging but achievable agenda for change."

—Patrick Callan, president, National Center for Public Policy and Higher Education

A college degree has become a minimum requirement for the best jobs, and most high school students aspire to attend college. Yet despite the demand in the labor market for educated workers, many institutions of higher education are reporting that degree completion is at an all-time low.

In *From High School to College* educational policy experts Michael W. Kirst, Andrea Venezia, and their contributors reveal why so many students are entering college unprepared for college-level work and often unable to complete a degree. This important book presents the findings of the Bridge Project—a major national research study conducted by Stanford University and funded by The Pew Charitable Trusts and the U.S. Department of Education. The researchers examined the fit between what high schools were doing to prepare students for college admissions and course work and what colleges considered when admitting and placing incoming freshmen. Based on hundreds of interviews with teachers and counselors, thousands of surveys with students and parents, and a thorough examination of the policies and practices in California, Georgia, Illinois, Maryland, Oregon, and Texas, *From High School to College* offers recommendations for bridging the gap between high school and college and for improving college admission and graduation rates.

Michael W. Kirst is professor of education and business administration at Stanford University. He also serves as co-director of Policy Analysis for California Education (PACE), a state education policy research group funded by the Hewlett Foundation.

Andrea Venezia is senior policy consultant and project director at the National Center for Public Policy and Higher Education.

Teaching for Understanding with Technology

Martha Stone Wiske with
Kristi Rennebohm Franz and Lisa Breit

Paper   ISBN: 0-7879-7230-4
www.josseybass.com

Teaching for Understanding with Technology shows how teachers can maximize the potential of new technologies to advance student learning and achievement. It uses the popular "Teaching for Understanding" framework that guides learners to think, analyze, solve problems, and make meaning of what they've learned. The book offers advice on tapping into a rich array of new technologies such as Web information, online curricular information, and professional networks to research teaching topics, set learning goals, create innovative lesson plans, assess student understanding, and develop communities of learners.

Teaching for Understanding with Technology is filled with useful tips, questions for reflection, and real-life examples from a range of educational settings that clearly show how teachers can make choices to plan curriculum that integrates new technologies, assemble the materials and assistance needed, manage classroom activities, and develop relationships with colleagues and collaborators within and beyond the classroom.

Martha Stone Wiske is lecturer at the Harvard Graduate School of Education where she co-directed the Educational Technology Center. Her research is concerned with the integration of new technologies and the incorporation of learner-centered teaching for understanding. She is coeditor of *Teaching for Understanding: Linking Research with Practice*.

Kristi Rennebohm Franz is an award-winning Washington State teacher who is known for her innovative use of new technologies in the classroom. Her classroom teaching has been filmed and featured in the PBS documentary "Digital Divide."

Lisa Breit develops professional development programs to help K–12 teachers design and implement curriculum with new technologies and consults with school leaders on how to cultivate leadership and provide institutional support as teachers and students gain proficiency.

Other Books of Interest

The Game of School: Why We All Play It, How It Hurts Kids, and What It Will Take to Change It

Robert L. Fried

Cloth   ISBN: 0-7879-7347-5

www.josseybass.com

Teachers, parents, and students of all grades and achievement levels participate in what has become the "game" of school—where students' natural curiosity and desire to learn are replaced with a frantic rush to please the teacher, cover the required material, and get the best grades and test scores. For too many students, school has become a place where the main lessons learned are how to follow the rules, find the easy way out, and get by.

In *The Game of School,* acclaimed educator Rob Fried argues that we have the power to change the rules of this game and bring joy back into the schoolhouse by

• Providing students with work that is useful and relevant

• Building on what students know

• Supporting intellectual risk-taking in the classroom

• Structuring meaningful communication between parents, teachers, and students

Combining his own wisdom and experience with insights from elementary, middle, and high school students, Rob Fried examines the problem and demonstrates what teachers, parents, and students can do to re-claim and re-focus the educational experience. He offers workable solutions for teachers that take into account the current climate of testing, accountability, and budget shortfalls.

Filled with stories, ideas, and practical advice, *The Game of School* will reinspire you to help your students find the joy of learning and awaken their passion for discovery.

Robert L. Fried, the author of the highly successful book *The Passionate Teacher* and its follow-up volume, *The Passionate Learner,* has been an English teacher, school principal, and board member. In addition, he consults with schools and speaks to teachers all over the country. He currently is an associate professor of education at Northeastern University and lives in Concord, New Hampshire.

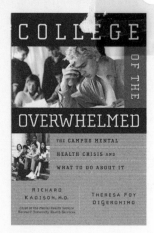

College of the Overwhelmed: The Campus Mental Health Crisis and What to Do About It

Richard Kadison, M.D., and
Theresa Foy DiGeronimo

Cloth   ISBN: 0-7879-7467-6

www.josseybass.com

With the intense media focus on the rising number of suicides on college campuses, there is a desperate need to understand what can be done to prevent serious emotional and mental health problems among students. In a national survey, more than 50 percent of college students reported feeling so depressed that it was difficult for them to function during the past academic year.

Written for parents, students, college counselors, and administrators, *College of the Overwhelmed* is a landmark book that explores the stressors that cause so many college students to suffer psychological problems. The book is filled with insights and stories about the current mental health crisis on our nation's campuses and offers a hands-on guide for helping students overcome stress and succeed in a college environment. Authors Dr. Richard Kadison, a national expert on the topic of campus mental health, and Theresa Foy DiGeronimo examine the effects of such commonplace stress factors as identity development, relationships, sexuality, roommate problems, academic pressures, extracurricular demands, parental expectations, and racial and cultural differences that affect self-worth. The book includes the personal stories of students under stress and describes how they overcame a variety of problems. The authors discuss the warning signs and symptoms of common problems, including depression, sleep disorders, substance abuse, anxiety disorders, eating disorders, impulsive behaviors, and suicide.

College of the Overwhelmed offers parents, college health services staff, and administrators a way to confront and deal with this ongoing crisis, showing them how to understand and recognize symptoms and act before it's too late. The book includes a how-to chapter for parents and shows how parents can be involved and proactive in guarding their college-age children's mental health. In addition, this vital resource offers students checklists, tips, and advice for reducing the day-to-day stresses of college life.

Richard Kadison, M.D., is the chief of the Mental Health Service at Harvard University Health Services. A board-certified psychiatrist, Kadison has specialized in campus mental health and student mental health treatment throughout his career.

Theresa Foy DiGeronimo is the author of more than thirty-five books in the fields of education and parenting. She is the coauthor of *How to Talk to Your Kids About Really Important Things* and *Launching Our Black Children for Success,* both from Jossey-Bass.